The Fulfillment of the
Davidic Covenant

A Hermeneutical and Exegetical Analysis of Three Evangelical Views

PATRICK W. NASONGO

WESTBOW
P R E S S®
A DIVISION OF THOMAS NELSON
& ZONDERVAN

Scripture taken from the King James Version of the Bible.

Scripture taken from the New King James Version®. Copyright © 1982 by Thomas Nelson. Used by permission. All rights reserved.

Scripture quotations taken from the New American Standard Bible® (NASB), Copyright © 1960, 1962, 1963, 1968, 1971, 1972, 1973, 1975, 1977, 1995 by The Lockman Foundation Used by permission.

This book is a work of non-fiction. Unless otherwise noted, the author and the publisher make no explicit guarantees as to the accuracy of the information contained in this book and in some cases, names of people and places have been altered to protect their privacy.

WestBow Press books may be ordered through booksellers or by contacting:

WestBow Press
A Division of Thomas Nelson & Zondervan
1663 Liberty Drive
Bloomington, IN 47403
www.westbowpress.com
1 (866) 928-1240

Because of the dynamic nature of the Internet, any web addresses or links contained in this book may have changed since publication and may no longer be valid. The views expressed in this work are solely those of the author and do not necessarily reflect the views of the publisher, and the publisher hereby disclaims any responsibility for them.

Any people depicted in stock imagery provided by Getty Images are models, and such images are being used for illustrative purposes only. Certain stock imagery © Getty Images.

ISBN: 978-1-9736-3502-4 (sc)
ISBN: 978-1-9736-3504-8 (hc)
ISBN: 978-1-9736-3503-1 (e)

Library of Congress Control Number: 2018908814

Print information available on the last page.

WestBow Press rev. date: 12/27/2018

To my lovely wife, Sylvia.
Without your cheerful smile, encouragement,
patience, and support, this work
could not have been possible.

And to my parents,
the late Samuel and Agnes Nasongo.
Thank you for motivating me to succeed.

Contents

List of Tables and Figures

Acknowledgments

I adapted this book from my PhD dissertation,[1] so I would like to begin by thanking my dissertation committee. First, I wish to express my deepest appreciation to Dr. Larry Tyler, whose skillful and insightful analysis, along with his patience and concern throughout the long process of development, gave this dissertation the needed clarity that would not have been possible otherwise. You mentored me through the course of this degree and shared much wisdom and knowledge with me. I will always appreciate your help. I also want to thank Dr. Frederick Bunts, whose suggestions helped lead me to my conclusion in this paper. You shaped the flow and direction of this work. I cannot thank you enough for investing your time in my dissertation.

I am also grateful to my external reader, Mr. Todd Parker, who helped me with my manuscript. You read both my initial proposal and my completed manuscript, spotting minute errors I failed to notice. May the Lord richly bless you. Fourth, I must thank my fellow students at Piedmont International University, as well as the faculty and staff—and the library staff in particular. Your counsel and recommendations for specific books during the course of my research and writing were critical to my success as a candidate.

But most importantly, I want to thank my Lord for saving me. His love and grace have guided me, especially during the challenge of the PhD program. I give all the glory to God alone.

Patrick W. Nasongo, PhD
June 26, 2018

---

1   Patrick W. Nasongo, "A Hermeneutical and Exegetical Analysis of the Fulfillment of the Davidic Kingdom in the New Testament from the Perspectives of Traditional Dispensationalism, Progressive Dispensationalism, and Postmillennialism" (PhD diss., Piedmont International University, 2016).

CHAPTER 1

Introduction

The Old Testament prophets foretold the coming of a golden age in which Israel's Messiah would reign over the entire earth (cf. Psalm 2; Isa. 2:1–4; 9:6–7). The last recorded question that Jesus' disciples asked him, "Lord, will You at this time restore the kingdom to Israel?" (Acts 1:6), shows that the inauguration of this kingdom was foremost in their minds. Because Jesus was the Son of David (Matt. 1:1; 21:9, 15), they expected his kingdom to be the one that God had promised to David (2 Sam. 7:4–17). But Jesus did not answer their question. Instead, he replied, "It is not for you to know times or seasons which the Father has put in His own authority" (v. 7). For almost two thousand years now, Christians have been asking this question and receiving the same answer. So, despite the coming of a man who claimed to be that Messiah and convinced many people that he was, the messianic kingdom has apparently not materialized. Were the prophets wrong, or is the kingdom different from what they thought it would be? Or has something else happened to change the situation?

In this study, we examine three views that evangelicals set forth to explain the situation. Prior to giving these views, we will look at the background of Israel's hope, the purpose of this study, the approach we will take in evaluating each of the views, and why this study is important.

Patrick W. Nasongo

Israel's Expectation of a Messianic Kingdom

Two central themes tend to dominate the Old Testament. The first is the hope that the Yahweh will come again; the second one is the expectation that the day of the Yahweh's coming is the day of Yahweh.[1] Israel's future restoration is the hub around which these two themes revolve. Daniel E. Gowan notes that the Old Testament prophetic hope for Israel means that "God must transform human society, restore Israel to the Promised Land, rebuild cities, and make Israel's new status a witness to the nations."[2] Furthermore, the Old Testament prophets believed that God's ultimate purpose for the Yahweh's coming was to establish a kingdom on the earth and then to rule over his people Israel (Jer. 23:5).

In the Old Testament, Yahweh was king over national Israel. Herman Ridderbos states, "The prophetic hope also put the kingship and reign of God in physical and national terms for Israel when world events had caused her national life to decline."[3] Therefore, the Old Testament promise of Yahweh's salvation centered on the future manifestation of his kingship. The prophesied kingdom was to take a political and national form for Israel. John the Baptist preached about the near fulfillment of that hope, and the angel Gabriel announced to Mary, "He will reign over the house of Jacob forever, and of His kingdom there will be no end" (Luke 1:33). The Jewish people, including Zachariah, Anna, and Mary, anticipated this hope.

The good news that the promised kingdom was about to be established is a recurring theme in the Gospels. The phrase, "kingdom of heaven," appears forty-eight times in the gospel of Matthew," and its synonym, "the kingdom of God," occurs thirty-four times in Luke. John the Baptist preached, "Repent, for the kingdom of heaven is at hand!" (Matt. 3:2). The kingdom is an important theme in Jesus' teaching. He rekindled the hope of the messianic kingdom when he publicly spoke the following words:

"Repent, for the kingdom of heaven is at hand" (Matt. 4:17). He preached "the gospel of the kingdom" (Matt. 9:35) and sent out the twelve apostles and the seventy disciples to announce that "the kingdom of heaven is at hand" (Matt. 10:7), or as Luke puts it, that "the kingdom of God has come near to you" (Luke 10:9). Jesus (Matt. 4:17) and the disciples (10:7) repeated John's proclamation verbatim in their preaching. Robert Gundry notes that "John the prototype, Jesus the teacher, the twelve disciples—all preach the same message."[4] In more than a third of the parables, Jesus says explicitly that the parables unfold the truth of the kingdom (Matt. 13:1–58). He also teaches the disciples to pray that the kingdom will come (Matt. 6:10). The preaching of the kingdom of heaven ends the period of the law and the prophets (Matt. 11:12; Luke 16:16), and Jesus portrays the kingdom as the great event of the future (Matt. 25:34).

While the kingdom is a central theme in Jesus' teaching, its meaning seems to vary widely, so we must properly understand it. What is the kingdom of God, that is, the messianic kingdom, and did the Jewish people understand this concept? At this point, we may presume that Jesus' audience was familiar with the concept of a messianic kingdom. John Bright observes that

> But for all his repeated mention of the kingdom of God, Jesus never once paused to define it. Nor did any hearer ever interrupt him to ask, "Master, what do these words 'Kingdom of God,' which you use so often, mean?" On the contrary, Jesus used the term as if assured it would be understood, and indeed it was. The kingdom of God lay within the vocabulary of every Jew. It was something they understood and longed for desperately.[5]

The concept occurs in the Old Testament, but not as clearly as it does in the New Testament—especially the Gospels. This does not mean that the concept of a messianic kingdom was nonexistent or that Jesus invented it, because the Old Testament depicts Yahweh as king. Bright explains the kingdom concept from a broader angle: "It involves the whole notion of the rule of God over his people, and particularly the vindication of that rule and people in glory at the end of history. That was the kingdom which the Jews awaited." He goes on to say that "the New Testament declared that Jesus was the Messiah who had come to set up His kingdom (Luke 1:32, 33)."[6]

Bright shows that the Old Testament background of Israel's messianic hope can help us arrive at a proper definition of the kingdom of God, but since it is such a broad topic, we can only discuss it briefly. Scholars have three theories regarding the origin of this concept in the Old Testament. First, the concept is part of the theme of promise that began in the book of Genesis. Second, it began with the promise of God to David, and since that time, the kingdom has had a central place in the whole promise plan of God. Third, the kingdom first appears in the prophets with the promise of a personal king reigning over all the nations from Jerusalem.[7] We will focus on the second option, which is the Davidic covenant.

If we briefly examine the Davidic covenant in 2 Samuel 7:9–16, we see many promises, but the prophet Nathan sums up the three primary elements in verse 16. First, God promised that David's house (dynasty) would last forever. Second, David's throne (i.e., the right for his family to rule) will last forever. Finally, David's kingdom would be established forever. This last element, in which God promised David that his kingdom would last forever, is the crucial issue in our study. John Walvoord points out that "the right to rule always belonged to David's seed." The term "kingdom" in this context refers to David's political reign over Israel because it was an earthly, political kingdom that was limited to Israel. Walvoord observes that the word "forever" signified that the Davidic authority to rule over Israel shall never be taken from David's posterity.[8] This promise is central to the kingdom.

The psalmist affirmed this when he wrote, "His seed shall endure forever, / And his throne as the sun before Me" (Ps. 89:36). David also gave his own testimony about this promise: "He has chosen my son Solomon to sit on the throne of the kingdom of the LORD over Israel" (1 Chron. 28:5).

Therefore, David's kingdom and throne were nothing less than Yahweh's throne and kingdom.[9] The future king who was a legitimate heir of this throne was "His Anointed" (Ps. 2:2). In this case, the anointed is any anointed king who sat on the throne of David. However, the phrase also refers to the future promised descendant of David. In Psalm 2:8, the writer quotes Yahweh as saying to his anointed one,

> Ask of Me, And I will give *You*
> The nations *for* Your inheritance,
> And the ends of the earth *for* Your possession.

Yahweh will graciously grant the future messianic king (Jesus) the promise of a worldwide rule as his inheritance. The prophet Daniel alludes to the fact that the kingdom will last forever. He writes, "The God of heaven will set up a kingdom which shall never be destroyed; and the kingdom shall not be left to other people; it shall break in pieces and consume all these kingdoms, and it shall stand forever" (Dan. 2:44). These passages instill hope for a future kingdom. God will restore Israel (Isa. 49:6; Rom. 11:26), rebuild the broken tent of David (Acts 15:16), and deliver the kingdom to his people Israel (Zech. 9:9; 12:10; Acts 1:6). The question is, "Did Jesus come to offer this kingdom?"

The Problem

Evangelicals agree that Jesus fulfills the Davidic covenant. So, the question under debate is, "How and when does he fulfill the promise of the messianic kingdom?" Different ways of interpreting the Scriptures lead to different views. Our purpose in this study, therefore, is to analyze and evaluate the hermeneutical approaches of three evangelical camps. The groups are postmillennialism, progressive dispensationalism, and traditional dispensationalism. Our goal is to find out which group's method best explains Jesus' fulfillment of the messianic kingdom, using two widely-accepted criteria. But to answer our main question, we also have to answer the following questions:

1) What is each group's hermeneutical approach?

2) What is each group's view on the following central issues related to the kingdom: (a) progressive revelation; (b) the priority of the testaments; (c) the church's status as a mystery in the Old Testament; (d) the relationship between Israel and the church; and (e) the nature of the kingdom?

3) Does each group's view of the priority of the testaments affect their understanding of the messianic kingdom, and if so, how?

4) How does the hermeneutical approach of each group affect their view of the following issues: (a) the time of the fulfillment of the messianic kingdom; (b) the recipient(s) of the messianic promises; and (c) the relationship between Israel and the church?

5) What are the Old Testament foundational passages for the messianic kingdom?

6) What is the New Testament concept of the fulfillment of the messianic kingdom?

7) What is the New Testament view on the time of its fulfillment?

8) Does biblical evidence exist for the postponement of the Davidic kingdom?

9) What are some objections raised against the teaching of the fulfillment of the messianic kingdom?

An Approach to Finding the Answer

First, we will allow the major proponents of each theological group speak for their position. Then I will apply what most evangelicals consider fair criteria in my evaluation of each view, namely, the grammatical-historical method of interpretation and the articles of *The Chicago Statement on Biblical Hermeneutics* (hereafter referred to as the *CSBH* see appendix 1).[10] After that, I will summarize my findings and draw some conclusions.

Analyzing the Three Views

In this section, I will discuss the reason for the order in which I deal with the three views, the sources I employ, the criteria I use for evaluating the views, and the content of the chapters.

The order of the views. The views in chapters 2–4 are not in chronological order, though the first view, postmillennialism, has a longer history than the other two views. The order is logical. Postmillennialism and traditional dispensationalism are at opposite ends of the spectrum regarding their view of the church and future events, while progressive dispensationalism stands somewhere between them and shares aspects in common with both of them. This explains the order of postmillennialism, progressive dispensationalism, and traditional dispensationalism.

The sources. In order to fairly analyze and evaluate each view, I look at the literature of authors who represent each view. My original goal was to consult contemporary scholars in order to have the most current research. However, some key proponents of these views have passed away recently, making it impossible to personally clarify their statements. Therefore, I will take their writings at face value. Also, I could not contact some of the contemporary scholars due to the nature of their work, so I was left to examine their literature as honestly as I could.

The criteria for evaluation. The grammatical-historical

method, as found in the *CSBH* (see appendix 1),[11] will be the sole criterion for evaluating each view. However, the authors of the *CSBH* present the essence of their grammatical-historical hermeneutic in eight articles, so for the sake of space, I only cite those articles in this study. They are as follows: Articles VI, VII, IX, XIII, XV, XVII, XVIII, and XIX. To make the evaluation more convenient, I cite the relevant portion of the article in the text. In the following paragraphs, I define and explain each criterion. I list the criteria in the order Gordon D. Fee states his exegetical steps: grammar, historicity (i.e., the historical-cultural background), genre, figures of speech, and context.[12] In table 4, I summarize each approach's adherence to these exegetical principles.

1) Grammar. In this study, the term "grammar" refers to the grammatical function of the words in a sentence and how this affects their meaning. Grammatical function focuses on the relationship between the words.[13] Terms have a range of meanings, but determining their grammatical function is the first step in arriving at their meaning in the immediate context. The goal is to limit the terms' meaning to their literal sense. In his explanation of Article XV in the *CSBH*, Norman L. Geisler states that "the English word literal carries some problematic connotations with it. Hence the words **normal** and **grammatical-historical** are used to explain what is meant."[14] J. I. Packer elaborates: "The literal sense of each passage should be sought by *the grammatical-historical method, that is, by asking* what is the linguistically natural way to understand the text in its historical setting."[15]

2) Historicity. Geisler adds regarding Article XV of the *CSBH*, "The literal sense is also designated by the more descriptive title grammatical-historical sense. This means the correct interpretation is the one which discovers the meaning of the text in its grammatical forms and in the historical, cultural context in which the text is expressed."[16] According to Fee, the historical-cultural background includes the circumstances surrounding the writing, as well as the culture, customs, and

worldview of the individuals involved.[17] Sidney Greidanus argues that what he terms "historical interpretation" enables the interpreter to understand the text better, maintain objectivity, and remain focused on the text.[18]

3) Genre. Roy B. Zuck points out that "*genre*, a French word from the Latin *genus*, means a literary type. 'Literary genre' refers to the category or the kind of writing characterized by a particular form(s) and/or content. Distinguishing the various genres (kinds of literature) in Scripture helps us interpret the Bible more accurately." He then notes that four of the *CSBH* affirmations mention literary form, and then he lists seven biblical genres: (a) legal literature; (b) narrative; (c) poetry; (d) wisdom literature; (e) the Gospels; (f) logical discussion (primarily in the epistles); and (g) prophecy.[19] Finally, he discusses the importance of considering the genre of a book of the Bible:

> An awareness of the literary genre or kind of literature of a given Bible book helps more in synthesis than detailed analysis. It helps give a sense of the overall thrust of the Bible book, so that verses and paragraphs can be seen in light of the whole. This helps prevent the problem of taking verses out of context. It also gives insight into the nature and purpose of an entire book as seen, for example, in the Book of Jonah.
>
> Structural patterns help us see why certain passages are included where they are. Also attention to literary genre keeps us from making more of the passage than we should or from making less of the passage than we should.[20]

4) Figures of speech. E. W. Bullinger defines a figure of speech as "simply a word or a sentence thrown into a peculiar *form*, different from its original or simplest meaning or use."[21] Earl D.

Rachmacher notes, however, that "behind every figure of speech is a literal meaning, and by means of the historical-grammatical exegesis of the text, these literal meanings are to be sought out."[22]

5) Context. This term and the need for using it as a criterion need no explanation or defense. However, we should understand that by "context" we mean the immediate context (i.e., the paragraph), the section, and the book in which the statement occurs, as well as the rest of the Scriptures.[23] Because of "the unity of Scripture and its self-interpreting ability" in Article XVII, Geisler points out that, "comparing Scripture with Scripture is an excellent help to an interpreter. For one passage sheds light on another. Hence the first commentary the interpreter should consult on a passage is what the rest of Scripture may say on that text."[24] Fee advises the exegete to think of the statement in terms of the paragraph in which it is located, and to focus on three questions regarding the paragraph: (a) "To whom is it being addressed?" (b) "What is the speaker or author talking about and what are they saying about it?" (c) "How does this statement or paragraph relate to what precedes it and what follows it? In other words, why did the author or speaker say this here?"[25] This strict approach regarding context involves traditional notions of biblical and systematic theology.[26]

The content of the chapters. I have shown the basic outline for chapter 5 in the table of contents. Chapters 2–4 include the following points of discussion, which serve as their outline:

1) An overview of the position. In each of the next three chapters, we will begin with an overview of the position. First, we will define the position's view as it relates to the kingdom in particular, and then we will look at a brief history of the position and the movements associated with it.

2) The position's beliefs about central issues. In chapters 2–4, we will explore each position's beliefs about the central issues that are related to interpreting passages regarding the messianic kingdom. They are as follows: (a) progressive revelation; (b) the

priority of the testaments; (c) the church's status as a mystery in the Old Testament; (d) the relationship between Israel and the church; and (e) the nature of the kingdom.

3) The position's hermeneutical approach. Each of these evangelical viewpoints apply different hermeneutical approaches when they interpret prophecies about the messianic kingdom. We will examine each approach with a view to evaluating it later in each chapter.

4) The position's view of the Davidic covenant. In each of the three chapters, we will first look at each position's view of the structure of the Davidic covenant, and then we will investigate their view of its fulfillment.

5) Traditional dispensationalism's distinctive view of the messianic kingdom. In chapter 4, we will discuss in detail the arguments for and against traditional dispensationalism's unique theory that the Old Testament contained prophecies about the postponement of the messianic kingdom. The other chapters do not have a section similar to this.

6) An evaluation of each position's hermeneutical approach. In this section of chapters 2–4, we will look at the evidence the proponents of each view present in their writings and evaluate it using the criteria of the grammatical-historical approach as stated in the *CSBH*.

7) A conclusion. At the end of each of these chapters, I will summarize our findings regarding each position's view of the fulfillment of the messianic kingdom.

Defining the Central Issues

In the following paragraphs, I explain how each of the central issues relates to the Davidic covenant. I put the issues in a logical order. The first three issues are hermeneutical assumptions that influence the interpreter regarding the last two issues.

Progressive revelation. According to Charles Ryrie,

"Progressive revelation is the recognition that God's message to man was not given in one single act but was unfolded in a series of successive acts and through the minds and hands of many men of varying backgrounds."[27] Not all the groups agree fully with this definition.

The priority of the testaments. Evangelical scholars generally agree that the New Testament fulfills some Old Testament prophecies, but they disagree about whether one testament has priority over the other when it comes to interpreting a prophecy.[28] This affects each group's view of the prophecies about the Davidic covenant.

Mystery. Leland Ryken claims this is "God's eschatological plan that was laid 'before the foundation of the world' (Eph. 1:4), that was formerly concealed and now has been revealed in Christ. ... The essential outline of the mystery is that the Gentiles are now fellow heirs, members of the same body, sharers in the promise with believing Israelites who have followed Jesus Christ (Eph. 3:6)."[29] We will examine closely the various definitions these three views give this term because it has a direct bearing on the each position's view of the last two central issues.

Israel and the church. Evangelicals also disagree on the relationship between Israel and the church. Is the church a continuation of Old Testament Israel, so that they belong to the same group? Are Israel and the church two different groups right now that God will merge into one group in the future? Or will they always be two different groups? If the church and Israel belong to the same group, then the church has a part in the Davidic covenant.

The nature of the kingdom. The options here are as follows: Is the kingdom only spiritual; is it currently spiritual but literal later; or will it only be literal later, though it may have spiritual requirements? A person's view of the other central issues determines their view of the kingdom.

Drawing Some Conclusions

In chapter 5, we will draw some conclusions about the three views. Its contents differ from the discussion in chapters 2–4. I will first summarize the findings in chapters 2–4, and then I will discuss the strengths and weaknesses of each hermeneutical approach. Finally, I will make a conciliatory statement about the entire issue.

The Importance of This Study

Many authors have written books on the Davidic covenant, but none of them address the hermeneutical methodology the three views apply to its fulfillment. The methodology a person uses determines the conclusion they will reach. This book will reveal each view's methods and conclusions so that you can decide which view is biblical.

---

1 Walter C. Kaiser Jr., "Kingdom Promises as Spiritual and National," in *Continuity and Discontinuity: Perspectives on the Relationship Between the Old and New Testaments—Essays in Honor of S. Lewis Johnson Jr.*, ed. John S. Feinberg (Westchester, IL: Crossway Books, 1988), 290.

2 Donald E. Gowan, *Eschatology in the Old Testament* (Philadelphia: Fortress, 1986), 2.

3 Herman Ridderbos, *The Coming of the Kingdom* (Philadelphia: Presbyterian and Reformed, 1962), 5.

4 Robert H. Gundry, *Matthew: A Commentary on His Literary and Theological Art* (Grand Rapids: Eerdmans, 1982), 43.

5 John Bright, *The Kingdom of God: The Biblical Concept and Its Meaning for the Church* (Nashville, TN: Abingdon Press, 1953), 17–18.

6 Bright, *The Kingdom of God*, 18.

7 Kaiser, "Kingdom Promises as Spiritual and National," 290.

8 John F. Walvoord, "Eschatological Problems VII: The Fulfillment of the Davidic Covenant," *Bibliotheca Sacra* 102, no. 406 (April 1945): 154, accessed 4/18/2018, http://www.galaxie.com/article/bsac102-406-03.

9 Kaiser, "Kingdom Promises as Spiritual and National," 292.

Patrick W. Nasongo

10 Norman L. Geisler, *Summit II Hermeneutics: Understanding God's Word—A Commentary*, with Exposition by J. I. Packer, ICBI Foundation Series 6 (Oakland, CA: International Council on Biblical Inerrancy, 1983), 19–25.

11 Geisler, *Summit II Hermeneutics*, 19–25.

12 Gordon D. Fee, *New Testament Exegesis: A Handbook for Students and Pastors*, 3rd ed. (Louisville, KY: Westminster John Knox Press, 2002), 15.

13 Fee, *New Testament Exegesis*, 3rd ed., 30–32.

14 Geisler, *Summit II Hermeneutics*, 12; bold orig.

15 Geisler, *Summit II Hermeneutics*, 30; italics orig.

16 Geisler, *Summit II Hermeneutics*, 12.

17 Fee, *New Testament Exegesis*, 3rd ed., 16.

18 Sidney Greidanus, *The Modern Preacher and the Ancient Text: Interpreting and Preaching Biblical Literature* (Grand Rapids: Eerdmans, 1988), 80–82.

19 Roy B. Zuck, *Basic Bible Interpretation: A Practical Guide to Discovering Biblical Truth* (Wheaton, IL: Victor Books, 1973), 126–35; italics orig.

20 Zuck, *Basic Bible Interpretation*, 135.

21 E. W. Bullinger, *Figures of Speech Used in the Bible: Explained and Illustrated* (repr., orig. pub. 1898; Grand Rapids: Baker Book House, 1968), xv; italics orig.

22 Earl D. Radmacher, "The Current Status of Dispensationalism and Its Eschatology," in *Perspectives on Evangelical Theology: Papers from the Thirtieth Annual Meeting of the Evangelical Theological Society*, ed. Kenneth S. Kantzer and Stanley N. Gundry (Grand Rapids: Baker Book House, 1979), 167.

23 Zuck, *Basic Bible Interpretation*, 106–112, 122.

24 Geisler, *Summit II Hermeneutics*, 13.

25 Fee, *New Testament Exegesis*, 34–35 [3rd ed., step 11].

26 Fee, *New Testament Exegesis*, 44. [3rd ed., step 12].

27 Charles C. Ryrie, *Dispensationalism*, 3rd ed. (Chicago: Moody Press, 2007), 36.

28 John S. Feinberg, "Systems of Discontinuity," in *Continuity and Discontinuity*, 75.

29 Leland Ryken, James C. Wilhoit, and Tremper Longman III, eds., *Dictionary of Biblical Imagery* (Downers Grove, IL: InterVarsity Press, 1998), 240-41.

CHAPTER 2

The Postmillennialist View

As stated in chapter 1, we will begin with an overview of postmillennialism. First, we will define their position, and then we will look at the historical and theological development of the views. Next, we will also discuss their hermeneutical approach and their view of the Davidic covenant. After that, we will evaluate their approach. Then I will state my conclusion.

An Overview of Postmillennialism

First, we will look at this group's definition and a description of its position, and then we will briefly discuss the various groups within postmillennialism.

A Definition of Postmillennialism

Loraine Boettner says postmillennialism "holds that the Kingdom of God is now being extended in the world through the preaching of the Gospel and the saving work of the Holy Spirit, that the world will eventually be Christianized, and that the return of Christ will occur at the close of the long period of righteousness and peace commonly called the Millennium."[1] Boettner's definition reveals the four basic themes of postmillennialism: the present reality of the kingdom, the necessity of the gospel, a hope for a future worldwide salvation, and the return of Christ after the millennium.

A Brief History of Postmillennialism

Postmillennialism was once a dominant view of eschatology. However, its adherents seemed to have lost their enthusiasm for it. Some evangelicals even consider it extinct. But it is back and regaining its former strength. We will examine postmillennialism's renewed popularity by looking at the aspects that made postmillennialism prominent in the past, and then comparing them to recent factors that have led to its resurgence.

An unfulfilled prophecy. For centuries, Christians have longed for Christ to return and establish a literal, one thousand-year kingdom on earth (i.e., the millennium), but it has not happened yet. As a result, the early church was divided regarding the meaning of Revelation 20:2–7, but postmillennialism eventually dominated Christianity for more than fifteen centuries.

Augustine's influence. At first, the great fourth-century theologian Augustine was a chiliast, but then he adopted the view that the present age is the millennium. He believed the kingdom of God is already manifested in the church and proclaimed that the period between the present age and the return of Christ is the millennium, thus advocating a figurative interpretation of Revelation 20:2–7. He defends his view as follows:

> Speaking of a part under the name of the whole, he [the apostle John] calls the last part of the millennium—which had yet to expire before the end of the world—a thousand years; or he used the thousand years as an equivalent for the whole duration of this world, employing the number of perfections to mark the fullness of time.[2]

Political events. Postmillennialism also gained prominence due to a political event. As Mal Couch notes, postmillennialism explained "the rise of Christendom and the merger of church and state with Constantine's declaration that Christianity was the new religion of the Roman Empire [AD 313])."[3] During the reign of Constantine, Christianity almost became an official religion of the Roman Empire. As a result, Christians developed the view that the church would conquer and overcome all other evil powers and reign for the Lord. The seventh-century Islamic uprising dealt a severe, yet not fatal, blow to this optimism.

The reformer's belief in the power of the gospel. Couch observes that the reformer's view of humanity's depraved nature would have led them to pessimism and despair, but they refused to embrace a negative view of the future. They held that the world will become better as a result of the spread of the gospel. The post-reformation theologians of the 1600s brought the idea of progress and optimism to its height. Postmillennialism's optimism stands out strongly in comparison to other end-time views. Apparently, those who believe that the gospel of Jesus Christ will exercise a dominant influence in the affairs of men is a postmillennialist. Again, Couch observes that "the idea of novelty rather than return is seen in the excited references to all the new manifestations of the age—the new lands, the new learning, the new books, the new missionaries."[4] The reformers outperformed Catholicism in missions, both in Europe and around the world. The Puritan postmillennialists flourished during this period. They held that the millennium would begin after the conversion of the Jews. Gentry states their position: "The millennial era proper will not begin until the conversion of the Jews, and will flower rather quickly, prevailing over the earth for a literal thousand years."[5]

Systematization of the view. Daniel Whitby (1638–1725) was a key scholar during this period. His principles for interpreting Revelation 20:2–7 appealed to both conservatives and liberals. Couch explains this situation, "Man's increasing knowledge of the world and scientific improvement which were coming could fit into this picture. On the other hand, the concept was pleasing to the liberal and skeptic. If they did not believe the prophets, at least they believed that man was now able to improve himself and his environment. They, too, believed a golden age was ahead."[6] Because the liberal scholars rejected the supernatural, they held that the world would be converted through humanistic and evolutionary processes,[7] such as education, social and economic progress, improved health programs, and better global relations.[8] But as Mal Couch points out, "Later, in the States, postmillennial decline awaited the turn of the century and was dealt a near-fatal blow by WWI and WWII and its identification with the social gospel and liberalism."[9]

Generic postmillennialists, also known as modern postmillennialists, existed from the late-nineteenth to mid-twentieth centuries. They did not hold to a future conversion of the Jews. Instead, they "believed that the Millennium spans all of the new covenant phase of the church history, developing incrementally from the time of Christ until his Second Advent."[10] Charles Hodge, B. B. Warfield, John Murray, Loraine Boettner, James Snowden, and John Jefferson Davis are some of the prominent scholars in this camp.

Christian Reconstructionism. Couch makes the observation that "only since the 1970s has postmillennialism begun to reassert itself, primarily through the reconstructionist movement."[11] This movement advocates enforcing God's law at all levels of government. Those involved in the movement believe that if the Ten Commandments are implemented, society's moral condition will improve and evil will decline. Also called theonomic postmillennialism,[12] this movement sees the gradual return to biblical norms of civil justice as a consequence of widespread success of the gospel through evangelism, missions, preaching, and Christian education. Gentry describes the movement's view in detail.

The judicial-political outlook of Reconstructionism includes the application of those justice-defining directives contained in the Old Testament legislation, when properly interpreted, adapted to new covenant conditions, and relevantly applied. With a core theological sub-structure firmly rooted in the absolute sovereignty of God (classic Calvinism), Christian Reconstructionists not only have a confident hope in the future (postmillennialism) but also a vision of how that optimistic future will operate in the area of social and political arenas (theonomy).[13]

Thomas Ice agrees with Gentry's explanation: "The Christian Reconstruction movement of the last three decades has been the primary catalyst for the recent resurgence of postmillennialism. ... Both postmillennialism and theonomy have sprouted in the soil of a strong Reformed revival."[14] But he also points out that sociological factors, such as the new age optimism—which began in the 1970s and has lasted until the present, have revived postmillennialism.

Prolific publication. Postmillennialism's recent resurgence is largely due to the publication of postmillennial literature in the 1970s and early 1980s by the Banner of Truth in Britain and the Christian Reconstructionist publishers, The Chalcedon Foundation and the Institute for Christian Economics, in America. The following individuals are key figures in this publishing revival: James DeJong, Iain Murray, Erroll Hulse, R. J. Rushdoony, Gary North, and Greg Bahnsen.[15] Postmillennialism has further flooded the evangelical landscape with books from the late 1980s through the first decade of the twenty-first century, including works by John J. Davis, David Chilton, Gary North, Gary DeMar, Kenneth Gentry, Alexander McLeod, Andrew Sandlin, Keith Mathison, and Greg Bahnsen.[16]

The popular speaker R. C. Sproul was a recent, noteworthy

convert to postmillennialism, and his position and influence seem to have stirred interest in Christian Reconstructionism among the emergent churches. Gentry list him among the notable contemporary leader.[17]

Postmillennialism and the Central Issues

In this section, we will discuss the views of postmillennialists regarding the central issues mentioned in chapter 1.

Progressive Revelation

Charles Hodge defines *progressive revelation* as a contrast between earlier and later revelation. He states, "The progressive character of divine revelation is recognized in relation to all the great doctrines of the Bible. ... What at first is only obscurely intimated is gradually unfolded in subsequent parts of the sacred volume, until the truth is revealed in its fullness."[18]

Benjamin B. Warfield identifies three modes of revelation: "theophany, prophecy, and inspiration." Theophany is God's outward manifestation. Warfield writes, "God spoke to men through their senses, in physical phenomena, as the burning bush, the cloudy pillar, or in sensuous forms, as men, angels, etc." Miracles are part of this category. Warfield then notes that God revealed himself "by means of inward prophetic inspiration." During the prophetic period, God spoke His Word through the prophets as the Holy Spirit guided them. Warfield observes that there were no external manifestations by this time, but internal revelation in the hearts of the prophets under the guidance of the Spirit. This category involves visions and dreams (Num. 12:3). Prophetic inspiration of the written Word characterized the final stage. Warfield notes, "The revealing Spirit speaks through chosen men as His organs, but through these organs in such a fashion that the most intimate processes of their souls become the instruments by means of which He speaks His mind." God made the revelation, regardless of the time. Warfield writes, "In whatever diversity of forms, by means of whatever variety of modes, in whatever distinguishable stages it is given, it is ever the revelation of one God, and it is ever the one consistently developing redemptive revelation of God."[19] Warfield also describes progressive revelation by how God overcame the sin-damaged mind and heart. He writes:

> But it has pleased him (God) to accomplish it only in the course of a process which extends through ages. He has first in a progressive revelation running through many generations, published the elements of a true religion and morality on his own authority, and embodied them in an authoritative record, which should stand for all time as the source and norm of the truth. He has then in the fullness of the times, sent His own Son to be the propitiation for the sins of the world. And he has then sent his Spirit into the world to work upon the hearts of men, framing in them faith in the sacrifice of the Son of God through which they might receive forgiveness of their sins, and cleansing their hearts, that they might understand and obey the truth as it had been delivered to them. This too, be doers. However, not all at once, but in a process extending through ages. Thus, it comes about that true religion and morality is only slowly made the possession of man. Objectively in the world is an authoritative revelation, it is subjectively assimilated by the world only if the kingdom of God is built up, step by step, slowly in the end.[20]

The Priority of the Testaments

While all postmillennialists give priority to the New Testament over the Old Testament, John J. Davis writes, "The New Testament is the key to the proper interpretation of the Old. The New Testament is the definitive revelation of Jesus Christ, and He is the true meaning of the Old Testament." Davis cites the following passages to support this view: (a) "You search the Scriptures. It is they that bear witness to me" (John 5:39); (b) "And beginning with Moses and all the prophets, he interpreted to them in all the Scriptures the things concerning himself" (Luke 24:27); and (c) "Jesus came not to abolish the law and the prophets but to fulfill them" (Matt. 5:17). Davis notes that, "The messianic prophecies of the Old Testament (e.g., Isa. 53:4–6, the suffering servant) find their true interpretation in the New (1 Pet. 2:24–25)." Postmillennialists emphasize the centrality of Jesus in biblical interpretation. Davis states that "the crucial link between the testaments is Jesus Christ himself, who is the fulfillment of all the promises of the old covenant." He observes that the "Christian exegete must allow the New Testament to interpret the Old Testament."[21] Theonomic postmillennialists in particular allege that the New Testament must take priority because the Old Testament's revelation is incomplete. Gentry makes the following comment, "This approach to biblical interpretation allows God's conclusive New Testament revelation authoritatively to interpret the incomplete revelation in the Old."[22]

The Meaning of "Mystery"

Gentry claims that the term "mystery" is not limited to the New Testament. He writes, "Certainly the revelation's *clarity* increases in the New Testament, and obviously the *audience* who hears it expands, but the revelation itself *was* given in the Old Testament."[23] He bases his argument on Ephesians 3:5–6, which reads, "[This mystery,] which in other ages was not made known to the sons of men, ... has now been revealed by the Spirit to His holy apostles and prophets: that the Gentiles should be fellow heirs, of the same body, and partakers of His promise in Christ through the gospel." According to Gentry, the salvation of the Gentiles was the mystery. God hid it from the Gentiles, but not from the Old Testament prophets. He cites Romans 16:25–26 in further support of this claim: "The revelation of the mystery, which was kept secret since the world began, but now is made manifest, and by the Scriptures of the prophets, according to the commandment of the everlasting God, made known to all nations for obedience of faith." Gentry concludes by stating that this "mystery ... [is] now made manifest ... [to] all nations—not just Israel."[24]

Israel and the Church

Israel. Gentry adopts his definition of *Israel* from the Westminster Confession of Faith (WCF). He says that "Old Testament Israel is the continuation of the New Testament Israel." In other words, Israel is "a church under age (WCF 19:3)." By this he means that Israel was the church as a child (cf. Gal. 3:23–26). In that case, Israel is equivalent to the church. Furthermore, Gentry notes that "Christians ... are grafted into Israel (Rom. 11:16–19) so that we become one with her, partaking of her promises (Eph. 2:11–20)." And as he points out again, "Gentiles are other sheep which must be brought in to make 'one flock' (Jn. 10:16)." Gentry teaches that Jesus "appointed the twelve apostles to be the spiritual seed of a New Israel, taking over for old covenants Israel's twelve sons."[25]

In an attempt to define the word "Israel," Keith Mathison provides four ways this word was applied. First, he notes that in the Old Testament, there were three categories of people: the Gentiles, national Israel, and true Israel (the "remnant"). Second, when Jesus was born, true Israel referred to the faithful remnant, such as Simeon and Anna. Third, during Jesus' public ministry, true Israel referred to His disciples apart from those who opposed Him (e.g., the Pharisees, the Sadducees, etc.). Finally, beginning from the day of Pentecost onwards, true Israel consists of those whom the Holy Spirit formed into a single body. This last category, which Mathison calls "the new community of believers,"[26] is the church. In other words, the church is "the true Israel." Therefore, the true Israel "includes believing Gentiles who are being grafted into this body along with faithful Jews (Rom. 11)."[27]

The church. Gentry and other postmillennialists describe the church as a spiritual Israel. He asks, "If Abraham can have Gentiles as his 'spiritual seed,' why may we not envision a spiritual Israel?" He notes that the church is the focus of Christ's kingdom (Matt. 16:18–19), the temple and house of God (1 Cor. 3:16), and the earthly expression of the city of God (Gal. 4:25–26). It sits on the hill to influence the world (Matt. 5:14; Heb. 12:22; Rev. 14:1; 21:10).[28]

The Nature of the Kingdom

Its establishment and current reality. Postmillennialists acknowledge that God confirmed the Davidic covenant with David (2 Sam. 7:12–16), but they believe that the Davidic kingdom was established during Jesus' earthly ministry.[29] Gentry points out that "postmillennialists maintain that Jesus established the Messianic Kingdom during His earthly ministry on earth. It was the kingdom prophesied in the Old Testament (Luke 17:20–21; Col. 1:13)."[30] Hodge calls it the "messianic or mediatorial kingdom of Christ." According to Hodge, there is no distinction between the messianic kingdom (the future kingdom where the Messiah, Jesus Christ reigns for a thousand years) and the mediatorial kingdom (the current work of Christ as a priest rather than as the king). He bases his argument on 1 Corinthians 15:24, where Paul says, "Then *comes* the end, when He delivers the kingdom to God the Father, when He puts an end to all rule and all authority and power." From this verse, Hodge concludes that "he shall deliver up to God even the Father, when his mediatorial work is accomplished." Because this kingdom relates to people on earth, Hodge calls it "the kingdom of grace." In this kingdom, the people under Christ's rule will "recognize him as their absolute proprietor and sovereign." After Christ accomplishes his work of redemption, this kingdom will be "the kingdom of glory and the kingdom of heaven in the highest sense of the words."[31] The kingdom of glory shall then last forever.

Hodge writes that "the kingdom of which the prophets speak began in its messianic form when the Son of God came in the flesh." He observes that the messianic kingdom is similar to the kingdom about which John the Baptist said, "It is at hand" (Matt. 3:2), and of which Jesus preached that "it is near" (Luke 10:9). Hodge further notes that "Jesus did not just preach about the kingdom of God, He was Himself the king of that kingdom." Furthermore, Jesus responded to Pilate, "You say *rightly* that I am a king. For this cause I was born, and for this cause I have come into the world" (John 18:37). According to the postmillennialists, this confirms that he is a king. In addition to this, the apostles preached the same kingdom (Acts 28:23). When all these people and groups preached about this kingdom, they invited individuals to embrace Christ as their king, so postmillennialists hold that the messianic kingdom is a present reality. Hodge states clearly that "nothing, therefore, can be more opposed to the plain teaching of the New Testament, than that the kingdom of Christ is yet future and is not to be inaugurated until his second coming."[32] Millard Erickson confirms the postmillennialists' belief that "the kingdom is not something to be introduced cataclysmically at some future time."[33]

Its realm. Postmillennialists argue that the kingdom is not a realm over which Christ reigns, but is the rule of Christ in the hearts of those who believe the gospel. Thus, they maintain that

Christ reigns from heaven in the hearts of those who believe in Him. They "teach that the sphere of the spiritual kingdom is in the heart of believers,"[34] and that "the fundamental nature of the kingdom is redemptive and spiritual, instead of being political and corporeal."[35]

Its progress. Postmillennialists hold that, through his death, burial, resurrection, and ascension, Christ conquered and defeated the devil. Satan is now bound and unable to deceive people and resist the spread of the gospel (Matt. 12:28–29).[36] As a result, Boettner states that "postmillennialists hold to a universal conversion of a large mass of people prior to Christ's return." He bases his assertion on the Great Commission by arguing that "the Great Commission will be accomplished because of the command that accompanies it."[37] The command is Jesus' claim, in which he states, "All authority has been given to Me in heaven and on earth" (Matt. 28:18).

However, the growth of the kingdom will be gradual,[38] as illustrated by the parable of the mustard seed, in which the smallest seed produces a large plant (Matt. 13:31–33). The presence of Christ himself and the power of the Holy Spirit working through His disciples enhance the kingdom's growth. Gentry notes, "We see the water of life flowing gradually deeper (Ezek. 47:1–12), and the kingdom of heaven slowly growing larger (Dan. 2:35) and taller (Ezek. 17:22–24); Matt. 13:31–32), permeating more fully (Matt. 13:33), and producing more fruitfully (Mark 4:1–8, 26–28)."[39] The kingdom's growth depends on the success of the gospel. Therefore, when the church preaches the gospel, and people believe in Christ, postmillennialists conclude that the kingdom of God is expanding. But as Gentry notes, "The ever-present Christ is directing kingdom growth from his throne in heaven, where he sits at God's right hand."[40]

Its duration. Once the world has been Christianized, postmillennialists anticipate a long period of earthly peace called the millennium (Isa. 11:6; John 14:27).[41] The Prince of Peace will provide this peace (Isa. 9:6). According to Boettner, the term "a thousand years is figurative indicating an indefinitely long period of time, a complete perfect number of years, probably not less than a literal one thousand years, in all probability, very much longer."[42] Postmillennialists call this period the "golden age." Gentry notes that "we can look forward to a great 'golden age' of spiritual prosperity continuing for centuries, or even for millenniums, during which Christianity shall be triumphant over all the earth."[43]

Its end. Postmillennialists believe that after the golden age, Christ will return personally, bodily, and visibly.[44] [The adherent of this view also believe in a general resurrection and judgment, followed by the eternal state.]

The Hermeneutics of Postmillennialism

In this section, we will analyze three key postmillennial hermeneutical concepts: the spiritual interpretation of prophecy, the claim that the church is the true or new Israel, and the fulfillment of the Davidic covenant at Christ's First Coming.

The Spiritual Interpretation of Prophecy

Postmillennialists feel free to interpret the Bible as they see fit. Boettner states, "We find no labels in the Scripture itself telling us, 'Take this literally,' or 'Take that figuratively.'" Therefore, Boettner urges, "The individual reader must use his own judgment, backed by as much experience and common sense as he can muster."[45] He goes on to assert that "since much of the Old and New Testament is written in figurative or symbolic language, the principle of figurative interpretation becomes valid." As an example, Boettner uses Malachi 4:5 to argue against the literal interpretation. It says, "Behold, I will send you Elijah the prophet / Before the coming of the great and dreadful day of the LORD." According to Boettner, literal interpretation is impossible in this passage "because Christ himself said that it was fulfilled in the person of John the Baptist (Matt. 11:14) who came in the Spirit of Elijah."[46] Boettner fails to apply the proper principles for interpreting figurative language. The words of the figures of speech are not interpreted literally, but the sense in the words of the figures provides the literal meaning. In this case, John is not Elijah, nor is he a spiritual Elijah. Donald A. Hagner notes, "What is meant here is not that John is actually Elijah *redivivus* (which is possibly what John denies according to John 1:21), but that he functions in the role that was ascribed to Elijah just preceding the end time."[47] One of Elijah's roles was to call Israel back to her faith. This is exactly what John the Baptist was doing. Isaiah 40:3–5 foretells the coming of John:

> The voice of one crying in the wilderness,
> "Prepare the way of the LORD;
> Make straight in the desert
> A highway for our God.
> Every valley shall be exalted
> And every mountain and hill brought low;
> The crooked places shall be made straight
> And the rough places smooth;
> The glory of the LORD shall be revealed,
> And all flesh shall see *it* together;
> For the mouth of the LORD has spoken."

Boettner notes that "the above verses were not certainly fulfilled by a highway-building program in Palestine but rather in the work of John the Baptist who prepared the way for the Lord."[48] He adds that the apostle "John himself said, 'For this is he who was spoken of by the prophet Isaiah when he said …,'" and proceeds to quote Matthew 3:1–3 and Luke 3:3–6.[49] Boettner then gives two more examples from the book of Exodus: Yahweh's statement to Moses, "You have seen what I did to the Egyptians, and *how* I bore you on eagles' wings and brought you to Myself" (Ex. 19:4), and his description of Canaan as "a land flowing with milk and honey" (Ex. 3:8). Boettner notes that these two passages use figurative language, which he interprets spiritually.[50]

Clearly, Boettner adheres to the spiritual interpretation of prophecy, as he himself admits: "To spiritualize certain prophecies or other statements does not mean that we explain them away. Sometimes their true meaning is to be found only in the unseen spiritual world."[51] He suggests two categories for interpretation. First, "the historical and more didactic portions should be interpreted literally. Second, other portions of Scripture should be understood in a figurative way."[52] As a result, one can determine whether prophecy is figurative or literal after it has been fulfilled. In summary, postmillennialists take a subjective approach to interpreting figures of speech, as Boettner states:

> Since the Bible gives no hard and fast rule for determining what is literal and what is figurative, we must study the nature of the material, the historical setting, the style and purpose of the writer and then fall back on what for lack of a better term we may call "sanctified common sense." Naturally the conclusions will vary somewhat from individual to individual for we do not all think alike nor see alike.[53]

Boettner says the following New Testament passages require a figurative or spiritual interpretation: "'Ye are the salt of the earth. Ye are the light of the world. Let your light so shine before men, that they may see your good works, and glorify your Father which is in heaven' (Matt. 5:13–16); Jesus' teaching to the disciples at the Lord's Super: 'This is my body … This is my blood' (Matt. 26:26); Paul's farewell speech to the elders of the church, 'I know that after my departure grievous wolves shall enter in among you, not sparing the flock' (Acts 20:29); and an exhortation from the apostle John, 'and they washed their robes, and made them white in the blood of the Lamb' (Rev. 7:14)."[54] The authors use figurative language in these passages, but Boettner spiritualizes them. Figurative language does not require that the interpreter spiritualize or seek a deeper meaning of the words. Jesus' reference to the disciples as the "salt of the earth" does not require a spiritual hermeneutic. While Boettner is right to take this phrase as a metaphor, and thus figuratively, he is mistaken when he interprets all figurative language as spiritual. When interpreting figures of speech, the words are taken figuratively but the sense of the words are interpreted literally. Tan notes, "Figures are interpreted, not from the literal words making up the figures but from the original, literal sense conveyed in the use of the figure."[55] Unlike commentators who focus on the characteristics of the real disciples, Boettner arrives at a spiritual meaning by focusing on the functions of the salt. But as a metaphor, salt refers directly to some qualities of the disciples. Hagner notes, "Thus, the disciples are vitally significant and necessary to the world in their witness to God and his kingdom."[56] Boettner's hermeneutic is not valid because it distorts the text's clear meaning.

In reference to the reign of Christ, Revelation 20:1–7 use the phrase "a thousand years" six times. Nevertheless, Boettner interprets this passage symbolically. He writes:

> The "thousand years" is quite clearly not to be understood as an exact measure of time but rather as a symbolical number. Strict arithmetic has no place here. The term is a figurative expression, indicating an indefinitely long period of time, a complete, perfect number of years, probably not less than a literal one thousand years, in all probability very much longer.[57]

By referring to the millennium as an indefinitely long period of time, Boettner discredits the literal interpretation, which takes reigning for a thousand years as a real eschatological event. Postmillennialists, however, interpret the reference to a thousand years in Revelation 20 as though it were an apocalyptic symbol because the book contains apocalyptic material.

The postmillennialist interpreter also spiritualizes New Testament prophecy because they claim the New Testament interprets Old Testament prophecies spiritually (Gal. 3:29; Rom. 2:28, 29; Phil. 3:3) and explains some scripture passages allegorically (Gal. 4:21–31). In conclusion, postmillennialists interpret many prophetic passages spiritually because "spiritual relationship is more important than, and takes precedence over, the physical."[58]

The Church as the New or True Israel

Postmillennial scholars equate the church with Israel. For example, Hodge highlights several features that show the similarities between Israel and the church as follows:

> (1) It is so called in Scripture. (Acts vii: 38.)
> (2) The Hebrews were called out from all the nations of the earth to be peculiar people of God. They constituted his kingdom. (3) To them were committed the oracles of God. They were Israelites; to them pertaineth the adoption, and the glory, and the covenants, and the giving of the law, and the service, and the promises. (Rom. ix. 4) Nothing more can be said of the Church under the new dispensation. They were selected for a church purpose, namely, to be witnesses for God in the world in behalf of the true religion; to celebrate his worship; and to observe his ordinances. ...

There is no authorized definition of the church, which does not include the people of God under the Mosaic law.[59]

Gentry also argues that the Scriptures apply old covenant terms to New covenant citizens. To support his arguments, he cites the following passages: "We are the 'seed of Abraham' (Rom 4:13–17; Gal. 3:6–9, 29),' 'the circumcision' (Ro 2:28–29; Php 3:3; Col 2:11), 'a royal priesthood,' (Ro 15:16; 1 Pe 2:9; Rev 1:6; 5:10; cf. Ex 19:6), 'twelve tribes' (Jas 1:1), '*diaspora*' (1 Pe. 1:1), the 'temple of God' (1 Co 3:16–17; 6:19; 2 Co 1:16; Eph. 2:21)."[60] From these passages, Gentry clearly states, "The New Testament applies these images to Christians."[61] Boettner likewise argues that Israel and the church are the same entity. He writes:

> In opposition to all this we shall undertake to prove that no earthly kingdom was offered to the Jews, that nothing in the Divine plan was postponed, and that the Christian Church is the fulfillment of that to which the Old Testament prophets, and indeed the entire Old Testament economy, looked forward.[62]

Boettner denies the offer of the earthly or Davidic kingdom; he denies the postponement theory and claims that the church fulfills Israel's promises. He goes on to write, "It may seem harsh to say that 'God is done with the Jews.' But the fact of the matter is that He is through with them as a unified national group having anything more to do with the evangelization of the world. That mission has been taken from them and given to the Christian church (Matt. 21:43)."[63]

The church took Israel's place after she was set aside. Boettner explains the logic behind the divine plan:

Old Testament Israel, as the congregation of God's people set aside from the Gentiles, was the forerunner of and developed into the Christian in which the earthly distinction between Jew and Gentiles disappears never to be re-instituted. To re-instate the old distinction between Jew and Gentiles after the New Testament era has dawned would be to reverse the forward march of the kingdom, and would be as illogical and useless as to go back to candle or lamp light after the sun has risen.[64]

The future restoration of Israel is a hotly debated issue among the three views. Hodge, for instance, argues against any hope for national Israel's future restoration because of the new relationship between Jews and Gentiles that Paul mentions in the book of Ephesians.[65] He states that

it is asserted over and over again that the middle wall of partition between Jews and Gentiles has broken down; that Gentile believers are fellow-citizens of the saints and members of the household of God; that they are built up together with the Jews into one temple (Eph. 2:11–22).[66]

According to Hodge, this distinction is based on the Scriptures themselves. He says that "all believers are one body in Christ, that all are partakers of the Holy Spirit." However, he concedes that some distinctions exist, "not in the virtue of national or social distinctions, but solely on individual character and devotion."[67]

Gentry further raises arguments against the distinction of the church and Israel. His first argument is also based on the Scriptures. He cites the following passages in which the apostle Paul indicates that distinctions are gone: "There is neither Jew nor

Greek ...; for you are all one in Christ Jesus" (Gal. 3:28). "There is neither Greek nor Jew, circumcised nor uncircumcised" (Col. 3:11). "For there is no distinction between Jew and Greek, for the same Lord over all is rich to all who call upon Him" (Rom. 10:12). Gentry concludes, "This principle of 'neither Jew nor Greek' explains why the Old Testament promises and prophecies can apply to Gentile Christians and the pan-ethnic new covenant Church."[68]

Gentry then argues that the church is indeed Israel. He affirms that "the new covenant Church is actually called Israel."[69] Gentry points out that Paul applies the term "Israel" to Christians in Galatians 6:16 when he writes, "And as many as walk according to this rule, peace and mercy *be* upon them, and upon the Israel of God." Gentry explains:

> Here, he is referring to Christians as "the Israel of God." The "and" preceding "the Israel of God," is *epexegetical*, which means that we should translate the verse "mercy upon them, that is, upon the Israel of God." Thus according to Paul "as many as walk according to this rule [Christian faith]" are the "Israel of God."[70]

The passage in Galatians 6:16 has always been a point of contention among evangelicals. I will provide a detailed response to this passage in the evaluation.

The Spiritual Fulfillment of the Davidic Kingdom at Christ's First Coming

The hermeneutical approach a person chooses determines their interpretation of any biblical text, especially if it is prophecy. Postmillennialists apply a spiritual hermeneutic for certain prophetic passages, which results in the belief that Old Testament prophecies regarding Israel and the Davidic covenant were fulfilled during Christ's First Coming. The church fulfilled other Old Testament prophecies regarding Israel as well.

Mathison insists that "Jesus inaugurated the Messianic Kingdom which is presently fulfilled through the Church."[71] Jesus established this kingdom at his First Coming, and so it does not need a Second Coming to be fulfilled, because the messianic kingdom is being fulfilled in the hearts of individual believers now. Postmillennialists also "teach that the Church has been appointed to fulfill Israel's covenantal promises."[72] Mathison asserts that "the Church is actually Israel, or a continuation of Israel, and in that case, the Church qualifies to fulfill Israel's prophecies."[73] Gentry writes, "Paul says we are grafted into Israel (Ro 11: 16–19) so that we become one with her, partaking of her promises (Eph. 2:11–20)."[74] Because the church and Israel are equal, and the church has replaced Israel, the church qualifies to fulfill Israel's promises. Several passages in the New Testament illustrate this postmillennialist view. First, by comparing Acts 15:15–17 with Amos 9:11–12, Gentry states, "God is rebuilding David's tabernacle through the calling of the Gentiles in the Church."[75] Second, Gentry notes that in Romans 15:8–12 the conversion of the Gentiles is one of Jesus Christ's ways in which he ensures the "confirming of the promises to the fathers."[76] Third, Gentry explains Paul's intent in Acts 26:6–7 as follows, "The preaching of the gospel touches on the very hope of the Jews, which was made to the fathers."[77] Fourth, Gentry cites Psalm 2, claiming that it "begins its fulfillment in the resurrection of Christ—not at the Second Advent (Acts 13:32–33)."[78]

Postmillennialism and the Davidic Covenant

We turn now to a discussion of the postmillennial view of the Davidic covenant. In chapter 1 we saw that the three primary promises God made to David were that his house (dynasty), throne (right to rule), and kingdom would last forever (2 Sam.

7:12–16, esp. v. 16; cf. Pss. 21, 72, 89, 110, 132). The Davidic covenant is found in 2 Samuel. 7:12–16 and in a parallel passage: 1 Chronicles 17. It is reiterated in Psalms 89, 110, and 132. The original statement is as follows:

> When your days are fulfilled and you rest with your fathers, I will set up your seed after you, who will come from your body, and I will establish his kingdom. He shall build a house for My name, and I will establish the throne of his kingdom forever. I will be his Father, and he shall be My son. If he commits iniquity, I will chasten him with the rod of men and with the blows of the sons of men. But My mercy shall not depart from him, as I took *it* from Saul, whom I removed from before you. And your house and your kingdom shall be established forever before you. Your throne shall be established forever. (2 Sam. 7:12–16)

First, we will look at postmillennialism's view of the structure of the covenant, and then we will examine their view of its fulfillment.

The Structure of the Davidic Covenant

Mathison provides a detailed structure of the Davidic covenant and maintains that "a key event in redemptive history is recorded in 2 Samuel 7. … The chapter records the events surrounding the establishment of the Davidic covenant"[79] because it "becomes the foundation for the messianic prophesies of the later prophets."[80] He then compares three major biblical covenants and concludes that "the Abrahamic covenant had promised a realm and a people for God's kingdom. The Mosaic covenant provided the law of the kingdom. The Davidic covenant now provides a human king for the kingdom."[81] As previously stated, the Davidic covenant demonstrated an element of perpetuity. In addition to this, Mathison notes that David wanted to build a permanent temple for the Lord, yet God promised to build a permanent dynasty (a house) for him.[82] The repetition of the word "forever" (עַד־עוֹלָם) eight times indicates its perpetuity. This repetition is a significant aspect of the Davidic covenant because it shows that stability is the main feature of the Davidic covenant.

The Fulfillment of the Davidic Covenant

A majority of evangelicals agree that Jesus fulfills the promise of the descendant of the "house" of David. The other two promises ("throne" and "kingdom") are still points of contention among evangelicals. This section will specifically address the postmillennialists view on the fulfillment of the throne and kingdom of David in the New Testament.

Christ established the messianic kingdom at his First Coming. Postmillennialists believe that Christ established the messianic kingdom during his First Coming. Boettner writes, "When Christ comes again, it will not be to reign in a millennial kingdom, He is now reigning in his mediatorial kingdom."[83] The kingdom is here now; it is not a future cataclysmic event. Postmillennialists claim that the New Testament teaches this. They present the following passages to prove that the messianic kingdom is a current reality:

1) Mark 1: 14–15. This passage says that "after John was put in prison, Jesus came to Galilee, preaching the gospel of the kingdom of God, and saying, 'The time is fulfilled, and the kingdom of God is at hand. Repent, and believe in the gospel.'" Gentry notes three factors from this passage. First, he points out that "the time has arrived." He says that in this passage the word "time" refers to "the prophetically anticipated time, the time of the coming of David's greater Son to establish his kingdom."[84] In other words, the messianic kingdom was established at Jesus' First Coming.

The second factor is that "the time is fulfilled."[85] According to Gentry, the fulfillment of time refers to "God-ordained time."[86] Third, "the kingdom of God is at hand."[87] Gentry says that the phrase, "at hand," means that "the kingdom of God is finally right at hand."[88] Gentry's point is that Jesus' First Coming was God's appointed time to establish the messianic kingdom.

2) Matthew 12:28. Jesus says, "But if I cast out demons by the Spirit of God, surely the kingdom of God has come upon you." According to Gentry, the act of casting out the devil was accomplished by Christ in his First Coming. Gentry claims this act "proves that the [messianic] kingdom came during Jesus' earthly ministry."[89] Postmillennialists maintain that Jesus defeated the devil during his First Coming.

3) Luke 17:20–21. Quoting this passage in block format in order to compare it with the Greek text is important for understanding Gentry's argument.

> Now when He was asked by the Pharisees when the kingdom of God would come, He answered them and said, "The kingdom of God does not come with observation; nor will they say, 'See here!' or 'See there!' For indeed, the kingdom of God is within you." (Luke 17:20–21)

The Greek text reads:

> Ἐπερωτηθεὶς δὲ ὑπὸ των φαρισαιων ποτε ἔρχεται ἡ βασιλεια του θεου μετὰ παρατηρησεως, οὐδὲ ἐρουσιν ἰδοὺ ὧδε ἡ Ἐκει ἰδοὺ γὰρ ἡ βασιλεια του θεου εντὸς ὑμων ἐστιν.

Gentry holds that Jesus' response to the Pharisees with present tense verbs "indicates that the kingdom is being established. The present tense verbs ἔρχεται and ἐστιν imply that the kingdom is in operation now, rather than being a future event. Thus Gentry asserts that "the kingdom exists spiritually now and among them."[90]

4) John 18:36–37a. In the conversation between Jesus and Pilate, "Jesus answered, 'My kingdom is not of this world. ...' Pilate therefore said to Him, 'Are You a king then?' Jesus answered, 'You say *rightly* that I am a king. For this cause I was born, and for this cause I have come into the world, that I should bear witness to the truth.'" (Cf. Matt. 27:11; Mark 15:2; Luke 23:3.) From this passage Gentry observes that "Jesus' kingdom is not of this world like the political kingdom of Pilate. Jesus' kingdom exists now, 'My kingdom' (John 18:36a)."[91] Gentry further concludes that "because of Jesus' claim to be king ('I am a king,' 18:37a), it establishes His purpose of coming into the world: to be a king (John 18:37b)."[92]

Christ is now reigning over the messianic kingdom. Postmillennialists also hold that Jesus is now the king of an established messianic kingdom because God promised in the Davidic covenant that a future descendant of David will be appointed king forever (2 Sam. 7:13, 16). This king was to rule from the throne of David. Evangelicals agree that Jesus is the promised king, but they disagree as to when he is or will be king. Postmillennialists maintain that Jesus is currently ruling in his kingdom with full authority because his claim to kingship fulfills his role as the king. They cite certain passages in support of their position.

1) Psalm 2:2. Gentry quotes this verse as follows and then comments on it: "'The kings of the earth set themselves, and the rulers take counsel together, against the LORD and against his anointed.' The Psalmist writes that the entire world is in opposition to God's authority and His Anointed One (מְשִׁיחוֹ)." In this case, the nations oppose the sovereign rule of God. He says verse 4 indicates that this opposition is "futile because the LORD is enthroned in heaven." Gentry rightly observes that the term,

"anointed one" (מָשִׁיחַ), "designates the great Deliverer and King, whom the Jews long expected (see John 1:20, 24–25, 41, 49). He is our Lord and Savior, Jesus Christ (Mark 8:29–30; 14:61–62)." The believers quote Psalms 2:2 in reference to the crucifixion (Acts 4:25–27). Psalm 2:6–7 state,

"Yet I have set My King
On My holy hill of Zion."

"I will declare the decree:
The LORD has said to Me,
'You *are* My Son,
Today I have begotten You.'"

In reference to verse 6, Gentry notes, "God does not speak of this installed one as 'a king' or 'the king' but as 'My King.'"[93] He continues: "Zion/Jerusalem transcends Old Testament realities, reaching heaven itself (Gal. 4:25–26); Heb. 12:21; Rev. 14:1). Thus, the center of the theocratic rule has been transferred to heaven, where Christ presently rules over his kingdom (John 18:36; Rev. 1:5)." Verse 7 is closely associated with the Davidic covenant, as Gentry points out. "The 'decree' is a pledge of adoption by God, a holy coronation rite establishing this king's legitimacy (see 2 Sam. 7:13–14; Ps. 89:26–27)."[94] According to Gentry, the phrase "this day" (or "today") means that the title of king is actually in effect. He writes:

> Rather than occurring at Second Advent, as many
> assume, the New Testament relates it once again
> to the first century—at the exaltation of Christ,
> the beginning with his resurrection. "[God] has
> fulfilled this for us, their children, by raising up
> Jesus. As it is written in the second Psalm: 'You
> are My Son, today I have become your Father'"

(Acts 13:33; cf. Rom. 1:4). Since the resurrection/ ascension Christ has been installed as the king (Rom. 1:4), ruling from God's right hand (Rom. 14:9–11; Eph. 1:20; Col. 1:18; 1 Pet. 3:22; Rev. 17:14; 19:16).[95]

2) Psalm 110:1–2. John Jefferson Davis views Psalm 110:1–2 as being messianic. The passage reads:

The LORD said to my Lord,
"Sit at My right hand,
Till I make Your enemies Your footstool."
The LORD shall send the rod of Your strength out of Zion.
Rule in the midst of Your enemies!

According to Davis, this Psalm was fulfilled in the resurrection and ascension of Jesus Christ. The New Testament confirms that it was fulfilled during this time (Acts 2:30–31, 33). Regarding Acts 3:34, Davis notes, "Peter specifically quotes Psalm 110:1 in relation to the resurrection and exaltation of Jesus as Lord and Messiah."[96] He says that Jesus now sits at the right hand of God. Edmund Kalt explains what this means, "Sitting at the right hand of God is a description taken from the judicial custom of the East and meant not only the highest honor thinkable but also unlimited participation in the world dominion of God. This heavenly act of solemn transfer introduces a new era in world history, the era of the kingdom of Christ over the whole world."[97] Davis takes this to mean that the right hand of God is "a location where Christ exercises his dominion," that is, the place from which Christ reigns in heaven. Davis cites passages to support this argument (Acts 2:33, 34; 5:31; 7:55–56; Rom. 8:34; Eph. 1:20; Col. 3:1; Heb. 1:3; 10:12; 1 Peter 3:22). He denies the notion that this throne represents a physical reign on earth. Concerning the time when Christ will subdue his enemies, Davis responds, "According to Psalm 110:1, Christ does not need to be physically present on earth to subdue his spiritual foes; this he does while still at the Father's right hand in heaven, Christ already has all power in heaven."[98]

Gregg Strawbridge bases his argument on 1 Corinthians 15:24–26, especially vv. 24–25,[99] which read:

> Then *comes* the end, when He delivers the kingdom to God the Father, when He puts an end to all rule and all authority and power. For He must reign till He has put all enemies under His feet. The last enemy *that* will be destroyed *is* death.

The Greek text reads as follows:

> εἶτα τὸ τέλος, ὅταν παραδιδῷ τὴν βασιλείαν τῷ θεῷ καὶ πατρί, ὅταν καταργήσῃ πᾶσαν ἀρχὴν καὶ πᾶσαν ἐξουσίαν καὶ δύναμιν. δεῖ γὰρ αὐτὸν βασιλεύειν ἄχρι οὗ θῇ πάντας τοὺς ἐχθροὺς ὑπὸ τοὺς πόδας αὐτοῦ. ἔσχατος ἐχθρὸς καταργεῖται ὁ θάνατος·

The context of this passage is the origin of death ("for as in Adam all die, even so in Christ all shall be made alive" [v. 22]). Strawbridge notes that the meaning of the word τελος (v. 24) is explained by two ὅταν clauses: the τελος in the first clause is "contemporaneous: the end is precisely when Christ delivers the kingdom." He claims this τελος implies "the kingdom is therefore a reality prior to the 'end.'" The τελος in the next clause refers to the abolition of all authority having already become a reality, so he maintains that this τελος "follows Christ's reign and thus the consummation of the kingdom, since the subjection of his enemies has previously taken place."[100]

First Corinthians 15:25 alludes to Psalm 110:1b: "Sit at My right hand, / Till I make Your enemies Your footstool." Strawbridge states, "Paul uses the word 'reign' in place of 'sit at My right hand' and portrays Christ as active in the role of subduing His enemies. Conceptually, 1 Corinthians 15:25 is identical to Psalm 110:1: the Lord is ruling until all enemies are subdued." He goes on to say that "βασιλεύειν is a present tense infinitive, indicating that the reign is a present reality to Paul." According to Strawbridge, verse 26 provides the clue as to when Christ's reign began. He writes, "We are told what the last enemy is—death (15:26) and we are told when death is 'swallowed up in victory' (15:54)—at the resurrection."[101] So, according to 1 Corinthians 15:24–26, Christ is reigning now. After Christ subdues his enemies completely, he will deliver the kingdom to the Father. This reign officially started after his resurrection when he conquered death.

3) Isaiah 9:6–7. According to postmillennialists, this passage indicates that Christ is king and is reigning from the throne of David. Isaiah writes,

> For unto us a Child is born,
> Unto us a Son is given;
> And the government will be upon His shoulder.
> And His name will be called Wonderful, Counselor, Mighty God,
> Everlasting Father, Prince of Peace.
> Of the increase of *His* government and peace
> *There will be* no end,
> Upon the throne of David and over His kingdom,
> To order it and establish it with judgment and justice
> From that time forward, even forever.
> The zeal of the LORD of hosts will perform this.

Gentry argues from this passage that "Christ was born to rule (cf. John 18:37; Luke 1:31–33),"[102] and rightly notes that "Isaiah 9:6–7 speaks of the Messianic Kingdom, the throne of David (Isa. 9:7b)."[103]

4) Acts 2:30–36. Citing this passage, Mathison explains what it means for Christ to be seated at the right hand of God: "The important point of our study is that the inauguration of the Messianic Kingdom does not await the future return of Christ. Jesus has already been seated at the right hand of God on the throne of David, and in fulfillment of Psalm 110, He will remain there until all of His enemies are made a footstool for His feet."[104]

5) Matthew 28:18. Postmillennialists maintain that the Great Commission indicates Christ's enthronement. Gentry observes that "Christ prefixes the actual commission with a bold—and necessary—claim: 'All authority in heaven and earth has been given to me.' This prefatory declaration dramatically contrasts with his previous humility: "I can do nothing of myself.""[105] In reference to the word "given," Gentry notes, "'Given' appears in the emphatic first position; its verb form *edothe* is in the aorist indicative, signifying point action in past time. Obviously the point when this occurs is at the resurrection."[106]

In conclusion, postmillennialists hold that Jesus has established the messianic kingdom. The Davidic throne has been transferred to heaven, and Jesus rules now sits on it, ruling with authority from heaven.

An Evaluation of the Postmillennialist Approach

In our evaluation of postmillennialism, we will focus on three issues: their spiritual hermeneutics, the church as the true or new Israel, and the spiritual fulfillment of the Davidic covenant at Christ's First Coming. The criteria for evaluating these three areas will be the *CSBH* and the grammatical-historical method.

The Spiritual Interpretation of Prophecy

Postmillennialists claim that many of the prophetic portions of the Scriptures should be interpreted spiritually. They also claim that biblical truth is hidden in the unknown spiritual world, and pride themselves in the view of their forerunners, such as Augustine and Origen. These ancient scholars championed the spiritual hermeneutics in their generation. While advocating for either a spiritual or a figurative hermeneutic, Boettner points out that the metaphors "salt of the earth" and "light of the world" in the beatitudes (Matt. 5:13–16) could be interpreted spiritually.[107] Matthew 5:13 states, "You are the salt of the earth" (ὑμεῖς ἐστε τὸ ἅλας τῆς γῆς). This phrase can be read literally as follows, "You, you are the salt of the earth." The pronoun "you" (ὑμεῖς) is first in the sentence, thus bearing strong emphasis and having the force of "you, you alone—you only and no one else."[108] The article on the predicate, τὸ ἅλας, makes it emphatic.[109] In this case, the subject and the predicate are identical. But who are the emphatic "you"? The immediate context points to the apostles and disciples of Christ listening to Him. Therefore, the metaphor of salt literally refers to the apostles, disciples, and all true believers.

The second person plural verb, "you are" (ἐστε), emphasizes the reality. The disciples or believers *are* the salt of the earth. It also denotes the continuing experience of those who are the salt. The believers are the salt and they continue to be salt. Boettner appears to hold to the misconception that figurative language only conveys a spiritual truth.[110] This view is invalid and unbiblical, as Zuck notes: "Figurative speech ... is a picturesque, out-of-the-ordinary way of presenting literal facts that might be otherwise be stated in a normal, plain, ordinary way."[111] Radmacher confirms Zuck's point, "Behind every figure of speech is a literal meaning, and by means of the historical-grammatical exegesis of the text, these literal meanings are to be sought out."[112] Zuck then concludes:

Figurative language then is not antithetical to literal interpretation; it is a part of it. Perhaps it is better not to speak of "figurative versus literal" interpretation, but of "ordinary-literal" versus "figurative-literal" interpretation. Therefore ... *figurative* means figurative-literal, and *literal* means ordinary-literal. ... Both are legitimate means of communicating literal truths—truths to be interpreted in their normal, historical, grammatical sense without making them say something not intended by the words.[113]

Jesus' use of figures of speech does not justify giving them a spiritual interpretation. It follows then that Jesus' use of the metaphor, "salt of the earth" (Matt. 5:13), conveys a literal meaning. Moreover, interpreting Malachi 4:5 about John the Baptist preparing the way for the Lord as spiritual rather than literal is unwarranted. The phrase, "prepare the way of the LORD" (Luke 3:3–4; Matt. 3:1–3), literally means to create a favorable environment for the one who is coming (i.e., Christ) to you (i.e., Israel) so he can operate in your life. In other words, John the Baptist prepared the way for Christ by preaching the baptism of repentance for the remission of sins. The words in the phrase have a figurative sense, but he completed his task literally. Therefore, Boettner's demand for a literal highway is unjustified. Boettner also claims that John the Baptist is Elijah in a spiritual sense, but the prophet Malachi writes:

> Behold, I will send you Elijah the prophet
> Before the coming of the great and dreadful day
> of the LORD.
> And he will turn
> The hearts of the fathers to the children,
> And the hearts of the children to their fathers,

Lest I come and strike the earth with a curse. (Malachi 4:5–6)

This Scripture clearly indicates that Elijah's role was that of calling Israel back to her faith. He was the first prophet to confront kings of both Israel and Judah and warn them of the consequences of leading Israel away from Yahweh. It may then be implied that Elijah's past career paves the way for his future ministry. In that case, John the Baptist, though he resembles Elijah in his role, is not a spiritual Elijah. Malachi clearly predicts that Elijah will come to the nation of Israel during the tribulation (Mal. 4:5), referred to here as "the great and dreadful day of the LORD." During the earthly life of Jesus, Elijah was joined by Moses at the transfiguration of Christ (Matt. 17:3). It is commonly held that Elijah and Moses are the two witnesses in the book of Revelation 11:3, as Thomas Ice notes:

> Malachi 4:5–6 foretells of an important role that Elijah will play in relation to the nation of Israel. Such language teaches that Elijah will play a future role during the tribulation in the conversion of the nation of Israel, before the second coming of Christ. Since Malachi's prophecy makes it clear that Elijah will play a role in end-time events, it is almost certain that this return of Elijah during the tribulation will be as one of the two witnesses spoken of in Revelation 11:3.[114]

This passage proves two things. First, that John the Baptist was not Elijah. Second, that John the Baptist does not fulfill the ministry of Elijah. In relation to this, Ice writes again:

> There are some who teach that the ministry of John the Baptist was a fulfillment of the prediction of

the coming of Elijah from Malachi 4:5 at Christ's first coming. This is not the case. John the Baptist fulfilled a different prediction, that of Malachi 3:1 and Isaiah 40:3–5. Yet, John the Baptist was said to be a forerunner, who would come in the spirit and power of Elijah (Lk. 1:17). ... In fact, when John the Baptist was asked directly, Are you Elijah? He clearly said, I am not (John 1:21). Thus, because of Israel's rejection, John the Baptist was John the Baptist (My messenger) and not Elijah. So Elijah is still to come.[115]

This approach also is inconsistent with Article XV of the *CSBH*, which states:

WE AFFIRM the necessity of interpreting the Bible according to its literal, or normal, sense. The literal sense is the grammatical-historical sense, that is, the meaning which the writer expressed. Interpretation according to the literal sense will take account of all figures of speech and literary forms found in the text.

WE DENY the legitimacy of any approach to Scripture that attributes to it meaning which the literal sense does not support.[116]

Postmillennialism practices an inconsistent hermeneutic. The advocates of this viewpoint might interpret the text literally, figuratively, or spiritually. Boettner writes:

It is admittedly difficult in many instances to determine whether statements in Scripture should be taken literally or figuratively. As regards prophecy, that often cannot be determined until after the fulfillment. Most of the Bible, however, particularly the historical and the more didactic portion, clearly is to be understood literally, although some figurative expressions are found in these. But that many other portions must be understood figuratively is also clearly evident.[117]

These variations are certain to produce an altered meaning for some passages. Lack of consistency in interpreting the Scriptures does not harmonize with Article XVII of the *CSBH*, which states, "WE AFFIRM the unity, harmony and consistency of Scripture and declare that it is its own best interpreter."[118]

Postmillennialists such as Boettner rely on the individual interpreter's skill and experience to arrive at their conclusions. This approach is subjective because it depends on human wisdom. Moreover, this principle does not recognize the principle of context. The context (commonly referred to as "Scripture interprets Scripture" or *Sola Scriptura*) grants authority to the Bible, thus, letting the Bible speak for itself. Instead, postmillennialists allow an individual interpreter to supersede the authority of the Scriptures, making them prone to conjecture. Boettner writes:

> Since the Bible gives no hard and fast rule determining what is literal and what is figurative, we must study the materials, the historical setting and style and purpose of the writer, and then fall back on what for lack of a better name we may call "sanctified common sense." If principles of interpretation are strictly followed, then any form of common sense will have no part. Naturally, the conclusions will vary somewhat from individual

to individual, for we do not all think alike nor see alike.[119]

The postmillennialists' approach violates Articles VI, VII, and XIX of the *CSBH*. Article VI states:

WE AFFIRM that the Bible expresses God's truth in propositional statements, and we declare that biblical truth is both objective and absolute. We further affirm that a statement is true if it represents matters as they actually are, but is an error if it misrepresents the facts.

WE DENY that, while Scripture is able to make us wise unto salvation, biblical truth should be defined in terms of this function. We further deny that error should be defined as that which willfully deceives.[120]

Article VII reads:

WE AFFIRM that the meaning expressed in each biblical text is single, definite and fixed.

WE DENY that the recognition of this single meaning eliminates the variety of its application.[121]

Article XIX states:

WE AFFIRM that any preunderstandings which the interpreter brings to Scripture should be in harmony with scriptural meaning and subject to correction by it.

WE DENY that Scripture should be required to fit alien preunderstandings, inconsistent with itself, such as naturalism, evolutionism, scientism, secular humanism, and relativism.[122]

The Church as the New or True Israel

As proof that Israel can be equated with the church, Hodge notes that certain terminology describing Israel also applies to the church. For example, Israel was a "peculiar people and to them belong a kingdom, the adoption, the glory, the covenants, the laws, and the service (Rom. 9:1–4)."[123] Similarly, Hodge notes, "The Church as a witness for God in the world, celebrates God's worship and ordinances."[124] In regard to the church being entitled to Israel's prophetic promises, Gentry argues, "The Church fulfills the prophecies which belong to national Israel."[125] But the view that the church spiritually fulfills Old Testament prophecies belonging to Israel lacks biblical support. Citing Galatians 3:29, Boettner notes, "Believing Gentiles are also the seed of Abraham."[126]

This argument fails because nowhere in the Scriptures are Gentiles referred to as "seed." Such a relationship is only attained through their position in Christ, not as children descended from Abraham. Ryken writes, "But Paul explains in Galatians that the true seed to which Abraham's family leads us is Jesus Christ (Gal. 3:15, 19). … Believers receive Abraham's family name and enter his line on their own through faith in Christ."[127] Therefore, it is illogical to overlook the Scriptures' clearly stated distinctions between Israel and Gentiles. Salvific unity does not nullify distinctions between these two institutions. It follows then that postmillennialists who use this argument are inconsistent with the Scriptures. Paul makes it clear in Romans that God has not revoked His promises to Israel by stating, "I say then, has God cast away His people? Certainly not! For I also am an Israelite, of the seed of Abraham, *of* the tribe of Benjamin. God has not cast away His people whom He foreknew" (Rom. 11:1–2a). Neither sin nor any form of infidelity could abrogate God's promises to Israel. This view therefore is not in harmony with Article XVIII of the *CSBH*, which states:

> WE AFFIRM that the Bible's own interpretation of itself is always correct, never deviating from, but rather elucidating, the single meaning of the inspired text. The single meaning of a prophet's words includes, but is not restricted to, the understanding of those words by the prophet and necessarily involves the intention of God evidenced in the fulfillment of those words.
>
> WE DENY that the writers of Scripture always understood the full implications of their own words.[128]

Postmillennialists—Gentry, Mathison, and Hodge in particular—insist that the phrase "Israel of God" (Gal. 6:16) refers to the church.[129] But they are committing an exegetical fallacy. Timothy George correctly identifies the referent of the phrase "Israel of God" when he notes that

> even though the grammatical structure is not clear, Paul is giving the particle **καὶ** its full connection sense ("and" or "also") rather than translating it as an intensive link ("even") with the preceding phrase. ... This could therefore be translated as: "May God give peace to all who will walk according to this criterion, and mercy also to his faithful people Israel."[130]

Therefore, postmillennialists should reconsider their exegesis of this passage. Their conclusion disregards the context of the Galatians, which upholds the view that Paul is referring to national Israel.

Gentry argues that the church existed in the Old Testament by interpreting Isaiah 2:2–4, especially the phrases "the mountain of the LORD's house" (הַר־בֵּית־יְהוָה [v. 2]) and "to the house of the God of Jacob" (אֶל־בֵּית אֱלֹהֵי יַעֲקֹב [v. 3]) as a reference to the church. However, rather than using הֵיכָל or קָהָל, which would be closer equivalents to the term "church," Isaiah uses the Hebrew word בֵּית. In this case, "house" and "Zion," when taken literally, have no reference to קָהָל at all. Therefore, equating "house" with "Zion" does not fit the context.

In summary, the church and Israel have some similarities. For instance, the church enjoys blessings that are similar to those promised to Israel. However, their distinctions remain. The terms that Gentry and Hodge claim refer to both the church and Israel are invalid analogies. When one reads the context, they will find that terms such as "a chosen generation," "a holy nation," and "His own special people" apply to Israel (1 Pet. 2:9). Finally, Peter addressed his first letter to the Jews in the diaspora. It is therefore appropriate for him to apply to Jewish Christians terms similar to the terms Paul uses in Romans 9:1–4 (e.g., "the adoption," "the glory," the covenants," "the laws," and "the service of God").

The Spiritual Fulfillment of the Davidic Kingdom at Christ's First Coming

Postmillennialists maintain that Christ spiritually fulfilled the promises of the Davidic covenant at his First Coming. They hold that Jesus' teaching indicates that he fulfilled the kingdom promises God made to David. For example, he says that "the kingdom is near" (Mark 1:15). Later on, the disciples fervently preached that the promises concerning the kingdom were fulfilled. In this section, I will respond to other passages postmillennialists claim teach that the Davidic kingdom and throne are a present reality.

1) Psalm 2:7. Postmillennialists hold that, according to Psalm 2 and its parallels in Acts, Christ is presently king. Christ received this honor at the resurrection-ascension event. He now sits at the right hand of God, a place of power, exercising this authority over the church, that is, the kingdom. The word "today" in Psalm 2:7 does not imply that Jesus is presently ruling, as Gentry argues.[131] Instead, it indicates that, since God is the Father of the Davidic king, "the relationship is confirmed at the moment of the coronation: 'Today I have become your Father.'"[132]

2) Daniel 2:44. Boettner interprets this verse to refer to the spiritual kingdom that Jesus set up during his First Coming. The context does not support this interpretation. The view that "the stone … cut out of the mountain without hands" refers to a spiritual kingdom that Jesus established while he was on earth is unfounded. Mathison claims that "the stone mentioned in Daniel 2:44 represents the Messianic Kingdom which Christ set up when He came.[133] He lists the following characteristics of this messianic kingdom: (a) it "was established during the Roman Empire"; (b) "it is a Kingdom that will never be destroyed"; (c) "it is destined to overcome all opposing kingdoms"; and (d) "the growth of the kingdom is gradual."[134] His arguments are unconvincing because an earthly kingdom was not established by Christ at his First Coming. When we examine the verse, we see that the kingdom is of divine origin ("the God of heaven will set up a kingdom" [v. 44]). We also find out that its origin is supernatural ("the stone was cut out of the mountain without hands"). The kingdom's coming is sudden and cataclysmic (vv. 34–35). It destroys earthly kingdoms and will become a kingdom that will fill the entire earth (vv. 34–5, 37–44). I must contend, therefore, that the kingdom spoken in this passage refers to an earthly reign of Christ that will be instituted at his Second Coming. The postmillennialists' claim that "the kingdom in Daniel is Christ's invisible, spiritual reign in

the hearts of believers established at his First Advent and evident in the Church"[135] is, therefore, both unbiblical and illogical.

3) Matthew 28:18. On the basis of this verse, postmillennialists claim that Christ was granted more authority after the resurrection than what he had before, but did not experience any change of state or authority on the day of Pentecost. This Scripture indicates that Jesus had already risen from the dead with a glorified body fifty days before Pentecost. Referring to the word "given" (ἐδόθη) in Matthew 28:18, Toussaint writes, "The aorist form of the verb "to give" (ἐδόθη) notes this as already given to Him."[136] Alfred Plumber also shares similar a thought. He writes, "Not merely power or might (δυναμις), such as a great conqueror might claim, but "authority" (ἐξουσία), as something which is His by right, conferred upon Him by One who has the right to bestow it (Rev. 2:27)."[137] In conclusion, postmillennialist's claim that Jesus received all authority after the resurrection is invalid.

4) Luke 17:20–21. Gentry refers to this passage in his claim that "the kingdom is spiritually fulfilled in the hearts of individuals. The noun παρατηρήσεως and preposition ἐντῶν [sic] are hapax legomena (Luke 6:7; 14:1; 20:20; and Acts 9:24)." However, John T. Carroll notes that in each occurrence of παρατηρέω, "the verb connotes a malicious watching directed at Jesus (or Paul)."[138] Therefore, μετὰ παρατηρήσεως in Luke 17:20 means "with malicious observation."[139] Jesus refuses to give signs to the Pharisees and anyone who rejects him and the signs that he performs,[140] so he responds negatively to the question of when the kingdom of God will come. He says, "The kingdom of God does not come with παρατηρήσεως." Therefore, the coming of the kingdom is an act directed by God himself. Jesus' response does not concur with a postmillennialist's view of a present spiritual kingdom. Instead, it implies that the kingdom will take place somewhere in the unpredictable future, as Carroll notes, "Luke

17:20 rejects all endeavors to forecast the advent of the kingdom of God by sign-watching."[141]

For the sake of argument, Luke 17:21 could be rendered as follows: "For look, the kingdom of God is ἐντὸς ὑμῶν." This verse is difficult to interpret because the preposition ἐντός occurs only here and in Matthew 23:26. It means "within you, in your hearts or among you, in your midst."[142] If ἐντός means "within your hearts," then the postmillennialist's concept of the kingdom being in the heart of the saints is correct. But the context does not allow this interpretation. Carroll notes that the meaning "inside you" is incorrect for two reasons. "First, nowhere else in Luke-Acts is the kingdom of God described as an inward, spiritual reality. Second, the object of the preposition (the Pharisees) is incompatible with that reading, for Luke has portrayed them in an increasingly negative light."[143] The Pharisees were unbelievers, and it was inconceivable for the kingdom to come in their hearts. Therefore, "the context, the contour of Luke's view of the kingdom, and the presence of a plural object of the preposition combine to dictate the translation 'among you' or 'in your midst.'"[144] In summary, the postmillennialists' view of a present, spiritual kingdom, or of a kingdom within the heart of believers, is unacceptable.

5) Acts 2:25–34 (cf. Pss. 16:8–11; 110:1). Gentry argues from this passage that Christ spiritually fulfilled the Old Testament prophecy in the apostolic period. He states that "Peter interprets the Davidic Kingdom prophecies in general (Acts 2:30) and Psalms 16:8–11 (Acts 2:25–28) and 110:1 (Acts 2:34–35) specifically as being fulfilled in Christ's ascension and session."[145] He also says that "God has fulfilled this for us their children, in that he has raised up Jesus. As it is also written in the second Psalm: 'You are My Son, today I have begotten You'" (Acts 13:32–34).[146] The promise was that Jesus would be raised from the dead as indicated in the Davidic covenant (2 Sam. 7:12). Gentry writes that this resurrection implies that Jesus is now Lord sitting on the throne: "Christ's resurrection fulfills David's promise to Israel."[147]

However, Gentry ignores the book context of this passage. In Acts 1:6, Jesus informed His disciples that the literal Davidic kingdom will be restored in the future, so when Gentry asserts that the kingdom is fulfilled, he is resorting to a spiritual hermeneutic and violating Article XV of the *CSBH*, which states:

> WE AFFIRM the necessity of interpreting the Bible according to its literal, or normal, sense. The literal sense is the grammatical-historical sense, that is, the meaning which the writer expressed. Interpretation according to the literal sense will take account of all figures of speech and literary forms found in the text.
>
> WE DENY the legitimacy of any approach to Scripture that attributes to it meaning which the literal sense does not support.[148]

6) Acts 2:29–35 (cf. Isa. 9:6–7). Gentry argues that Isaiah 9:6–7 indicates that the Davidic throne is fulfilled in the book of Acts. He writes, "In Acts 2:29–35 Peter preaches at Pentecost that Christ is the ultimate fulfillment of the Davidic promise and that he has ascended to the right hand of God, far above even David himself (vv. 33–34)."[149] Acts 2 is not a fulfillment of Isaiah 9:6–7, so Jesus sitting on the Davidic throne is not fulfilled in the book of Acts. The Davidic throne was earthly, not heavenly; it will be physical, not spiritual (Rev. 20:2–6). Therefore, Christ will reign on David's throne when he comes in the future to establish the messianic kingdom.

7) Acts 15:15–18. This passage relates to the Davidic covenant. James quotes part of Amos 9:11–12, and then adds a paraphrase from either Isaiah (cf. Isa. 45:21; 46:10) or Daniel (cf. Dan. 2:22, 28):

And with this the words of the prophets agree, just as it is written:

> "After this I will return
> And will rebuild the tabernacle of David, which has fallen down;
> I will rebuild its ruins,
> And I will set it up;
> So that the rest of mankind may seek the LORD,
> Even all the Gentiles who are called by My name,
> Says the LORD who does all these things."

Known to God from eternity are all His works. (Acts 15:15–18) Gentry interprets this passage to mean that God is now calling the Gentiles to fulfill the promises of national Israel.[150] Since postmillennialists teach that the New Testament church is the New Israel, the church is fulfilling the Old Testament prophecies concerning the kingdom. Gentry's interpretation overlooks the literal element in the passage. As a result, he applies a spiritual hermeneutic, which in turn dissolves the distinction between Israel and Gentiles. This approach violates Article XVII of the *CSBH*, which contains the following statements:

> WE AFFIRM the unity, harmony and consistency of Scripture and declare that it is its own best interpreter.

> WE DENY that Scripture may be interpreted in such a way as to suggest that one passage corrects or militates against another. We deny that later writers of Scripture misinterpreted earlier passages of Scripture when quoting from or referring to them.[151]

Furthermore, Gentry's view overlooks the literal meaning. "Israel" always means Israel; it does not refer to the church. God has a separate plan for Gentiles and Jews. In this case, James was speaking about a future restoration of Israel, as well as a future salvation of the Gentiles.

8) 1 Corinthians 15:24–26. In this passage, Strawbridge's argument that the kingdom is a present reality is not convincing.[152] Paul is not teaching about the present kingdom. He has a time-sequence in mind (cf. v. 23) that postmillennialists fail to grasp. W. Harold Mare notes, "We assume that in vv. 24ff. he continues with further time-sequences, as shown by the particle *eita* ('then'). That is, at the time of Christ's second coming and the resurrection of the blessed dead (cf. Rev. 20:4–6), next ('then') in order will come the process of handing over … the kingdom to God."[153] This involves the future conquest of earthly kingdoms, as described in Daniel 2:44–45. Furthermore, when the Son hands the kingdom over to God, that is, to the Father (1 Cor. 15:24), Paul distinguishes between Christ's Davidic kingdom and the Father's eternal kingdom. Therefore, this passage reveals two kingdoms that take priority at different times. Verse 25 alludes to Christ's reign (i.e., the millennial kingdom). Revelation 20:4–6 records this reign. It lasts until its enemies are destroyed (Ps. 110:1). Postmillennialists correctly note that the last enemy to be destroyed is death (v. 26),[154] which parallels Revelation 20:2–15, but this happens at Jesus' Second Coming, not at the First Coming—as Strawbridge claims.[155]

Conclusion

Having examined postmillennialism and its hermeneutic in detail (see also table 4), we must commend them for their great effort to evangelize the world. It is needed in times like these, when many are failing in this responsibility. But they are motivated by an optimistic view that the world will get better. However, the goal of evangelizing the whole world is unrealistic because it is unbiblical. Paul (2 Tim. 3:1–13), Peter (2 Pet. 3:1–7), and Jude (vv. 17–19) all state clearly that the religious situation will grow worse at the end of this age. They base their statements of what Jesus and the other apostles taught.

Postmillennialism promises a golden age for all believers, but they will usher this period in through human effort, rather than recognizing that Christ will establish the millennial kingdom before he hands over to the Father his sole right to rule on earth (1 Cor. 15:24).

I also commend Gentry's view that there will be "future, massive conversions among the Jews."[156] However, postmillennialists should remember that believing Jews are part of the church today. Even though many of them will be saved in the future, they are now within the reach of grace, just as believing Gentiles are (Rom. 10:9, 10). Regarding the future salvation of the nation of Israel, Zechariah 12:10 states, "And I will pour on the house of David and on the inhabitants of Jerusalem the Spirit of grace and supplication; then they will look on Me whom they pierced. Yes, they will mourn for Him as one mourns for *his* only *son*, and grieve for Him as one grieves for a firstborn." The context indicates that this will take place after the battle of Armageddon (vv. 1–6) when Yahweh rescues the nation of Israel from her enemies (vv. 7–9). Table 4 summarizes postmillennialism's noncompliance with the *GSBH* principles.

---

1   Loraine Boettner, *The Millennium* (Philadelphia: Presbyterian and Reformed, 1957), 4.

2   St. Augustine, *The City of God*, trans. Marcus Dods (New York: The Modern Library, 1950), 720. However, evangelicals are divided as to whether Augustine held this view because it lacks the optimistic element.

3   Mal Couch, ed., *Dictionary of Premillennial Theology: A Practical Guide to the People, Viewpoints, and History of Prophetic Studies* (Grand Rapids: Kregel, 1996), 308.

4   Couch, *Dictionary of Premillennial Theology*, 308–309.

5   Kenneth L. Gentry Jr., "Postmillennialism," in *Three Views on the Millennium and Beyond*, Counterpoints: Bible and Theology, ed. Darrell Bock and Stanly N. Gundry (Grand Rapids: Zondervan, 1999), 18.

6   Couch, *Dictionary of Premillennial Theology*, 309.

7   Jim Willis and Barbara Willis, *Armageddon Now: The End of the World A to Z* (Detroit: Visible Ink Press, 2006), 396-97.

8   Lorraine Boettner, "Postmillennialism," in *The Meaning of the Millennium: Four Views*, ed. Robert G. Clouse (Downers Grove, IL: IVP Academic, 1977), 138.

9   Couch, *Dictionary of Premillennial Theology*, 309. Couch is referring to postmillennialism's identification with the social gospel and liberalism. The two world wars were not identified with these two theological views.

10   Gentry, "Postmillennialism," 18.

11   Couch, *Dictionary of Premillennial Theology*, 10.

12   *Theonomy* stands for the Greek term θεόνομος, which is a compound of θεός ("God") and νομός ("law"). It means "God's law."

13   Kennedy L. Gentry, "Recent Development in Eschatological Debate," *Reformation Online*, "Theology" (May 16, 2018), accessed October 9, 2015, http://www.reformationonline.com/debate.htm.

14   Thomas Ice, "The Unscriptural Theologies of Amillennialism and Postmillennialism," *Pre-TribResearchCenter* (paper presented at the 26th Annual Conference, December 4–6, 2017), 7, 03/20/2016, http://www.pre-trib.org/articles/view/unscriptural-theologies-of-amillennialism-and-postmillennialism.

15   James A. DeJong, *As the Waters Cover the Sea: The Millennial Expectations in the Rise of Anglo-American Missions 1640–1810* (Kampen, Neth.: Kok, 1970); Iain Murray, *The Puritan Hope* (Edinburgh: Banner of Truth, 1971); Erroll Hulse, *The Restoration of Israel*, 3rd ed. (Worthing, Sussex: Henry E. Walter, 1982); Rousas John Rushdoony, *Thy Kingdom Come: Studies in Daniel and Revelation* (Fairfax, VA: Thoburn Press, 1970); Rushdoony, *God's Plan for Victory: The Meaning of Post Millennialism: A Chalcedon Study* (Fairfax, VA: Thoburn Press, 1977); Gary North, "The Economics Thought of Luther & Calvin," *The Journal of Christian Reconstruction* vol. ii, no. 1 (Summer, 1975): 97–136, accessed 6/27/2018: https://chalcedon.edu/store/40089-jcr-vol-2-no-1-symposium-on-christian-economics. Greg L. Bahnsen, "Double Jeopardy: A Case Study in the Influence of Christian Legislation," *The Journal of Christian Reconstruction* vol.2, no. 2 (Winter, 1975): 57.–77, accessed 6/27/2018: https://chalcedon.edu/store/40091-jcr-vol-2-no-2-symposium-on-biblical-law.

16 John Jefferson Davis, *The Victory of Christ's Kingdom: An Introduction to Postmillennialism* (Moscow, ID: Canon Press, 1996); David Chilton, *Paradise Restored: A Biblical Theology of Dominion* (Fort Worth, TX: Dominion Press, 1987); Gary North, *Millennialism and Social Theory* (Tyler, TX: Institute for Christian Economics, 1990; Gary DeMar, *Last Days Madness: The Folly of Trying to Predict When Christ Will Return* (Brentwood, TN: Wolgemuth and Hyatt, 1991); Kenneth L. Gentry, Jr., *He Shall Have Dominion: A Postmillennial Eschatology* (Draper, VA: ApologeticsGroup Media, 2009); Alexander McLeod, *Messiah, Governor of the Nations* (Elmwood Park, NJ: Reformed Presbyterian Press, 1992); Andrew Sandlin, *A Postmillennial Primer* (Vallecito, CA: and Beyond, Counterpoints: Bible and Theology (Grand Rapids: Zondervan, 1999).

17 Gentry, *He Shall Have Dominion*, 107. R. C. Sproul is listed here as a voice of postmillennialism through the numerous books published under Ligonier Ministry: https://www.ligonier.org/about/rc-sproul/rcs-book-release-timeline/. Accessed 6/27/2018.

18 Charles Hodge, *Systematic Theology*, 3 vols. (Peabody, MA: Hendrickson, 1999), 1:446.

19 Benjamin B. Warfield, *The Inspiration and Authority of the Bible* (Philipsburg, NJ: Presbyterian and Reformed, 1948), 82–84.

20 David P. Smith and June Corduan, *B. B. Warfield's Scientifically Constructive Theological Scholarship*, The Evangelical Society Monograph Series 10 (Eugene, OR: Pickwick, 2011), 241.

21 John Jefferson Davis, *Foundations of Evangelical Theology* (Grand Rapids: Baker, 1984), 257, 259.

22 Gentry, *He Shall Have Dominion*, 156.

23 Kenneth L. Gentry, *Postmillennialism Made Easy* (Draper, VA: ApologeticsGroup Media, 2009), Kindle, loc. 1562-1563 of 2794; italics orig.

24 Gentry, *Postmillennialism Made Easy*, loc. 1578.

25 Gentry, *He Shall have Dominion*, 167–68.

26 Keith A. Mathison, *Dispensationalism: Rightly Dividing the People of God?* (Philipsburg, NJ: P and R Publishing, 1995), 39-41.

27 Mathison, *Dispensationalism*, 30.

28 Gentry, *He Shall Have Dominion*, 168, 207.

29 Mathison, *Postmillennialism*, 120.

30 Kenneth Gentry Jr., "The Postmillennial Vision of Christian Eschatology," *Criswell Theological Review* 11, no. 1 (Fall 2013): 92.

31 Hodge, *Systematic Theology*, 3:856.

32 Hodge, *Systematic Theology*, 3:857.

33 Millard J. Erickson, *A Basic Guide to Eschatology: Making Sense of the Millennium*, 2nd ed. (Grand Rapids: Baker Books, 1998), 55.
34 Boettner, "Postmillennialism," 121.
35 Gentry, *He Shall Have Dominion*, 82.
36 Gentry, "The Postmillennial Vision of Christian Eschatology," 92.
37 Boettner, *The Millennium*, 22.
38 James H. Snowden, *The Coming of the Lord: Will It Be Premillennial?*, 2nd ed. (Repr.; orig. pub. 1919; Whitefish, MT: Kessinger, 2007), 72-85.
39 Gentry, "Postmillennialism," 30.
40 Gentry, *He Shall Have Dominion*, 83.
41 Snowden, *The Coming of the Lord*, 257-263; Boettner, *The Millennium*, 53.
42 Boettner, *The Millennium*, 64.
43 Gentry, *He shall Have Dominion*, 83.
44 Cf. Hodge, *Systematic Theology*, 3:792-800.
45 Boettner, *The Millennium*, 83.
46 Boettner, "Postmillennialism," in *The Meaning of Millennium: Four Views*, 134.
47 Donald A. Hagner, *Matthew 1-13*, Word Biblical Commentary 33A, ed. Bruce Metzger (Nashville, TN: Thomas Nelson, 1993), 308.
48 Boettner, "Postmillennialism, 134.
49 Boettner, "Postmillennialism, 136.
50 Boettner, "Postmillennialism, 137.
51 Boettner, "Postmillennialism," 137.
52 Boettner, "Postmillennialism," 137
53 Boettner, "Postmillennialism," 138.
54 Boettner, *Millennium*, 85.
55 Paul Lee Tan, *Literal Interpretation of the Bible* (Rockville, MD: Assurance Publishers, 1978), 51.
56 Hagner, *Matthew 1-13*, 99.
57 Boettner, *Millennium*, 64.
58 Boettner, "Postmillennialism," 92.
59 Hodge, *Systematic Theology*, 3:548-549.
60 Gentry, *He Shall Have Dominion*, 167.
61 Gentry, *He Shall Have Dominion*, 167.
62 Boettner, *Millennium*, 47.
63 Boettner, *Millennium*, 89-90.
64 Boettner, "Postmillennialism," 241.
65 Hodge, *Systematic Theology*, 3:810.
66 Hodge, *Systematic Theology*, 3:810.
67 Hodge, *Systematic Theology*, 3:810.
68 Gentry, *Postmillennialism Made Easy*, loc. 1662.

69   Gentry, *Postmillennialism Made Easy*, loc. 1626.
70   Gentry, *Postmillennialism Made Easy*, loc. 1627.
71   Mathison, *Postmillennialism*, 120.
72   Gentry, *He Shall Have Dominion*, 171.
73   Mathison, *Dispensationalism*, 40.
74   Gentry, *He Shall Have Dominion*, 167.
75   Gentry, *He Shall Have Dominion*, 171.
76   Gentry, *He Shall Have Dominion*, 167.
77   Gentry, *He Shall Have Dominion*, 171.
78   Gentry, *He Shall Have Dominion*, 171.
79   Keith Mathison, "The Davidic Covenant—The Unfolding of Biblical Eschatology," *Ligonier Ministries: The Teaching Fellowship of R. C. Sproul* (March 5, 2012), ¶3, accessed May 18, 2015, http://www.ligonier.org/blog/davidic-covenant-unfolding-biblical-eschatology.
80   Mathison, "The Davidic Covenant," 7.
81   Mathison, "The Davidic Covenant," 6.
82   Mathison, "The Davidic Covenant," 7.
83   Boettner, "Response," in *The Millennial Kingdom*, 103.
84   Gentry, *Postmillennialism Made Easy*, loc. 456.
85   Gentry, *Postmillennialism Made Easy*, loc. 458.
86   Gentry, *Postmillennialism Made Easy*, loc. 461.
87   Gentry, *Postmillennialism Made Easy*, loc. 474.
88   Gentry, *Postmillennialism Made Easy*, loc. 478.
89   Gentry, *Postmillennialism Made Easy*, loc. 489.
90   Gentry, *Postmillennialism Made Easy*, loc. 489.
91   Gentry, *Postmillennialism Made Easy*, loc. 489.
92   Gentry, *Postmillennialism Made Easy*, loc. 507.
93   Gentry, "Postmillennialism," 33.
94   Gentry, "Postmillennialism," 35.
95   Gentry, "Postmillennialism," 34–35
96   Davis, *The Victory of Christ's Kingdom*, 28.
97   Edmund Kalt, ed., *Herder's Commentary on the Psalms* (Westminster, MD.: Newman Press, 1961), 429.
98   Davis, *Victory*, 32.
99   Gregg Strawbridge, "An Exegetical Defense of Postmillennialism from 1 Corinthians 15:25-26: The Eschatology of the DIXIT DOMINUS" (paper presented at the 51st Annual Meeting of the Evangelical Theological Society, Danvers, MA, November 17–19, 1999), 4, http://www.wordmp3.com/files/gs/postmill.htm.
100 Strawbridge, "An Exegetical Defense of Postmillennialism," 4.
101 Strawbridge, "An Exegetical Defense of Postmillennialism," 4.

102 Gentry, *Postmillennialism Made Easy*, loc. 350.

103 Gentry, *Postmillennialism Made Easy*, loc. 349.

104 Keith A. Mathison, *Postmillennialism: An Eschatology of Hope* (Philipsburg, NJ: P and R Publishing, 1999), 118.

105 Gentry, *He Shall Have Dominion*, 222.

106 Gentry, *He Shall Have Dominion*, 222.

107 Boettner, *The Millennium*, 85.

108 Daniel B. Wallace (*Greek Grammar Beyond the Basics: An Exegetical Syntax of the New Testament* [Grand Rapids: Zondervan, 1996], 320–23) might classify this as "subject focus for emphasis." but claims such classifications are notoriously difficult.

109 Wallace (*Greek Grammar Beyond the Basics*, 222–23) may classify this as an article "*Par Excellence.*" He says this "article is frequently used to point out a substantive that is, in a sense, 'in a class by itself.' It is the only one deserving of the name."

110 Boettner, *The Millennium*, 85.

111 Zuck, *Basic Bible Interpretation*, 147.

112 Radmacher, "The Current Status of Dispensationalism and Its Eschatology," 167.

113 Zuck, *Basic Bible Interpretation*, 147; italics orig.

114 Thomas Ice, "Elijah is Coming," *Pre-TribResearchCenter* (paper presented at the 26th Annual Conference, December 4–6, 2017), 1. March 3, 2018, http://www.pre-trib.org/articles/view/elijah-is-coming.

115 Ice, "Elijah is Coming," 2.

116 Geisler, *Summit II Hermeneutics*, 23.

117 Boettner, *Millennium*, 98.

118 Geisler, *Summit II Hermeneutics*, 23.

119 Boettner, "Postmillennialism," 138.

120 Geisler, *Summit II Hermeneutics*, 21.

121 Geisler, *Summit II Hermeneutics*, 21.

122 Geisler, *Summit II Hermeneutics*, 24.

123 Hodge, *Systematic Theology*, 3:548-549.

124 Hodge, *Systematic Theology*, 3:548-549.

125 Gentry, *He Shall Have Dominion*, 171.

126 Boettner, *Millennium*, 98.

127 Ryken, Wilhoit, and Longman, *Dictionary of Biblical Imagery*, 267.

128 Geisler, *Summit II Hermeneutics*, 23.

129 Gentry, *He Shall Have Dominion*, 82; Mathison, *Postmillennialism*, 129.

130 Timothy George, *Galatians: An Exegetical and Theological Exposition of Holy Scripture*, The New American Commentary 30, ed. E. Ray Clendenen (Nashville, TN: Broadman and Holman, 1994), 440.

131 Gentry, *He Shall Have Dominion*, 202.

132 Willem VanGemeren, "Psalms," in *The Expositor's Bible Commentary*, 12 vols., ed Frank E. Gaebelein (Grand Rapids: Zondervan, 1991), 5:70.

133 Mathison, *Postmillennialism*, 93.

134 Mathison, *Postmillennialism*, 94.

135 Rushdoony, *Thy Kingdom Come*, 18.

136 Stanley D. Toussaint, *Behold the King: A Study of Matthew* (Grand Rapids: Kregel, 1980), 317.

137 Alfred Plummer, *An Exegetical Commentary on the Gospel According to S. Matthew* (New York: Charles Scribner's Sons, 1910), 428.

138 John T. Carroll, *Response to the End of History: Eschatology and Situation in Luke-Acts*, Society of Biblical Literature Dissertation Series 92 (Atlanta, GA: Scholars Press, 1988), 77.

139 Hobert K. Farrell, "The Eschatological Perspective of Luke-Acts" (PhD diss., Boston University, 1972), 54-56.

140 Carroll, *Response to the End of History* [or: "Response to the End of History,"], 77.

141 Carroll, *Response to the End of History* [or: "Response to the End of History,"], 78.

142 F. Wilbur Gingrich, *Shorter Lexicon of the Greek New Testament*, 2nd ed., ed. Frederick W. Danker (Chicago: University of Chicago Press, 1983), s.v. "ἐντός."

143 Carroll, *Response to the End of History* [or: "Response to the End of History,"], 79.

144 Carroll, *Response to the End of History* [or: "Response to the End of History,"], 79.

145 Gentry, *He Shall Have Dominion*, 148.

146 Gentry, *He Shall Have Dominion*, 149.

147 Gentry, *He Shall Have Dominion*, 149.

148 Geisler, *Summit II Hermeneutics*, 23.

149 Gentry, *He Shall Have Dominion*, 209.

150 Gentry, *He Shall Have Dominion*, 171.

151 Geisler, *Summit II Hermeneutics*, 23.

152 Cf. Strawbridge, "An Exegetical Defense of Postmillennialism," 4.

153 W. Harold Mare, "1 Corinthians," in *The Expositor's Bible Commentary*, 10:285.

154 Cf. Strawbridge, "An Exegetical Defense of Postmillennialism," 4.

155 Strawbridge, "An Exegetical Defense of Postmillennialism," 4.

156 Gentry, *Postmillennialism Made Easy*, loc. 693.

CHAPTER 3

The Progressive Dispensationalist View

Traditional dispensationalism preceded progressive dispensationalism, but we are dealing with progressive dispensationalism here because it has some aspects in common with both postmillennialism and traditional dispensationalism. In a sense, it falls between them in the hermeneutical spectrum. As with chapter 2, we will follow the outline we laid out in chapter 1.

An Overview of Progressive Dispensationalism

First, we will seek to define progressive dispensationalism and state its essential nature, and then we will examine the movement's development.

A Definition of Progressive Dispensationalism

Progressive dispensationalism has never been precisely defined. Blaising and Bock only state that they gave "patterns of dispensationalism, but they did not provide a definition of the view."[1] In an attempt to define the view by implication, Robert Saucy describes it as "a mediating position between non-dispensationalism and traditional dispensationalism that provides a better understanding of Scripture." He further describes it as follows: "It advocates for a natural reading of Scripture, it recognizes Israel's future role, it advocates for unity within history, and it denies a radical discontinuity between the Church and the Messianic Kingdom."[2] Progressive dispensationalism therefore maintains continuity between Israel and the church.

Blaising and Bock provide the following description of progressive dispensationalism. "It strongly affirms the authority of Scripture"; it approaches the Scripture "by means of historical, literary hermeneutics, which includes grammar, lexicography, compositional matters, genre, and intertextual features such as typology"; it recognizes "the role of biblical theology as manifested by progressive revelation as it impacts the interpretation of any individual passage"; and it has "a conscious awareness of the role of tradition in the interpretation and is cognizant of the interplay of preunderstanding, text, and community in the hermeneutical process."[3]

Progressive dispensationalist's adherents claim that the past and present dispensations have a progressive relationship, and that the present and future dispensations do as well. (See appendix 2.) Blaising and Bock state that the term "progressive" refers to "a progressive fulfillment of God's plan in history." They hold to "a continuation between Israel and the Church,"[4] and write that "it is continuity through *progress*: the progress of promissory fulfillment. But it is also the progress of the *novum*, the new."[5] Thus, progressive revelation brings a now development, and sets it apart from former revelation. Blaising and Bock note that

> the label *progressive dispensationalism* is being suggested because of the way in which this dispensationalism views the interrelationship of divine dispensations in history, their overall orientation to the eternal kingdom of God (which is final, eternal dispensation embracing God and humanity), and reflection of these historical and

eschatological relations in the literary features of Scripture.[6]

A Brief History of Progressive Dispensationalism

Progressive dispensationalism began in 1985 as an attempt by a couple of traditional dispensationalists to develop more cordial relations with covenant theologians, but it eventually developed into an almost complete departure from traditional dispensationalism. The departure includes "a number of modifications" and "sufficient revisions."[7] In fact, some progressive dispensationalists initially supported the *CSBH*. Robert Saucy, a founder and key leader of progressive dispensationalism, signed the *CSBH*. Sadly, he abandoned the articles.[8] The adherents of progressive dispensationalism drifted away from traditional dispensationalism after they alluded to its hermeneutics as deficient, so they do not subscribe to the three essentials of traditional dispensationalism: the distinction between the church and Israel, a literal hermeneutic, and the glory of God as the central theme of the Scriptures.[9] Blaising writes, "Consistently literal exegesis is inadequate to describe the essential distinctive of [traditional] dispensationalism."[10] They advocate what they call "complementary hermeneutics." This approach allows for changes, additions, and advancement in the meaning of God's original Word. It teaches that God's revelations in the Old Testament can have a new and different fulfillment in the New Testament.[11] The view has become popular due to its "already" not "yet" eschatology regarding the kingdom of God, as well as the publications and regular conferences that promote it. It permeates theological seminaries and churches across the United States and other parts of the world.[12]

Patrick W. Nasongo

Progressive Dispensationalism and the Central Issues

As with postmillennialism, we will look first at progressive dispensationalism's premises regarding the three hermeneutical issues of progressive revelation, the priority of the testaments, and the meaning of the term "mystery." Then we will examine their conclusions concerning the relationship between Israel and the church and the nature of the kingdom.

Progressive Revelation

Progressive dispensationalism's entire hermeneutical system is built on their principle of progressive revelation. Bock describes his view of progressive revelation in these terms:

> God's promises are initially presented in general terms, but as God works in history He progressively reveals and provides the specifics of His promises. Words, then, may take on an extended sense of meaning when an Old Testament text is recontextualized in the New Testament by an author who was influenced by his historical milieu and the progress of revelation. The New Testament can tell us more about God's promise but does not say less than the Old Testament did [13]

According to Bock, then, God reveals his truth in portions over a period of time, but he maintains that, as revelation moves from the general Old Testament revelation to specific New Testament revelation, these promises are altered, changed, or given additional information to make them relevant to the new context. The changes that take place in the initial promises are significant. Bock asks, "Does the expansion of meaning entail a change of meaning?" He responds to this question in two ways.

First he says, "To add to the revelation of a promise is to introduce 'change' to it through addition." And then he adds, "Progressive dispensationalists believe that by progressive revelation, referents are added to the scope of a previously given promises." Again, Bock indirectly elevates the New Testament over the Old Testament. He asks, "If the promise were present with its full meaning from the start, then where would the revelatory progress of promise reside? ... There would be no progression, only a re-presentation of meaning." Therefore, Bock holds that the interpreter can expect the process of progressive revelation to alter or change the original promises. When these changes occur, an author can derive new meanings, realize new referents, and sometimes cancel initial promises. Bock writes, "Progress and expansion can emerge as more pieces of the promise are brought together into a unified whole or as more of its elements are revealed." He summarizes progressive revelation by saying that "the disclosure and nature of [the] promise is not a static, but dynamic process of progressive revelation about God's covenant."[14] This approach allows changes to God's original statements.

Bock's second response is that "an expansion of meaning is not a change in meaning, for the original features of the promise are ultimately retained." In this case, Bock employs a partial fulfillment of the promise in the context of the progress of revelation. He observes that the interpreter must keep in mind both the partial fulfillment and the progress of revelation when examining these passages. He concludes, "Biblical revelation of promise does not stop with Malachi, nor does NT revelation ignore what the OT promised. Rather, the NT presents and develops OT hope."[15]

The Priority of the Testaments

Progressive dispensationalists define this concept as "a presuppositional preference of one text over the other that determines a person's literal historical-grammatical hermeneutical starting point."[16] According to Bock, the "New Testament does not have a priority. Rather it has a place, a completing (complementary) one, in contributing evidence as a continuance piece of the canon that addresses God's covenant promise and advances our understanding of it as a result."[17] He states that this hermeneutical method shows "an expansion within the boundaries of the covenant backdrop and message of Old Testament passages [that is] also based on a complementary reading in New Testament usage."[18] This expanded meaning is conditioned on Christ's present work but also affirms the Old Testament reading in the future millennial kingdom. In his approach, "there is no 'restoring' of Old Testament meaning, but there is the affirming of that meaning as applying ultimately to the later period of fulfillment, while affirming also what the New Testament says about the initial realization of such promises."[19]

As to whether the New Testament completes the Old Testament, Blaising and Bock ask, "Does the New Testament complement Old Testament revelation?" Their answer is affirmative: "The New Testament does introduce change and advance; it does not merely repeat Old Testament revelation. In making complementary additions, however, it does not jettison old promises. The enhancement is not at the expense of the original promise."[20]

The Meaning of "Mystery"

In defining the term "mystery," Bock claims that its meaning "in the New Testament is tied to the concept of mystery in Daniel 2:18, 19, 27–30, 47." The word for "mystery" or "secret" in the passages in Daniel is the Aramaic phrase (2:18עַל־רָזָה). Bock asserts that this term has a Semitic root. According to Bock, this term "finds conceptual parallels at Qumran (1QH 5:36; lQpHab 7:5, 8, 14; 1Q27 1:1, 2–4)." Mystery is therefore that which "involves a revelation whose import is directly disclosed by God. The mystery (*raz*) is a 'secret' because before its contents were supernaturally revealed, the message was not fully understood." "Mystery" or "revelation," according to Blaising and Bock, is "either new, as in the interpretation of existing dreams or is a fresh declaration of truth about an older message."[21]

Bock also states that "the revelatory roots behind the רָז, *raz* can be recent or old, depending on the case in question." Some features in the mystery may be new, while others develop Old Testament themes. So "the content and connection of each 'revealed secret' must be considered." Bock cites Colossians. 1:26–27 and Ephesians. 3:6–9, in which he suggests that the truth revealed is completely new because the OT nowhere declares either the indwelling of Gentiles by the Messiah or the total equality of Jews and Gentiles in one new body. Furthermore, "the meaning of those texts is clear since the contexts in which they appear highlight the fact of concealment from previous times and generations."[22] This definition of "mystery" therefore makes it both an Old Testament and New Testament concept.

In a similar manner, Saucy observes that in the Septuagint the word "mystery" is first used in Daniel 2. It is translated in Aramaic as רָז. He observes that "the term 'mystery' is also frequently used in apocryphal writings to refer to various kinds of secrets which consist of human and divine." He notes that another word for "'mystery' סוֹד, *sod*, is found in canonical Scriptures for 'God's secrets' (Amos 3:7; Ps. 25:14; Prov. 3:32; Job 15:8), but the word used in these passages is not μυστήριον." Saucy observes that "the word μυστήριον (LXX) is used in Daniel. 2:18 as an eschatological mystery."[23]

Saucy notes that the term "mystery" (μυστήριον) "appears twenty-eight times in the New Testament, with twenty-one of those appearances in Pauline epistles." He identifies three categories of "mystery." First, it stands for "the divine plan of salvation that is now revealed in Christ. This includes the teaching of Christ about the kingdom of heaven (Mark 4:11) and the apostolic teaching related to God's dealing with Israel and the Gentiles (Rom. 11:25)." Second, the term is used for various divine secrets that are divulged to given individuals, for example, knowing and speaking mysteries in 1 Corinthians 13:2 and 14:2.[24] Third, "mystery" is used for hidden meaning found in symbols and types. The seven stars and lampstands (Rev. 1:20), mystery Babylon (Rev. 17:5, 7), and marriage (Eph. 5:31–32) are examples of this kind of mystery.[25] Saucy concludes that the term "mystery" in the New Testament is centered on Christ and the gospel.[26]

Israel and the Church

As the result of their view of the first three central issues, progressive dispensationalism's view of the relationship between Israel and the church is a hybrid of the postmillennial position and the traditional dispensational interpretation.

Israel. Saucy explains that the term "Israel" is "a name of honor divinely bestowed on Jacob following his struggle with God at Peniel (Gen. 32:28)." Jacob was called this throughout his life, and even after his death (Gen. 35:21; Ex. 32:13). It was applied to Jacob's twelve sons, and then came to refer to his descendants (Exod. 1:7) and eventually to the nation that was formed after them (the twelve).[27] After the kingdom split, the northern kingdom took the name "Israel," and the southern kingdom became Judah (1 Sam. 11:8). Despite the different uses of the name, all these groups were called "Israel." Saucy explains this situation by defining Israel as follows:

> In the Old Testament teaching, therefore, "Israel" signifies a community of people with a special relationship to God. This community is marked off from other peoples, first by its religious relationship with the true God, but also by its

physical descendants. While it was possible for those who were not biological descendants from Abraham through Jacob to become part of the commonwealth of Israel as proselytes, the physical element is never discarded in favor of a purely religious definition of Israel.[28]

Though Saucy's statement indicates that both physical and religious elements are required for one to be an Israelite, he emphasizes the religious aspect as the most important factor. In addition to this, Saucy's preference to the word "community" removes distinctions.

Saucy observes that in the New Testament the term "Israel" occurs sixty-eight times (mostly in Matthew, Luke, and Paul). In every instance, it refers to the "national covenanted people of the Old Testament." Saucy points out that the apostle Paul also uses the term "Israel" to refer to the "historic people, as do the three references in Hebrews."[29] Therefore, the New Testament uses the term "Israel" to refer to the ethnic nation of the Old Testament. However, Saucy's interpretation of the term "Israel" in Galatians 6:16 and Romans 9:6 appear to challenge the literal usages of Israel in the Scripture.[30] He writes, "Christian scholars for centuries have understood the New Testament to teach that the church is, in fact, the 'new Israel.'" Speaking of these scholars, Saucy observes, "They have tended to base this view more on a broad reading of Scripture rather than on specific texts that use the term 'Israel' or 'Jew.'"[31]

The church. Saucy defines the church as a "spiritual organism alive with the resurrection life of Christ through the presence of the Spirit. It is the new humanity, the firstfruits after Christ of the new creation. ... It is possible to describe the church as the eschatological community of God's people."[32] This definition contains some concepts that progressive dispensationalists consider important: the Spirit, the resurrection of Christ, the new community (which includes both believing Gentiles and believing Jews), and the people of God. Blaising defines it as "redeemed humanity itself (both Jews and Gentiles) as it exists in this dispensation prior to the coming of Christ."[33] It is apparent, then that progressive dispensationalists see both a national Israel and a spiritual Israel, and that this spiritual Israel includes the church.

The Nature of the Kingdom

The Davidic kingdom is the kingdom that God established in his covenant with David (2 Sam. 7:12–16; 1 Chr. 17; and Ps. 89:4, 32–36). Saucy writes that a "royal dynasty and kingdom would be given to David forever" (2 Sam. 7:11–16).[34] The promise of a permanent dynasty and eternal kingdom are the important features of this kingdom, as Saucy notes:

> The promise of a royal dynasty entailed a "kingdom" and "throne" (2 Sam. 7:16). The nation over which David ruled had been designated as a "kingdom" since the very beginning (Ex. 19:6; Num. 24:7). Yahweh was a theocratic ruler over the nation of Israel before King Saul and before the establishment of a monarchy under David (1 Sam. 8:7; 12:12). The demand of a king seemed a sinful act (1 Sam. 8:5), however, it was in fulfillment of God's original intent. Yahweh had promised a king to the tribe of Judah before then (Gen. 49:10), and later through Moses (Deut. 17:14ff.). However, the ultimate promise of a true king was to be realized in David. The promise to David, therefore, carried forward the divine purpose of a human monarchy designating a permanent kingly line from the lineage of David.[35]

Still, "the appointment of a human king did not alter Yahweh's status as the king over His people Israel." Saucy observes, "Even in the prophecy announcing 'his kingdom' and 'throne,' David was also called the 'ruler over my people Israel' (2 Sam. 7:8)." In the same thought, he writes that the Messiah who is designated to fulfill the Davidic promise "was called a 'prince,' indicating that he 'is not an autonomous Ruler. ... He is responsible to a higher figure.'"[36] We will examine the progressive dispensationalist view of the fulfillment of the Davidic kingdom later in the chapter.

The Hermeneutics of Progressive Dispensationalism

Progressive dispensationalists adopt their own system of hermeneutics based on what Bock calls the "historical-grammatical-literary-theological approach,"[37] and Blaising writes, "Consistently literal exegesis is inadequate to describe the essential distinctive of dispensationalism."[38] As a result, Bock suggests a three-leveled reading of the Scriptures that leads to a complementary hermeneutic. These three levels are as follows:

1) The "historical-exegetical reading." In this level, the context of the event is viewed as a fairly self-contained unit. This level has some limitation, but its advantage lies in giving the immediate impact of an event. It "preserves the sense of progress in the story and allows one to appreciate how the story builds as time passes and revelation progresses."[39]

2) The "biblical-theological reading." In this level, Bock says that "a text is read in the context of the whole book in which it falls." For example, one might read the book of Romans as a reader in Rome might have read it, that is, without having access to any of Paul's other writing to help him figure out Paul's meaning. In other words, the person reads Romans as if it stands alone. Bock illustrates his point by referring to the seed of Abraham in Genesis. In the early chapters of Genesis, this seed focuses on Isaac. As the story continues in the book, the seed focuses on Jacob

and his sons. And in the rest of Genesis, the seed becomes the nation of Israel. Furthermore, Genesis nowhere mentions Jesus as the seed. In conclusion, Bock states that the revelation of the seed concept narrows down. He writes, "Only the movement of the story of promise beyond Genesis begins to show the possibility for such narrowing in the concept of the king as representative of the nation."[40]

3) The "canonical-systematic level." At this level, the interpreter looks at the larger picture.[41] Bock writes, "This reading takes the passage in light of the whole, either through all of an author's writing, through the lens of a given period, or most comprehensively, in light of the whole of the canon."[42] For instance, Jesus fulfilled the promise of the seed of Abraham. Bock notes that "Jesus as Christ—the promised king of the line of David—fulfills promises to Abraham and bestows the Spirit of God. Jesus brings the initial manifestation of the kingdom (John the Baptist announcement of the 'one to come')."[43] The seed aspect does not end with Jesus. Bock states, "For those who are 'in Christ' also become 'the seed,' as Galatians 3:39 shows."[44] He prefers the canonically-systematical method because it "brings the Bible's message together."[45]

Progressive dispensationalists hold to an "already" and "not-yet" approach, which involves two forms of fulfillment, especially in relation to the kingdom of God passages. Bock explains how this works, "It is possible to get fulfillment 'now' in some texts while noting that 'not yet' fulfillment exists in other passages."[46] He refers to this "approach as inaugurated eschatology."[47] We will observe the "already" and "not-yet" aspects in this study "in relation to the inauguration and institution of the Messianic Kingdom," as Bock puts it.[48]

Progressive dispensationalists use complementary hermeneutics. The result is that they differ from the other two approaches in three areas: the expanded meaning of the

Scriptures, the church as redeemed humanity, and the "already" and "not-yet" aspects of the Davidic kingdom.

Expanded Meaning

Progressive dispensationalists assert that they have shifted away from a consistently literal interpretation to an approach that involves a more sophisticated literal interpretation. Blaising writes, "This literal interpretation then developed from the 'clear, plain' method of attaching to words whatever meaning 'seemed clear' to the interpreter to a more critical awareness of how bias (or pre-understanding) conditions our intuitions, our impressions of certainty, and clarity of interpretation."[49] He notes the significance of this broadened grammatical-historical approach:

> From an early emphasis on the grammatical analysis of words, interpretation broadened to include syntactical, rhetorical, and literary study. Historical interpretation expanded beyond dates and chronologies to include the historical setting and development of themes, words, and ideas. It also came to bear on the history of interpretation, the matter of tradition, and the historical context of the interpreter.[50]

The preceding discussion indicates that progressive dispensationalists no longer hold to the essentials of traditional dispensationalism. It is evident that the historical aspect of grammatical-historical interpretation is expanded. I believe that this expansion may cause them to miss the divine and human authorial intent. However, Blaising defends such a move by affirming that "it is a development of 'literal' interpretation into a more consistent historical-literary interpretation."[51] In addition to this, Bock argues that his literal approach produces a stable meaning. He writes, "A progressive dispensational hermeneutic is committed to stable meaning as it is progressively revealed across the canon and across the dispensations."[52] We will revisit this statement in the evaluation.

Consequently, progressive dispensationalists advocate a complementary hermeneutic. This method has become their grid for biblical interpretation. We will consider several areas in which they apply the complementary method. First, in an attempt to interpret new revelation in the New Testament, Blaising and Bock write, "The New Testament does introduce change and advance; it does not merely repeat Old Testament revelation. In making complementary additions, however, it does not jettison old promises. The enhancement is not at the expense of the original promises."[53] Words such as change, expansion, additions, and development are characteristic of complementary hermeneutics. Second, in progressive revelation, Bock explains that complementary hermeneutics "introduces a fresh note of continuity in the progress of revelation without resulting in an alteration of ultimate meaning of the Old Testament passages."[54] "Progress" and "expansion" are key features in progressive dispensationalism's hermeneutic, so at this point we will consider these terms, especially as they relate to the fulfillment of the Davidic covenant.

Expansion of meaning and progressive revelation. First, Bock asks a fundamental question about the issue of "expansion in meaning" with regard to the progress of revelation: "Does the expansion of meaning entail a change of meaning?"[55] His question shows that progressive dispensationalists do not adhere to single meaning. He responds with a two-fold answer:

> The answer is both yes and no. On the one hand, to add to the revelation of a promise is to introduce "change" to it through addition. But that is precisely how revelation progresses, as

referents are added to the scope of a previously given promise. If the promise were present with its full meaning from the start, then where would the revelatory progress of promise reside? There would be no progression, only a re-presentation of meaning.[56]

This response reveals that Bock advocates an "expansion" of meaning. He goes on to say that "since a promise is forward-looking, it automatically lays the ground for 'expansion' without requiring that all elements of the covenant be present from the beginning for realization."[57] Then he notes that

progress and expansion can emerge as more pieces of the promise are brought together into a unified whole or as more of its elements are revealed. These additions can occur without undercutting a consistency of meaning, which is necessary for texts to be understandable and hermeneutics to be stable. In sum, the disclosure and nature of promise is not a static, but a dynamic process of progressive revelation about God's covenants.[58]

On the other hand, Bock takes a second approach, which he calls "promise-fulfillment." He holds that biblical promises are dynamic because they are the result of the progressive nature of revelation. He illustrates this point by using Genesis 12:3, in which the Gentiles' blessings are associated with the seed of Abraham. According to Bock, the promise of the "seed" progresses through Abraham, David, and Christ (Rom. 1:2–4; Gal. 3), which means it had multiple referents, including "Isaac, Jacob, the twelve sons, and the nation of Israel." Bock claims, however, that the "expansion in meaning does not change meaning."[59] This approach is neither traditional dispensationalist, nor is it biblical. In this case, Bock writes:

> We must, then, allow for partial fulfillment of promise texts in the context of the progress of revelation. Both the partiality of fulfillment and the progress of revelation must be kept in mind in examining these passages. Biblical revelation of promise does not stop with Malachi, nor does NT revelation ignore what the OT promised. Rather, the NT presents and develops OT hope. Promise can develop beyond the limits of the OT and yet those developments are still to be connected to the original promise.[60]

Expansion of meaning and the context. Progressive dispensationalists advocate an expansion of the meaning of a text, which is contrary to the principle of progressive revelation. But they expand a text's meaning in other ways. First, they expand meaning when it comes to the historical aspect. Traditionally, the term "history" means the text's original historical setting. This setting involves the author, dialogue they record, and the original audience. As much as is possible, the interpreter must determine the meaning that the author or speaker intended and that the audience understood. An Berkhof notes, "The interpreter must place himself on the standpoint of the author, and seek to enter into his very soul, until he, as it were, live his life and think his thoughts."[61] Progressive dispensationalists do not take this approach. Instead, Bock advocates "a multilayered reading of the text, which underlies the complementary hermeneutics." He proposes the following three layers of readings: the original historical setting, a literal reading of the whole book, and reading the statement in light of the entire biblical canon. He writes:

One can read the passage in two complementary ways. One can look at the event itself and/or read it in light of following events. Both readings are legitimate and impact appropriately the meaning of the passage. … In addition, the reading that emerges is not at the expense of the original reading, but is a complementary one. In other words, God may promise more than He originally promised but never less.[62]

Therefore, those who use complementary hermeneutics view the text from the standpoint of later events as well as the original setting. Because of their view of progressive revelation, they do not compare a later text with the earlier text. Bock concludes, "Subsequent revelation can always expand on previous revelation. … Subsequent texts to which the earlier text is related supply an additional detail to the concept already presented unless cancellation is explicitly noted."[63] Bock confirms his view when he says that "meaning is not static but dynamic, always changing."[64] In summary, the progressive dispensationalists' understanding of the "historical" aspect drifts away from the context of the original setting. As a result, they promote the view that a text can take on a different meaning when it is used in a different context at a later time.

Progressive dispensationalists also teach that a text has more than one meaning, and they expand a statement's meaning by identifying how its meaning is to be interpreted in a text. Bock states that "interpretation is not a matter of seeing one rule or approach applied to every text, it involves appreciating the variety of ways in which God weaves together His message." In using complementary hermeneutics, he advocates more than one meaning because "an additional angle of the text reveals an additional element of its message or a fresh way of relating the parts of a text's message."[65]

Furthermore, progressive dispensationalists expand meaning by giving the New Testament priority when interpreting the Old Testament. Bock urges readers to begin in the Old Testament but practice a complementary historical-grammatical hermeneutic.[66] He alleges that the apostles changed the meaning of Old Testament statements when they interpreted them in the New Testament. In his conclusion, Bock notes that "New Testament authors use and adopt concepts and ideas that were part of first century religious thinking."[67] In saying this, he appears to argue that words develop new meanings over time. For instance, due to its usage the word "Israel" has changed meaning over a period of time.

Summary. The progressive dispensationalists' complementary hermeneutic involves an expansion of meaning because of their view of the New Testament writers' use of the Old Testament. The result is that they advocate multiple meanings in progressive revelation and in their understanding of the original historical context.

The Church as Redeemed Humanity

Progressive dispensationalists undermine any distinction between the church and Israel. They place the one people of God, that is, Israel and the church, in two dispensations: the former and present dispensations. In the former dispensations "the divine blessings were poured out upon Israel while Gentiles were alienated or subordinated." In the present dispensation, the "divine blessings of the Spirit are going to Jews and Gentiles equally while national blessings are in abeyance."[68] According to Blaising and Bock, the two dispensations merge very well with the fulfillment of the future kingdom dispensation. Their view accounts for the equality of Jews and Gentiles in the regenerating, renewing, Christ-uniting ministry of the Holy Spirit, which brings about glorification. The blessing of the one new covenant unites both dispensations. According to Blaising and Bock, "These dispensations continue through redemption without replacement of peoples nor parallels." Progressive dispensationalists promote a unity that harmonizes the two groups in a unique way. Blaising and Bock assert that this model "promotes the principle of unity in Christ, in whom humanity and deity have not been rendered indistinct but have been harmonized in the oneness of his person in a way that challenges the limits of human language."[69]

Robert Saucy calls the church and Israel "one people of God." According to Saucy, there was prophetic anticipation of the "one people of God." He writes, "Although the term 'people of God' begins with Israel, … there is already in the prophet the anticipation that some outside of Israel will come under its purview."[70] Saucy observes that the Scriptures include the Gentiles in this phrase. He writes, "The concept 'the people of God' is extended to the Gentile nations in the Old Testament without their becoming a part of Israel."[71] This phrase embraced both Israel and Gentiles before the New Testament was written. Saucy concludes by saying, "The people of God are one people because all will be related to him through the same covenant salvation."[72]

Blaising and Bock, on the other hand, list several distinctive features of what the church is in progressive dispensationalism, as opposed to traditional dispensationalism. First, the church is not an anthropological category, as opposed to Israel, nations, Jews, and Gentiles.[73] Second, the church is neither a race of humanity (Jews or Gentiles) nor a competing nation.[74] Third, the church is not a group of angel-like humans destined for the heavens; instead it is "redeemed humanity itself (both Jews and Gentiles) as it exists in this dispensation prior to the coming of Christ."[75] According to Blaising and Bock, "the Church is one "new man" in Ephesians. 2:15, the redeemed humanity."[76] This means that in Christ the distinction between Jew and Gentile does not exist. The church is composed of people with racial, political, or national differences, so when Paul says in Galatians 3:28 that "there exists no difference between Jews and Gentiles,"[77] he means that "the blessings of the

Spirit which constitute the church as the new dispensation are given equally without ethnic, gender or class distinction."[78] Paul states that prophetic promises envision Christ ruling forever over the redeemed nations.[79] The church is composed of one people of God, as Blaising and Bock write, "Those Jews and Gentiles who compose the church prior to Christ's coming join the redeemed Jews and Gentiles of earlier dispensations to share equally in the resurrection glory."[80] The pre-church age redeemed Jews and Gentiles will be brought to the same level of complete fulfillment when they are raised from the dead.

J. Lanier Burns also rejects the distinction between Israel and the church, even though he examines in detail each entity's distinctive qualities, starting with Israel (Rom. 9–11). He gives Paul's list of seven distinctives (Rom, 9:5): "(a) adoption; (b) chosen; (c) dwelling of the glories: (d) received covenant of promise; (e) received the revelation of the law; (f) temple worship; and (g) messianic promises."[81] However, Burns claims that, "despite Israel's blessings and privileges, her memory had been marred by a majority persistent unbelief."[82] But God's mercy was not withdrawn from Israel, as seen by Paul's emphasis on the themes of total depravity and divine mercy (Rom. 11:30–36). Burns points out two arguments Paul raised regarding God's mercy. First, "God's justice is grounded in His sovereign mercy (Rom. 9:15–29)." Paul's second point, on which Burns focuses, is that "God's justice is proven by faith alone."[83] He notes, "By faith, Gentiles obtained righteousness while unbelieving Jews did not."[84] Burns argues that the inheritance of the world is not through the law [Jews], but through the righteousness that comes by faith. He quotes Romans 4:16–17:

> Therefore it is of faith, that it might be by grace; to the end the promise might be sure to all the seed; not to that only which is of the law, but to that also which is of the faith of Abraham; who is the father

of us all, (As it is written, I have made thee a father of many nations,) before him whom he believed. (Rom. 4:16, 17).[85]

This Scripture leads Burns to rule out the distinction between Israel and the church. He writes:

> This passage, in a word, forbids any discussion of a people of God apart from the principle of righteousness by faith alone. Israelites that will receive divine promises necessarily believe Jesus. The point has sometimes been obscured by well-meaning people who overgeneralized Israel/church distinctions; the focus is to be on physical seed of faith rather than mere descent from Abraham.[86]

Burns observes that "Christ is the end of the Messianic line (Rom. 9:5), Zion's stumbling stone (v. 33), and 'the end of the Law' (Rom. 10:4)." He adds that "this portion ends with an emphasis of the 'Word of faith' which states that 'there is no difference between Jew and Gentiles. For the same Lord is Lord of all and richly blesses all who call on Him' (Rom. 10: 8–9, 12)."[87] Burns indicates that since the coming of Jesus Christ, faith has been made available to everyone. Again, the Jewish people had their opportunity of righteousness, but they did not take advantage of it. He writes, "Chapter 10 closes with Old Testament citations that demonstrate that Israel had the messianic word of righteousness but had maintained an obstinate rejection of God's provision (Isa. 65:2)." Later in his discussion on Romans 11:11–29, Burns reveals that "God will bless Gentiles to their 'fullness' as a means of fulfilling His promises through Israel's full Salvation." Burns portrays Israel's unbelief as severe, but, by recognizing God's election of the nation, he falls short of declaring that they are completely rejected. He echoes Paul's conclusion: "However, consistent with his following arguments about the 'non-rejection of God's people' and the irrevocability of patriarchal roots, 'the people' in Isaiah maintain their chosen status in spite of their unbelief."[88] Therefore, Burns holds that there is no distinction between Jews and Gentiles. Israel squandered their opportunity to be blessed through their faith, so God is extending the blessing to everyone who believes, whether they are a Jew or Gentile.

Burns also focuses on the church's distinctives, but at the same time he undermines the distinction between Israel and the church. Again, he bases his arguments on Romans 9–11 and observes that the relationship between Israel and the church centers on three topics: "(a) Paul's use of the Old Testament, (b) his focus on Jew/ Gentile relationships rather than on Israel/church contrasts; and (c) the centrality of Christ in crucial passages." He asks rhetorically why Paul and his fellow apostles quoted from the Old Testament, and why Paul used Israelite references in Romans 11. And then he asks, "Is Israel and the church unconnected or antithetical?" Burns notes that if the answer is affirmative, "he would have de-emphasized Jewish precedents in favor of new revelation about the church. He (Paul) is not doing this in Romans 9–11."[89] Burns argues that God did not contradict himself, and so he asks, "If the purpose of the divine plan is doxological (11:33–36), then why must the mutually edifying relationships of Jews and Gentiles (11:30–32) be distinguished in purpose to the point that the single tree is diminished?" In summary, Burns writes, "We should advance a proper moderation and avoid 'false dichotomies.'"[90]

Burns's second topic concerns Paul's focus on the relationship between the Jews and Gentiles, rather than on the contrasts between Israel and the church. Burns writes that "a primary distinctive of the church is the equal acceptance and organic union of Jews and Gentiles in the body of Christ."[91] Evangelicals accept this truth as undisputed because it is supported by Ephesians 2:11–22 and Galatians 3:27–29. The passage in Ephesians 2 contrasts the

Gentiles' past status ("once ... at that time" [Eph. 2:11, 12]) with their present one ("but now" [Eph. 2:13]). Paul makes this clear in Romans 9:4, where he describes the Gentiles as uncircumcised and "separate from God" by their birth and identity. In Romans 11:24, Paul describes them metaphorically as branches "cut out of the wild olive tree which is wild by nature." But the Gentiles' status changed at the coming of Jesus Christ, as Ephesians 2:13 clearly indicates ("But now ..."). All these passages affirm that "Hebrew Christians should fully accept Gentile believers in the church based on the precedent of faith and the accomplishment of Christ."[92]

Up to this point, Burns argues that the continuity between Israel and the church is based on Christ's work on the cross, so that Burns agrees with the traditional dispensational view. However, Burns is against the notion of distinction of these two entities based on the phrase, "the people of God," in Peter's first epistle, where the apostle states:

> But you *are* a chosen generation, a royal priesthood, a holy nation, His own special people, that you may proclaim the praises of Him who called you out of darkness into His marvelous light; who once *were* not a people but *are* now the people of God, who had not obtained mercy but now have obtained mercy. (1 Pet. 2:9–10)

Burns argues that this passage upholds continuity and invalidates "false dichotomies" by the use of the phrase "people of God" in reference to Israel and the church.[93] He points out that Peter's description of Israel as God's elect people "are transferred to his readers with the constant assurance that they were now God's people and aliens in the world. ... Finally the nation of 'aliens and strangers' has been transferred from a position 'outside of the holy nation' to a call to be holy in opposition to the cosmos system."[94] Burns gives a brief definition and explanation of the words γένος ("generation"), ἔθνος ("nation"), and λαὸς ("people"). According to Burns, these terms equate Israel in the Old Testament with the church (cf. Exod. 19:5; Isa. 43:20).[95] Third, Burns argues for continuity based on the centrality of Christ. All dispensationalists agree on this point. Christ is the fulfillment of the Law and of the promises regarding the Jewish Messiah. Burns concludes by explaining why progressive dispensationalists do not maintain a distinction between Israel and the church:

> Therefore, Paul's use of the Old Testament, his focus on Jewish/Gentile relationships in Christ by faith, and the centrality of Christ for all dispensations are continuities that keep us from distinguishing Israel and the church, at the same time, recognizing the continuities of progressive revelation from Genesis to the Revelation.[96]

The Already and Not-Yet Fulfillments of the Davidic Kingdom

Progressive dispensationalists propose that biblical interpretation has dual aspects that allow a "both/and fulfillment option," which results in an "already" and "not-yet" dichotomy. This is "a scenario that has often been applied to the kingdom."[97] While postmillennialists see only a future earthly kingdom in which Christ reigns from heaven, Bock holds to both a present aspect of the kingdom, in which Christ reigns from heaven, and a future one in which he reigns for a thousand years on earth. He accepts a "'both-and' perspective without denying either side of the present-future relationship," and maintains that "it is possible to get fulfillment 'now' in some texts, while noting that 'not yet' fulfillment exists in other passages."[98] Bock claims the kingdom is said to be "near" or to have "arrived" in "Luke 10:9, 18–19; 11:20–23; 17:21; 19:14–15, while in other texts, the kingdom is consummated or anticipated." He points out that "Luke 11:20–23; 17:21; and 22:69 make it clear that Luke placed the coming of the kingdom in an 'already'/'not yet' form. He did not look at the kingdom as an 'either/or' affair. ... Rather it comes in stages."[99]

Bock goes on to explain that "the uniqueness of an 'already/not yet' tension is basically a complementary hermeneutic which insists that the 'New Testament fulfillment does not resignify OT meaning." This means that both the Old Testament promise and its New Testament connection should be studied in their own contexts before the two testaments are related to each other. In this case, the interpreter will recognize the complementary result. Bock writes, "New teaching develops promise by coming alongside the old promise, except in these cases where old promise is explicitly set aside."[100]

With this creation of the "already" and "not-yet" tension, progressive dispensationalists see the fulfillment of the Davidic promise both as a present fulfillment and a future one centered in Christ. Bock affirms that "Jesus is the hub of fulfillment, and his future position as King of Israel, reigning from Zion over all the earth, will fulfill the central role given to Israel in God's kingdom and covenant plan (Luke 1:31–33)."[101] Progressive dispensationalists use this "already" and "not-yet" scenario to argue for Israel's future. It could also be used theologically to argue for the phases of salvation, as Bock notes:

> I am saved now when I trust in Jesus, but God is going to complete that salvation in the future. In one sense salvation has arrived; in another I wait it. ... To note the presence of one aspect of the relationship is not to deny the other part of its realization.[102]

Bock concludes by saying that the "already" and "not-yet" teaching "links both the plan of God into a unified whole. It allows one to see the continuity and discontinuity in the outworking of God's promises."[103]

Progressive Dispensationalism and the Davidic Covenant

The Davidic covenant is found in 2 Samuel. 7:12–16 and in its parallel, 1 Chronicles 17:7–15. It is reiterated in Psalms 89, 110, and 132. The original statement is as follows:

> When your days are fulfilled and you rest with your fathers, I will set up your seed after you, who will come from your body, and I will establish his kingdom. He shall build a house for My name, and I will establish the throne of his kingdom forever. I will be his Father, and he shall be My son. If he commits iniquity, I will chasten him with the rod of men and with the blows of the sons of men. But My mercy shall not depart from him, as I took *it* from Saul, whom I removed from before you. And your house and your kingdom shall be established forever before you. Your throne shall be established forever. (2 Sam. 7:12–16)

The Structure of the Davidic Covenant

Blaising and Bock divide the Davidic covenant into two main parts. The first part concerns the establishment of David's house, while the second part concerns the relationship between God and David's descendants.[104] We will focus on the first part. Saucy lists four elements of the Davidic covenant: "(a) a great name (2 Sam. 7:9); (b) a place (v. 10); (c) rest from Israel's enemies (v. 10–11); and (d) a royal dynasty and kingdom that will be given to David forever (vv. 11–16)."[105] We will develop these four elements alongside Blaising and Bock's two-fold structure of the Davidic promise.

The first element is the promise to build the house of David. Blaising and Bock state that "the promise is repeated four times in 2 Samuel 7:12, 13, 16 and 1 Chronicles 17:11–12, 14, alternating the term kingdom and throne for emphases." They point out that the implication of each passage forms the basis of the Davidic covenant. They claim the passages do this in the following ways. First, by using the phrases "your house," "your throne," and "your kingdom," Yahweh emphasizes the continuity of the Davidic rulership (2 Sam. 7:16). Second, by setting the phrases "his throne shall be established forever" and "I will settle him in my house and in My kingdom forever" in parallel, the author of 1 Chronicles stresses the establishment of the kingship of David's descendants within Yahweh's kingly rule over Israel and the nations (1 Chron. 17:14). Third, Nathan recalls Yahweh's covenant promise to establish David's descendants and David's throne (Psa. 89:4, 29, 36–37). Blaising notes that the promise of a "house" signifies physical lineage.[106]

According to Saucy, "the promise of a royal dynasty involved a 'kingdom' and 'throne' (2 Sam. 7:16)." He writes that the human monarchy began with Saul, but the covenant was established with David, promising him an enduring dynasty (2 Sam. 7:16). But Saucy traces the background of a king from Jacob (Gen. 49:10) to the prophecy by Moses which looked forward to a future king (Deut. 18:17–18). He notes that "the promise to David carried forward the divine purpose of a human monarchy designating a permanent kingly line from the lineage of David."[107] However, Blaising points out that "the appointment of a human king did not change the status of Yahweh as king over His people"[108] because God refers to David as "a ruler over my people Israel" (2 Sam. 7:8).

Blaising and Bock confirm that the Davidic covenant is unconditional because of the kind of covenant it is:

Like the covenant with Abraham, the covenant with David is a grant covenant. It is the formal establishment of a grant or gift to David, the servant of the Lord. It consists of promises to David. … As a covenant of grant, the Davidic covenant is unconditional. David, a man of faith, receives these promises believing that God will fulfill them. God declares His intentions to carry out these blessings to David as an act of His grace.[109]

Saucy also holds to the unconditional nature of the Davidic covenant. He observes that "the covenant is frequently described as 'eternal' (2 Sam. 7:13, 16; 23:5; Ps. 89:4, 28, 36–37)." However, regarding these passages, Saucy notes that "while the word 'eternal' or 'forever' does not itself demand immutability or permanence, the context indicates that this is the case with God's word to David."[110]

The Fulfillment of the Davidic Kingdom in the New Testament

The Davidic covenant has three provisions: the Davidic house (i.e., the dynasty), the kingdom (the realm), and the throne (the right to rule [2 Sam. 7:12, 13, 16]). Progressive dispensationalists maintain that the fulfillment of the Davidic covenant begins in Jesus. Blaising and Bock write, "The fulfillment of the Davidic covenant is the means for bringing to fulfillment all of the great covenant promises of God, the consideration of Jesus' Davidic kingship will reveal Him to be the fulfillment of the biblical covenants."[111] At this point, we will consider progressive dispensationalism's view of each provision.

The first promise concerns a royal dynasty. The Gospels begin with a strong emphasis on the coming of Jesus as a descendant of David. This theme is dominant in the genealogies

(Matt. 1:1, 6, 17, 20; Luke 1:27, 32, 69; 2:4, 11; 3:31). As a result, Saucy notes that "the genealogies are significant since they show that the promise of the Davidic seed had come to fruition [i.e., fulfillment]." Jesus is therefore recognized as the promised seed of David or son of David, an accepted messianic title in Jesus' days (Matt. 9:27; 12:23). Jesus himself accepted the title of "Son of David" (Matt. 21:16). Furthermore, Saucy writes that "the early church declared that the risen Jesus was the fulfillment of the promised seed of David."[112] Saucy interprets Peter's statement on the day of Pentecost, "God has made this Jesus ... both Lord and Christ" (Acts 2:36), to mean that God's promise to seat one of David's descendants on the throne had been fulfilled. Saucy states that "the promise of an everlasting dynasty and kingdom were bound up in him."[113]

The fulfillment of the Davidic dynasty reaches its climax in the book of Revelation. According to Saucy, the phrase, "who holds the key of David" (Rev. 3:7), means "Christ has been given full authority over the Davidic Messianic Kingdom." Again, in reference to throne scenes where the seals of the scrolls are broken (Rev. 5:5), Saucy writes that, "because He 'has triumphed' at the cross, but also because He is the 'Lion of the tribe of Judah, the root of David,'" Jesus has authority to break the seals of the scroll. Saucy makes a final reference to the Davidic dynasty: "I am the root and the Offspring of David (Rev. 22:16)." In this verse, Saucy states that "Jesus identifies Himself to the waiting churches as the prophesied Messiah through whom God has promised it all to fruition."[114]

Progressive dispensationalists maintain that some provisions of the Davidic covenant have already taken place in an inaugural fulfillment. Bock states:

> The progressive argument is that the New Testament treats a wide scope of provisions as realized in the current era, while also noting

the fundamental shifts in the administrative structure and operation of God's promise in this era. These provisions and shifts are proclaimed in terms that point to the realization and advance of the promises of God. They show that a covenantal stage has been reached as a result of Jesus' coming that is directly connected to the promises of old. In sum, some of what was promised in the covenants has come and has been instituted. The sheer scope of this covenantal language points to initial realization.[115]

We will now examine some of the provisions that progressive dispensationalists consider fulfilled. The Gospels, and Luke in particular, establish the fact that Jesus fulfills the Davidic promise. To support this claim, Blaising and Bock cite Luke 1:32–35:

> He shall be great, and shall be called the Son of the Highest: and the Lord God shall give unto him the throne of his father David. And he shall reign over the house of Jacob for ever; and of his kingdom there shall be no end. Then said Mary unto the angel, How shall this be, seeing I know not a man? And the angel answered and said unto her, The Holy Ghost shall come upon thee, and the power of the Highest shall overshadow thee: therefore also that holy thing which shall be born of thee shall be called the Son of God. (Luke 1:32–35).[116]

According to Blaising and Bock, this passage demonstrates that "the Davidic promise has been transferred to Jesus because both aspects of the Davidic promises (the Davidic house, the throne, and the kingdom) are present." They cite Luke 1:69–72, which portrays Jesus as the 'horn of salvation' which God has 'raised up' ... in the house of David His servant."[117] In their comment on this passage, Blaising and Bock write that it "recalls the Davidic covenant promises in Psalm 89:17, 24 and 132:17 regarding the horn of David as well as the promise about 'raising up' a descendant in 2 Samuel 7:12." In addition to this, he claims Jesus' baptism is an analogy of "raising up" in 2 Sam. 7:12, so that it "revealed that Jesus is the Christ, the Davidic king."[118]

Furthermore, progressive dispensationalists teach that the initial fulfillment of the Davidic covenant is also realized in Jesus' death, resurrection, and ascension. Blaising says that these events "renewed and affirmed the faith of many that He was and is indeed the prophesied king, the ultimate fulfillment of the promises to David."[119] As for the resurrection, Blaising and Bock note that "the apostles preached that Acts 2:22–36 has reference to the fulfillment of the covenant promise to 'raise up,' a promise which parallels David's descendants (2 Sam. 7:12)." They write that "the promise to 'raise up' a descendant in 2 Samuel 7:12 is connected with the promise to establish His kingdom." Therefore, Blaising concludes that "as a result of the resurrection, Jesus has now been enthroned. The enthronement has taken place upon the entrance of Jesus into heaven, in keeping with the language of Psalms 110:1 that describes the seating of David's son at God's right hand."[120] Blaising applies this directly to Jesus by making this psalm messianic and interpreting the title "Adonai" to refer to enthroned kings. In his view, "Jesus has been made Lord over Israel and Christ by virtue of the fact that he has acted from that heavenly position on behalf of his people to bless them with the gift of the Holy Spirit."[121] This aspect of the Davidic promises encompasses the raising up of Jesus Son of David from the dead, Jesus attaining the title the Son of God, His enthronement at the right hand of God, and His activity of blessing Jews and all other people. Blaising notes that "the New Testament repeatedly proclaims these as presently fulfilled."[122] Progressive dispensationalists, Blaising in particular, maintain that "Jesus' present position (enthroned at the right hand of God) and activity is a fulfillment of promises of the Davidic covenant."[123]

Furthermore, progressive dispensationalists believe that the throne on which Christ sits in heaven is the Davidic throne. Saucy argues, "Christ fulfilled it by sitting on Davidic dynasty."[124] Blaising relates the heavenly throne scenes (Rev. 5:5; 22:16) to David as a confirmation that Christ is fulfilling the Davidic throne aspect in heaven.[125] According to Saucy, "the messianic throne has been transferred from Jerusalem to heaven, and Jesus has begun His messianic reign as the Davidic king."[126]

What does the "right hand of God" mean, and what are its implications? Progressive dispensationalists maintain that the throne of God is closely related to the "right hand of God." According to Saucy, "the right hand of God" indicates a "fulfillment of Psalms 110:1 and proved that Jesus had been installed as the Messiah (Acts 2:36)." He interprets the phrase "the right hand of God" in Psalm 110:1 and Acts 2:33 to mean the position of Messianic authority, the throne of David.[127] To sum up their view, Saucy states, "This interpretation of the exaltation of Jesus to the right hand of God in fulfillment of the Davidic messianic promise therefore allows for the inaugural fulfillment of those promises in distinction from the total postponement of the Davidic promise in traditional dispensationalism."[128] Blaising confirms this with the following statement: "Repeatedly, the New Testament declares that He is enthroned at the right hand of God in fulfillment of the promise given in Psalm 110:1."[129] There are "already" and "not-yet" aspects in this passage. Therefore, progressive dispensationalists hold that Christ sitting at the right hand of God is symbolic of His ruling roles. He is "already" exercising authority over cosmic forces and ministering to people (Heb. 1:3–4, 13; 8:1; 10:12). The "not-yet" aspect is stated in Hebrews 10:13, where Christ will fully defeat the enemies in terms of Psalm 110:1, which is yet to come. Blaising and Bock cite Acts

2, which explicitly mentions the throne seating (Ps. 132:11) and also alludes to the throne language of 2 Samuel 7. Therefore, Blaising believes that Jesus is neither inactive nor passive as he awaits the final defeat of enemies at the "right hand." Bock states the following:

> No comparison can be made to the Old Testament example of David's being anointed and reigning later—because Jesus is active at the right hand of God. He is performing messianic activities. In Acts 5 it is in the offer of repentance to Israel and the availability of forgiveness. In Acts 2 it is distributing the promised Spirit of God, the ultimate sign of the arrival of the period of fulfillment in conjunction with new covenant hope.[130]

In summary, progressive dispensationalism maintains that Jesus is the king now, that is, he is ruling from His throne in heaven.

An Evaluation of the Progressive Dispensationalist Approach

In this evaluation of progressive dispensationalism's hermeneutic, we will focus on their views of expanded meaning, the church as the new humanity, and the fulfillment of the Davidic covenant at Christ's Second Coming.

Expanded Meaning

Progressive dispensationalists state that a grammatical-historical hermeneutic is no longer adequate. They employ the grammatical-historical-literary-theological method. In this approach, they use complementary hermeneutics to justify the expansion of meaning.

This is not in harmony with the affirmation of Article XVIII of the *CSBH*, which states, "WE AFFIRM that the Bible's own interpretation of itself is always correct, never deviating from, but rather elucidating, the single meaning of the inspired text."[131]

We have made clear the fact that progressive dispensationalists defend the view that a text can have multiple meanings. They claim a text should be read in a series of layers. They reject the fact that a text has only one meaning. Bock writes, "Interpretation is not a matter of seeing one rule or approach applied to every text; it involves appreciating the variety of ways in which God weaves together His message."[132] Therefore, Bock proposes that interpreters use a complementary hermeneutic. This method allows additions, changes, and expansion of the text as the result of the progress of revelation. However, when progressive dispensationalists add to or broaden a text from what it originally meant, they are violating Article VII of *CSBH*. This article states that

> WE AFFIRM that the meaning expressed in each biblical text is single, definite and fixed.
>
> WE DENY that the recognition of this single meaning eliminates the variety of its application.[133]

Complementary hermeneutics therefore imposes on the text a meaning that the original author did not intend. By doing so, it violates the established principles of the grammatical-historical method. (See table 4.) The Word of God is fixed, and no one may add or subtract from it. John severely cautions those who do:

> For I testify to everyone who hears the words of the prophecy of this book: If anyone adds to these things, God will add to him the plagues that are written in this book; and if anyone takes away from the words of the book of this prophecy, God

shall take away his part from the Book of Life, from the holy city, and *from* the things which are written in this book. (Rev. 22:18–19)

The progressive dispensationalists do not heed to this warning when they employ their complementary hermeneutic. The progressive dispensational hermeneutical method also contains some serious internal conflicts. The system promotes ambiguity. Blaising and Bock adamantly claim to reject a spiritual or allegorical hermeneutic, yet in their approach they employ spiritual interpretation. For instance, Saucy writes, "The throne of David has been transferred to heaven."[134] This is an allegorical hermeneutic. Bock is quick to deny that he practices this kind of interpretation, but it is implied. He writes, "Such a multilayered reading is not allegorizing or spiritualizing the text; it simply reflects the depth and the diversity of biblical message as more and more context is examined."[135] If this is the case, progressive dispensationalists do not adhere to the grammar or literal meaning underlying the grammatical-historical method. As a result, they violate Article XV of the *CSBH* which states:

WE AFFIRM the necessity of interpreting the Bible according to its literal, or normal, sense. The literal sense is the grammatical-historical sense, that is, the meaning which the writer expressed. Interpretation according to the literal sense will take account of all figures of speech and literary forms found in the text.

WE DENY the legitimacy of any approach to Scripture that attributes to it meaning which the literal sense does not support.[136]

Progressive dispensationalists approach the text with a bias that is based on human limitations and preunderstanding. These are the starting points for their interpretations. To be specific, Bock's hermeneutic of partial fulfillment begins with an unfounded premise. He writes, "If a promise contains many elements, it is possible to have a partial fulfillment by having some of those elements realized. In other words, to have an initial fulfillment is distinct from having total fulfillment."[137] Bock presupposes that when several elements of an Old Testament promise appear in a New Testament text, it constitutes an initial fulfillment. This conclusion is based on an unproven presupposition, not on a biblical text. This approach is therefore subjective rather than objective. It violates Article XIX of the *CSBH*, which states:

> WE DENY that Scripture should be required to fit alien preunderstandings, inconsistent with itself, such as naturalism, evolutionism, scientism, secular humanism, and relativism.[138]

In the progressive dispensationalists' case, their preunderstanding renders the interpretation of the text subjective. If the truth contained in the text is compromised, then it promotes relativism. This is the unfortunate result with which Bock is left in doing what he is trying to accomplish.

Progressive dispensationalists also misinterpret figures of speech. According to Saucy, the "right hand of God" refers to a "fulfillment of Psalms 110:1 and proved that Jesus had been installed as the Messiah (Acts 2:36)."[139] The phrase is figurative. Normally, the meaning of figures of speech is not derived from the literal words that form the figures, but from the literal sense conveyed by the figure.[140] That is, the sense behind the figures should be understood literally. Therefore, the "right hand of God" implies a future, literal, and earthly Davidic throne. It does not refer to a spiritual throne, as progressive dispensationalists claim. When they speak of figurative language, Bock writes,

> Interpretation of apocalyptic is not a matter of literal versus figurative/allegorical approaches, but of how to identify and understand the reference of the figure in question. Often the case is that more narrowly defined images of the Old Testament have been expanded to cover a wider scope in Revelation, but not at the expense of the original emphasis of the term; rather, such expansion is in addition to the original image.[141]

When Blaising and Bock expand figures of speech in this way, the figures no longer have the literal meaning intended in the context. Therefore, this interpretive method does not harmonize with Article XV of the *CSBH*, which states:

> WE AFFIRM the necessity of interpreting the Bible according to its literal, or normal, sense. The literal sense is the grammatical-historical sense, that is, the meaning which the writer expressed. Interpretation according to the literal sense will take account of all figures of speech and literary forms found in the text.
>
> WE DENY the legitimacy of any approach to Scripture that attributes to it meaning which the literal sense does not support[142]

The Church as Redeemed Humanity

We commend progressive dispensationalists for holding that Christ will return to earth to reign over a literal thousand-year kingdom. However, their claim that they maintain a distinction between Israel and the church is doubtful, because they also believe in continuity between Israel and the church. This position is inconsistent and makes the relationship between Israel and the church ambiguous. This inconsistency violates the affirmation of Article XVII in the *CSBH*, which states, "WE AFFIRM the unity, harmony and consistency of Scripture and declare that it is its own best interpreter."[143]

Furthermore, Blaising and Bock hold that God will fulfill his promises to Israel in the future. They write, "An OT promise made to a specific recipient must benefit that recipient, even if the promise is later expanded to include others. The only way to exclude the original recipient is to have specific revelation that makes clear that the promise now permanently excludes the original recipient."[144] But Bock has not cited any specific revelation that makes clear that the original promise includes the church and Israel. These two institutions have always been separate entities. Because Bock's argument lacks evidence, we can conclude that he wrote this to support his system of complementary hermeneutics. However, progressive dispensationalists violate this principle. They hold that the church fulfills Israel's promises, but Carl Hoch Jr., a progressive dispensationalist, notes that "The believing remnant of Israel within the Church share in promises of Israel, they experience promised blessings in which Gentiles also participate."[145] This statement contradicts Bock's claim and violates Article XVIII of the *CSBH*:

> WE AFFIRM that the Bible's own interpretation of itself is always correct, never deviating from, but rather elucidating, the single meaning of the inspired text. The single meaning of a prophet's words includes, but is not restricted to, the understanding of those words by the prophet

and necessarily involves the intention of God evidenced in the fulfillment of those words.

WE DENY that the writers of Scripture always understood the full implications of their own words.[146]

Because progressive dispensationalists teach the continuity of Israel and the church in past, present, and future dispensations, they minimize the church's uniqueness. Despite the rich background and definition they provide on the term "mystery," they teach that the mystery concept of the church was unrealized in the Old Testament rather than being unrevealed. According to Bock, "the church is an 'already' or 'sneak preview' of the kingdom."[147] Therefore, progressive dispensationalists conclude that God does not have separate plans for Israel and the church. This view contradicts the evidence in Matthew and Acts, which show that the church is unique. Furthermore, progressive dispensationalists consider the church to be "the new Israel." They take this view from 1 Peter 2:9, where Peter describes the church in terms that originally applied to Israel (e.g., "chosen," "nation," and "people"). But does his application of these terms to the church mean that it is the "new Israel"? The authorship, date, and recipients of the letter reveal otherwise. We have to answer two questions regarding this passage: First, who are the recipients of 1 Peter, and how is this passage interpreted?

In response to the first question, Peter addressed the letter to believing Jews despite strong Gentile allusions. The phrase, "the pilgrims of the Dispersion" (1 Pet. 1:1), is strongly Jewish. Peter's focus is on the Jewish mission (Gal. 2:7), and several Old Testament quotations allude to the Jewish audience. But some scholars hold that he addressed the letter to Gentile Christians because of his reference to their "futile way of life" (1 Pet. 1:18, NASB) and the fact that in the past they "were not a people"

(2:10). However, W. Edward Glenny points out that "many of the arguments used to suggest the church is a new Israel replacing the nation are based on parallels and correspondences between the two; an obvious error is the belief that such a correspondence or parallel proves identity."[148] Vlach's argument against applying such terms as "chosen," "nation," and "generation" to the church in 1 Peter 2:9 also deserve consideration. He makes the following observation: "There are occasions in Scripture in which 'Israel' imagery is applied to non-Israelites without these non-Israelites becoming Israel. Isaiah 19:24–25, for instance, predicts that Egypt would someday be called 'my people.' Yet the context makes clear that Egypt is distinct from Israel since Egypt is mentioned alongside 'Israel my inheritance.'"[149]

The final question concerns the exegesis of this passage. Does the interpreter employ a literal or spiritual hermeneutic? If they employ the latter method, then they will designate the church as "new Israel." However, nowhere in the Scriptures is the church referred to as the "new Israel." Israel has always denoted the literal ethnic Israel, that is, the seed of Abraham. When a literal interpretation is observed, the words of the original text do not change their meaning over time as progressive dispensationalists allege. The hermeneutical system that changes the words of the Scriptures to mean something other than how they are plainly presented is a spiritual hermeneutic. In conclusion, therefore, this hermeneutic violates the grammatical-historical principles (see table 4) and is not in harmony with Article IX of the *CSBH*, which states:

> WE DENY that the message of Scripture derives from, or is dictated by, the interpreter's understanding. Thus we deny that the "horizons" of the biblical writer and the interpreter might rightly "fuse" in such a way that what the text communicates to the interpreter is not ultimately

controlled by the expressed meaning of the Scripture.[150]

The Already and Not-Yet Fulfillments of the Davidic Kingdom

The "already" and "not-yet" eschatology is based on the assumption that the church is the initial phase of the fulfillment of the promises of the Davidic covenant. It is dialectic in its approach because it portrays the kingdom as present ("already") and future ("not-yet") at the same time. At some point, the two realities will be merged into one, so that the current church age and the future kingdom age are ultimately indistinguishable. Using this approach, progressive dispensationalists argue that Jesus is currently reigning from the throne of God. The "already" and "not-yet" approach to biblical interpretation is invalid because it appears to be a forced hermeneutic. Furthermore, it is not in harmony with Article XIII of the *CSBH*. It states,

> WE AFFIRM that awareness of the literary categories, formal and stylistic, of the various parts of Scripture is essential for proper exegesis, and hence we value genre criticism as one of the many disciplines of biblical study.

> WE DENY that generic categories which negate historicity may rightly be imposed on biblical narratives which present themselves as factual.[151]

We can note several shortcomings of this approach. First, this form of fulfillment makes the interpretation of texts unstable. Johnson observes that the original meaning of the author is lost when the text is altered or broadened.[152] In this case, it violates Article VII of the *CSBH*, which states, "WE AFFIRM that the meaning expressed in each biblical text is single, definite and fixed."[153] Second, this model relies upon an expansion of the original meaning in order to reframe a text in a new context. Johnson writes, "The expansion is not the result of anything found in the original text but is determined by the 'already' context of progressive fulfillment."[154] As a result, an Old Testament text means one thing for now and yet has another textually literal meaning for the future. Third, the interpreter who uses this method

> advocates for unique interpretations of New Testament apostles. To argue that an apostle has the right to interpret the expanded meanings is to confuse revelation and interpretation. An apostle reveals new truths in addition to the truth revealed originally in the Old Testament. This new truth is often referred to as "mysteries" (Matt. 13; Eph. 3) when spoken of in the New Testament. To introduce a new freedom for apostles reusing Old Testament texts is to confuse categories of what is interpreted and what is revealed.[155]

Consequently, this principle is not in harmony with Article XVII of the *CSBH*, which states:

> WE DENY that Scripture may be interpreted in such a way as to suggest that one passage corrects or militates against another. We deny that later writers of Scripture misinterpreted earlier passages of Scripture when quoting from or referring to them.[156]

Fourth, this model of fulfillment oversimplifies the variety of promises in progressive revelation because it "relies upon a partial fulfillment to determine what is already fulfilled. The concept of 'partial fulfillment' often equivocates on what is meant by 'partial.'"[157] This partial fulfillment is subjective because it is based on human preunderstanding. Therefore, this principle is not in harmony with Article XIX of the *CSBH*:

> WE DENY that Scripture should be required to fit alien preunderstandings, inconsistent with itself.[158]

The "already" and "not-yet" dualism has become part of progressive dispensationalist's hermeneutic. It means that the Davidic kingdom is partially fulfilled in the present (the initial fulfillment, i.e., the "already" aspect) and will be consummated in the future (in the millennial kingdom, i.e., the "not-yet" aspect). Is this teaching clearly taught in the Scriptures? If not, what is its shortcoming? Hal Harless alludes to the progressive dispensationalists' problem as being semantic.[159] The semantic problem basically has to do with the meaning of the word "fulfill." Progressive dispensationalists prefer the term "fulfill" because it is broad enough to fit their concept of the initial or partial fulfillment of the kingdom. To put the issue in perspective, *Webster's Third New International Dictionary* (hereafter *Webster's*) defines "fulfill" as follows: (a) "to make full: FILL; (b) to supply the missing parts: make whole; and (c) to carry out: ACCOMPLISH, EXECUTE."[160]

We noted previously that the Davidic kingdom has three elements: a house, a throne, and a kingdom. Normally, all the elements must be in place in order to consider a covenant fulfilled. In this case, the first definition: carry out: fill, is applicable. But Bock appears to use the third definition. He writes, "In this writer's view one can speak of initial fulfillment when any of the aspects are realized."[161] This contradicts the Scriptures, which deny partial fulfillment (cf. Josh. 23:14; 1 Kings 8:15–24; Neh. 9:8; Jer. 34:18; Luke 4:21). Despite this fact, Hal Harless notes,

> The corrective is to realize that although covenant
> is established at a given point, the stipulations of
> the covenant may be instituted at different times.
> This is not an initial versus final fulfillment. Each
> individual stipulation will be completely fulfilled
> in its own time and the covenant will be fulfilled
> when all of the stipulations are fulfilled.[162]

In this case, progressive dispensationalists have succumbed to a semantic problem involving their understanding of the word "fulfill."

Conclusion

Progressive dispensationalism is still developing its hermeneutic. However, by using this approach, they have drifted away from traditional dispensationalism's essential beliefs, namely, "grammatical-historical interpretation, the distinction of Israel and the Church, and the purpose of God (which is doxological)."[163] Their writers claim to be dispensationalists, but their shifting interpretive trend (i.e., complementary hermeneutics) betrays them.

Progressive dispensationalists have many weaknesses. First, they present a non-biblical view of the progress of revelation. They maintain that it changes or expands the meaning of the original promises in order to change the divine author's meaning. As a result, they render the text fallible. God's nature is the biblical basis for understanding God's Word. He is immutable, and so the meaning of his words do not change. The psalmists note that "the words of the LORD *are* pure words" (Psa. 12:6); they quote Yahweh as saying, "My covenant I will not break, / Nor alter the word that has gone out of My lips" (Ps. 89:34); and they proclaim, "Forever, O LORD, / Your word is settled in heaven" (Ps. 119:89). Therefore, the meaning of God's words do not change as progressive dispensationalists allege when they use progressive revelation in their hermeneutic.

Secondly, they also have a false concept of the term "mystery." They hold that "mystery" is not new revelation. It refers to something that existed in the Old Testament but was "unrealized." Bock for instance, explores the background of this word in extrabiblical records, particularly those from Qumran, to prove that this word was in use.[164] Because of this, they fail to recognize that the church was not revealed in the Old Testament. Hence, they teach that the church is a continuation of Israel. This view is both invalid and unbiblical.

Finally, in progressive revelation, a statement can only have one referent. But progressive dispensationalists hold that the Davidic promises have two reference points: the church and Israel. The Scriptures are clear, however, that Israel is the only referent for the Davidic promises. The church is not a referent but is blessed with similar blessings that are of a spiritual nature. These "spiritual blessings are not the same as the covenant promises that God made to David and Israel since that would be a logical fallacy."[165] The two-referent view is based on eisegesis and is therefore subjective and unbiblical.

In summary, progressive dispensationalists use complementary hermeneutics to interpret Old Testament prophecies. This approach has the authors of the New Testament altering, adding, and canceling Old Testament promises. It is based on the premise that the Davidic kingdom has been inaugurated in a so called "already" aspect, in which the kingdom is operating in the present in a spiritual form. The "not-yet" aspect means that the Davidic kingdom will be consummated in the future when Jesus returns. Progressive dispensationalists hold that the kingdom is revealed progressively. They also believe that the church fulfills Israel's promises. According to this view, the church is spiritual Israel. It is not a New Testament revelation, but existed in the Old Testament dispensation.

In chapter 4, we will focus on the traditional dispensationalist view of the fulfillment of the Davidic covenant. This position has never been as popular as the other views. We are discussing it last for two reasons. First, on the hermeneutical spectrum it is farthest from the postmillennial view and closest to the progressive dispensationalists view. Second, my goal is to defend the traditional dispensationalist view, so the logical approach is to discuss the opposing views first, and then present the option I feel is best. So now we will look at it in detail.

1   Craig A. Blaising and Darrell L. Bock, "Dispensationalism, Israel and the Church: Assessment and Dialogue," in Craig A. Blaising and Darrell L. Bock, *Dispensationalism, Israel and the Church: The Search for Definition* (Grand Rapids: Zondervan, 1992), 379.

2   Robert L. Saucy, *The Case for Progressive Dispensationalism: The Interface Between Dispensationalism and Non-Dispensational Theology* (Grand Rapids: Zondervan, 1993), 27.

3   Blaising and Bock, "Assessment and Dialogue," 380.

4   Blaising and Bock, "Assessment and Dialogue," 380.

5   Blaising and Bock, "Assessment and Dialogue," 381.

6   Blaising and Bock, "Assessment and Dialogue," 380.

7   Craig A. Blaising and Darrell L. Bock, *Progressive Dispensationalism*, 22-23.

8   List of Signees of CSBH, Accessed 6/7/2018, http://library.dts.edu/Pages/TL/Special/ICBI_1_typed.pdf. Saucy's name appears in the second page, its 12th on far right column. It is assumed Saucy rejected the CSBH affirmation VII of single meaning by adopting a Complimentary hermeneutics of Progressive Dispensationalism.

9   Ryrie, *Dispensationalism: Revised and Expanded*, 46-48.

10 Craig Blaising, "Developing Dispensationalists Part 2: Development of Dispensationalism by Contemporary Dispensationalists," Bibliotheca Sacra 145, no. 579 (July 1988): 272, accessed June 8, 2018: http://www.galaxie.com/article/bsac145-579-02.

11 Darrell L. Bock, "Hermeneutics of Progressive Dispensationalism," in Three Central Issues in Contemporary Dispensationalism, 97.

12 R. J. Rushdoony, Chalcedon Foundation, is focused on publications of Christian Reconstruction resources. For more information, check the http:chalcedon.edu/about.

13 Blaising, "Development of Dispensationalism by Contemporary Dispensationalists," 272.

14 Darrell L. Bock, "Current Messianic Activity and OT Davidic Promise: Dispensationalism, Hermeneutics, and Fulfillment," *Trinity Journal* 15, no. 1 (Spring 1994): 71, http://www.galaxie.com/article/trinj15-1-04.

15 Bock, "Current Messianic Activity," 72.

16 Herbert W. Bateman IV, "Dispensationalism Yesterday and Today," in *Three Central Issues in Contemporary Dispensationalism*, ed. Herbert W. Bateman IV (Grand Rapids: Kregel, 1999), 38.

17 Darrell L. Bock, "Covenants in Traditional Dispensationalism: Response by Darrell Bock," in *Three Central Issues in Contemporary Dispensationalism*, 157.

18 Bock, "Covenant in Traditional Dispensationalism," in *Three Central Issues*, 157.

19 Bock, "Covenants in Traditional Dispensationalism: Response by Darrell Bock," 158.

20 Blaising and Bock, "Assessment and Dialogue," 392-3.

21 Blaising and Bock, "Assessment and Dialogue," 81. They differ in their definition of mystery with traditional dispensationalists, who understand "mystery" as "something new, never revealed before."

22 Bock, "Current Messianic Activity," 81.

23 Robert L. Saucy, "The Church as the Mystery of God," in *Dispensationalism, Israel and the Church*, 137.

24 Saucy, "The Church as the Mystery of God," 139.

25 Saucy, "The Church as the Mystery of God," 139.

26 Saucy, "The Church as the Mystery of God," 139.

27 Saucy, *The Case for Progressive Dispensationalism*, 191.

28 Saucy, *The Case for Progressive Dispensationalism*, 192.

29 Saucy, *The Case for Progressive Dispensationalism*, 194.

30 Saucy, *The Case for Progressive Dispensationalism*, 195–198.

31 Saucy, *The Case for Progressive Dispensationalism*, 195.

32 Saucy, *The Case for Progressive Dispensationalism*, 208.

33 Craig A. Blaising, "The Extent and Varieties of Dispensationalism," in Craig A. Blaising and Darrell L. Bock, *Progressive Dispensationalism* (Wheaton, IL: BridgePoint, 1993), 49.

34 Saucy, *The Case for Progressive Dispensationalism*, 60.

35 Saucy, *The Case for Progressive Dispensationalism*, 61.

36 Saucy, *The Case for Progressive Dispensationalism*, 61.

37 Darrell L. Bock, "Interpreting the Bible—How Texts Speak to Us," in *Progressive Dispensationalism*, 77.

38 Blaising, "Development of Dispensationalism by Contemporary Dispensationalists," 272.

39 Bock, "How Texts Speak to Us," 100.

40 Bock, "How Texts Speak to Us," 100.

41 Bock, "How Texts Speak to Us," 101.

42 Bock, "How Texts Speak to Us," 100.

43 Bock, "How Texts Speak to Us," 101.

44 Bock, "How Texts Speak to Us," 100-103.

45 Bock, "How Texts Speak to Us," 102.

46 Bock, "How Texts Speak to Us," 98.

47 Bock, "How Texts Speak to Us," 98.

48 Bock, "How Texts Speak to Us," 96-100.

49 Blaising, "The Extent and Varieties of Dispensationalism," 52.

50 Blaising, "The Extent and Varieties of Dispensationalism," 52.

51 Blaising, "The Extent and Varieties of Dispensationalism," 52.

52 Bock, "How Texts Speak to Us," 97-98.

53 Blaising and Bock, "Assessment and Dialogue," 392-93.

54 Darrell L. Bock, "Hermeneutics of Progressive Dispensationalism," in *Three Central Issues in Contemporary Dispensationalism*, 97.

55 Bock, "Current Messianic Activity," 71.

56 Bock, "Current Messianic Activity," 71.

57 Bock, "Current Messianic Activity," 72.

58 Bock, "Current Messianic Activity," 72.

59 Bock, "Current Messianic Activity," 72.

60 Bock, "Current Messianic Activity," 72.

61 Louis Berkhof, *Principles of Biblical Interpretation: Sacred Hermeneutics* (Grand Rapids: Baker Book House, 1950), 115.

62 Darrell L. Bock, "The Son of David and the Saints' Task: The Hermeneutics of Initial Fulfillment," *Bibliotheca Sacra* 150 (October–December 1993): 445-6, accessed April 6, 2015, http://web.a.ebscohost.com/ehost/pdfviewer?

63 Bock, "Son of David." 447.

64 Bock, "Current Messianic Activity," 71.

65 Bock, "Interpreting the Bible—How We Read Texts," in *Progressive Dispensationalism*, 68.

66 Bock, "How Texts Speak to Us," 76-105.

67 Bateman, "Dispensationalism Yesterday and Today," 40.

68 Blaising and Bock, "Assessment and Dialogue," 383.

69 Blaising and Bock, "Assessment and Dialogue," 384.

70   Saucy, *The Case for Progressive Dispensationalism*, 188

71   Saucy, *The Case for Progressive Dispensationalism*, 189.

72   Saucy, *The Case for Progressive Dispensationalism*, 190.

73   Blaising, "The Extent and Varieties of Dispensationalism," 49.

74   Blaising, "The Extent and Varieties of Dispensationalism," 49.

75   Blaising, "The Extent and Varieties of Dispensationalism," 49.

76   Blaising, "The Extent and Varieties of Dispensationalism," 50.

77   Blaising, "The Extent and Varieties of Dispensationalism," 50.

78   Blaising, "The Extent and Varieties of Dispensationalism," 50.

79   Blaising, "The Extent and Varieties of Dispensationalism," 50.

80   Blaising, "The Extent and Varieties of Dispensationalism," 50.

81   J. Lanier Burns, "Israel and the Church of a Progressive Dispensationalist," in *Three Central Issues in Contemporary Dispensationalism*, 266.

82   Burns, "Israel and the Church of a Progressive Dispensationalist," 266.

83   Burns, "Israel and the Church of a Progressive Dispensationalist," 268.

84   Burns, "Israel and the Church of a Progressive Dispensationalist," 268.

85   Burns, "Israel and the Church of a Progressive Dispensationalist," 269.

86   Burns, "Israel and the Church of a Progressive Dispensationalist," 269.

87   Burns, "Israel and the Church of a Progressive Dispensationalist," 270.

88   Burns, "Israel and the Church of a Progressive Dispensationalist," 271.

89   Burns, "Israel and the Church of a Progressive Dispensationalist," 283.

90   Burns, "Israel and the Church of a Progressive Dispensationalist," 283.

91   Burns, "Israel and the Church of a Progressive Dispensationalist," 284.

92   Burns, "Israel and the Church of a Progressive Dispensationalist," 284.

93   Burns, "Israel and the Church of a Progressive Dispensationalist," 286.

94   Burns, "Israel and the Church of a Progressive Dispensationalist," 286.

95   Burns, "Israel and the Church of a Progressive Dispensationalist," 286.

96   Burns, "Israel and the Church of a Progressive Dispensationalist," 288.

97   Bock, "Current Messianic Activity," 69.

98   Bock, "How Texts Speak to Us," 97.

99   Bock, "Evidence from Acts," 184.

100 Bock, "Current Messianic Activity," 70

101 Bock, "Current Messianic Activity," 70.

102 Bock, "Current Messianic Activity," 98.

103 Bock, "Current Messianic Activity," 98.

104 Craig A. Blaising, "The Structure of the Biblical Covenants: The Covenants Prior to Christ," in *Progressive Dispensationalism*, 159.

105 Saucy, *The Case for Progressive Dispensationalism*, 60.

106 Blaising, "The Structure of the Biblical Covenants," 160.

107 Saucy, *The Case for Progressive Dispensationalism*, 60, 61.

108 Blaising, "The Structure of the Biblical Covenants," 163.

109 Blaising, "The Structure of the Biblical Covenants," 163.

110 Saucy, *Case for Progressive Dispensationalism*, 65.

111 Craig A. Blaising, "The Fulfillment of the Biblical Covenants through Jesus Christ," in *Progressive Dispensationalism*, 175.

112 Saucy, *Case for Progressive Dispensationalism*, 67.

113 Saucy, *Case for Progressive Dispensationalism*, 65.

114 Saucy, *Case for Progressive Dispensationalism*, 68.

115 Bock, "Covenants in Traditional Dispensationalism: Response by Darrell L. Bock," 157.

116 Blaising and Bock, "The Fulfillment of the Biblical Covenants Through Jesus Christ," in Progressive Dispensationalism, 175

117 Blaising, "The Fulfillment of the Biblical Covenants," 175.

118 Blaising, "The Fulfillment of the Biblical Covenants," 175–6.

119 Blaising, "The Fulfillment of the Biblical Covenants," 177.

120 Blaising, "The Fulfillment of the Biblical Covenants," 175.

121 Blaising, "The Fulfillment of the Biblical Covenants," 177.

122 Blaising, "The Fulfillment of the Biblical Covenants," 178.

123 Blaising, "The Fulfillment of the Biblical Covenants," 180.

124 Saucy, *The Case for Progressive Dispensationalism*, 68. He claims that Christ holding the key of David (Rev. 3:7) means "Christ has been given full authority over the Davidic Messianic Kingdom." In other words, Christ is already the king. However, this passage gives the titles of Christ, not His current function.

125 Blaising, "The Fulfillment of the Biblical Covenants," 177.

126 Saucy, *Case for Progressive Dispensationalism*, 70.

127 Saucy, *Case for Progressive Dispensationalism*, 70.

128 Saucy, *Case for Progressive Dispensationalism*, 76.

129 Blaising, "The Fulfillment of the Biblical Covenants," 182.

130 Bock, "Covenants in Progressive Dispensationalism," 200.

131 Geisler, *Summit II Hermeneutics*, 23.

132 Bock, "How We Read Texts," 68.

133 Geisler, *Summit II Hermeneutics*, 21.

134 Saucy, *The Case for Progressive Dispensationalism*, 70.

135 Bock, "The Son of David and the Saints' Task," 445.

136 Geisler, *Summit II Hermeneutics*, 23.

137 Bock, "Current Messianic Activity," 72.

138 Geisler, *Summit II Hermeneutics*, 24.

139 Saucy, *Case for Progressive Dispensationalism*, 70.

140 Tan, *Literal Interpretation*, 51.

141 Bock, "How Texts Speak to Us," 93.

142 Geisler, *Summit II Hermeneutics*, 23.

143 Geisler, *Summit II Hermeneutics*, 23.

144 Bock, "Current Messianic Activity," 67.

145 Carl B. Hoch Jr., "The New Man of Ephesians 2," in *Dispensationalism, Israel and the Church*, 126.

146 Geisler, *Summit II Hermeneutics*, 23–24.

147 Darrell L Bock, "The Reign of the Lord Jesus Christ," in *Dispensationalism, Israel and the Church*, 53.

148 W. Edward. Glenny, "The Israelite Imagery of 1 Peter 2," in *Dispensationalism, Israel and the Church*, 183, n. 126.

149 Michael J. Vlach, *Has the Church Replaced Israel?* (Nashville, TN: B and H Academic, 2010), 149.

150 Geisler, *Summit II Hermeneutics*, 21.

151 Geisler, *Summit II Hermeneutics*, 22.

152 Elliott E. Johnson, "A Traditional Dispensational Hermeneutic," in *Three Central Issues in Contemporary Dispensationalism*, 75.

153 Geisler, *Summit II Hermeneutics*, 21.

154 Johnson, "Hermeneutics of Progressive Dispensationalism" response in, Three Essential Issues, 103

155 Johnson, "A Traditional Dispensational Hermeneutic," 75.

156 Geisler, *Summit II Hermeneutics*, 23.

157 Johnson, "A Traditional Dispensational Hermeneutic," 75-6.

158 Geisler, *Summit II Hermeneutics*, 24.

159 Hal Harless, *How Firm a Foundation: The Dispensations in the Light of the Divine Covenants*, Studies in Biblical Literature 63 (New York: Peter Lang, 2004), 158.

160 *Webster's Third New International Dictionary of the English Language, Unbridged and Seven Language Dictionary* (hereafter, *Webster's*), 3 vols. (Chicago: Encyclopedia Britannica, 1993), s.v. "fulfill"; all capitals orig.

161 Bock, "The Son of David and the Saints' Task," 454.

162 Harless, *How Firm a Foundation*, 158.

163 Ryrie (*Dispensationalism*, 46-48) clearly states the essential features of traditional dispensationalism as distinction of church and Israel, literal hermeneutics, and the purpose of God in the world (also called doxology).

164 Bock, "Current Messianic Activity," 72.

165 William Sanford LaSor, *Israel: A Biblical View* (Grand Rapids: Eerdmans, 1976), 95.

CHAPTER 4

The Traditional Dispensationalist View

Traditional dispensationalism is a system of biblical interpretation that distinguishes between distinct periods (dispensations) in biblical history. The proponents of this view claim to adhere to a grammatical-historical interpretation of Scripture and argue for a consistent literal interpretation of all portions of Scripture, including those that are prophetic.[1] In particular, they hold that all the promises God made to Abraham and David will be fulfilled literally in the millennial kingdom.

An Overview of Traditional Dispensationalism

In the following sections, we will discuss the essence of the traditional dispensationalist hermeneutic and its use throughout church history.

A Definition of Traditional Dispensationalism

Traditional dispensationalists use the grammatical-historical method, also known as literal interpretation. This means they take God's Word in both testaments literally or plainly, that is, as the original authors meant it.[2] They are committed to three essentials: the distinction between the church and Israel, the literal meaning of

Patrick W. Nasongo

the Scriptures, and the doxological purpose of God as opposed to a purpose that is soteriological (postmillennialist) or Christological (progressive dispensationalist).[3] As a result, the adherents of this view recognize various dispensations through which God works in the affairs of his people.[4] Traditional dispensationalists also maintain that God has not fulfilled the grant covenants (i.e., the Abrahamic, Davidic, and New covenants) during the church age, but that he will fulfill them in the future to the restored nation of Israel.[5] The proponents of this view also agree with the *Chicago Statement of Biblical Hermeneutics* established in 1978.[6]

A Brief History of Traditional Dispensationalism

Dispensationalists have refined their views many times and may be on the verge of another refinement. However, their hermeneutical principles have not changed. They simply attempt to more consistently apply their principles. In the following paragraphs we will briefly discuss these refinements.

Early forms of dispensationalism. As early as the second century, many Christians have held to some form of dispensationalism, though most of the early approaches were just basic outlines. For instance, Justin Martyr (110–165), Irenaeus (130–200), Clement of Alexandria (150–220), Augustine (354–430), and Joachim Fiore (ca. 1135–1202) believed that God worked in different ways with different groups of people throughout human history.[7]

The beginnings of systemization. Pierre Poiret (1646–1719), Jonathan Edwards (1637–1716), and Isaac Watts (1647–1748) each developed dispensational frameworks that closely resemble the dispensations to which later dispensationalists hold. In fact, Ryrie points out that Scofield's outline resembles Isaac Watt's framework more than it does John Nelson Darby's.[8]

Darby's dispensationalism. In the nineteenth century, John Nelson Darby systematized dispensationalism and spread his teachings throughout the world.[9] He introduced the basic elements of a dispensation: God's government, human responsibility, God's revelation to humanity, a test, a failure, and a judgment.[10] His dispensational framework was complicated, which may explain why Scofield did not use it.[11] Darby also held that the church was so distinct from Israel that it did not participate in the millennial kingdom. As far as he was concerned, the church would remain in heaven during the millennial reign of Christ.[12]

Classical dispensationalism. Dispensationalism experienced phenomenal growth occurred during the first seven decades of the twentieth century as the result of the publication of *The Scofield Reference Bible*, the establishment of Dallas Theological Seminary, a fervent commitment to God's Word, and the publication of traditional dispensationalism's principles. The name classical dispensationalism distinguishes this phase from the preceding and following stages. Lewis Sperry Chafer, professor of systematic theology at Dallas Theological Seminary, played a major role in educating the second generation of dispensationalists in the United States.[13] Classical dispensationalism sought to explain how the church could participate in the kingdom in what may have been a reaction to Darby's extreme view of the church.

Essential dispensationalism. In the 1960s, the second-generation dispensationalists still struggled with the church's relationship to the New covenant and the kingdom. This group, which included such men as Charles Ryrie, John Walvoord, and Roy Zuck, held to what has been variously known as traditional dispensationalism, normative dispensationalism, essential dispensationalism, and revisionist dispensationalism. Ryrie developed the three essentials of dispensationalism stated above, which led the progressive dispensationalists to call this group "essential dispensationalists."[14] This may be the best name of this phase of dispensationalism. As with the classical dispensationalists, the majority of traditional dispensationalists maintain that the church is the mystery form of the kingdom Jesus alluded to in the parables in Matthew 13.[15]

Consistent dispensationalism. Some third-generation traditional dispensationalists, such as Christopher Cone, are calling for a more consistent application of the grammatical-historical hermeneutic that traditional dispensationalists claim they implement.[16] The challenge may be based on Ryrie's own words: "Hermeneutics is the science that furnishes the principles of interpretation. These principles guide and govern anybody's system of theology. They ought to be determined *before* one's theology is systematized, but in practice the reverse is usually true."[17] The implications of this challenge remain to be worked out, but such implications could change traditional dispensationalists' views of the church's relationship to the kingdom, as well as of many books and passages in the Scriptures that may only apply to national Israel. The movement is so recent that it is out of the scope of our discussion to pursue it.

Traditional Dispensationalism and the Central Issues

As with postmillennialism and progressive dispensationalism, we will look first at traditional dispensationalism's presuppositions regarding the three hermeneutical issues of progressive revelation, the priority of the testaments, and the meaning of the term "mystery." Then we will examine their conclusions concerning the relationship between Israel and the church, as well as the nature of the kingdom.

Progressive Revelation

Ryrie defines progressive revelation as "the recognition that God's message to man was not given in one single act but was unfolded in a series of successive acts and through the minds and hands of many men of varying background."[18] In addition to this, Ryrie notes that "in the process of revealing His message to man, God may add or even change in one era what He had given in another."[19]

Ryrie's words, "adding" and "changing," do not refer to altering the author's original meaning as presented in the Old Testament. Instead, he is talking about ceremonial issues such as eating pork (cf. Mark 7:19; Acts 10:15). Thomas D. Bernard also develops this concept of progressive revelation by stating that the Bible presents "not the exposition of a revelation completed, but the records of a revelation in progress."[20]

Roy Zuck also explains progressive revelation: "In later Scriptures, God added to what He had given in earlier portions." He asserts that "progressive revelation does not mean that the Old Testament is less inspired than the New or that the Old Testament is less clear than the New." Furthermore, God's unchanging character (i.e., his immutability) applies to his inspired Word as well.[21]

Here we can give some biblical examples of progressive revelation. For instance, in the Sermon on the Mount, Jesus did not encourage His disciples to break the Law. Instead, he said to them, "Do not think that I came to destroy the Law or the Prophets. I did not come to destroy but to fulfill" (Matt. 5:17). The Law was given as a guide to basic morality, but the Lord brought out its spiritual aspect. Alfred Plummer states:

> Such an expression implies that He knew that there was danger of their thinking so, and possibly that some had actually said this of Him. The Pharisees would be sure to say it. He disregarded the oral tradition which they held to be equal in authority to the written laws; and He interpreted the written law according to its spirit, and not as they did, according to the rigid letter. … He neglected the traditional modes of reading and preached in a way of His own.[22]

Paul's sermon to his audience on Mars Hill also illustrates progressive revelation. He says, "Truly, these times of ignorance God overlooked, but now commands all men everywhere to repent" (Acts 17:30). Thomas Ice makes the following observation:

> Paul's phrase "the times of ignorance" is a parallel concept to God's having not revealed the mystery in past times (see Rom. 16:25; Eph. 3:6; Col. 1:26). Paul's declaration that "God is now declaring to men that all everywhere should repent," is similar to his statements that the gospel message is now going global, for all men everywhere (see Rom. 16:26; Eph. 3:6; Col. 1:27). Paul is now announcing a new global accountability for all men because of the introduction of the gospel.[23]

The apostle John also illustrates this point: "For the law was given through Moses, *but* grace and truth came through Jesus Christ" (John 1:17). This passage points to a contrast: The Law led up to Christ but it could not save anyone. Kenneth Boa states:

> The Law could only bring someone to a point of seeing God's perfection and righteous requirements but nobody could keep the Law. The Law was never intended to save people. It instead was designed to be a schoolmaster to drive us to dependence upon the One that God would send—the Lamb of God who would take away the sin of the world. He alone fulfilled the perfect and righteous requirements. Now it is possible for us to be righteous before God because Christ offers His very life to those who would follow Him. The perfection of Christ is placed in our account.[24]

Furthermore, in Galatians 4:4, Paul divided up God's dealings with human beings into two periods—before Christ and after Christ. The period before Christ was a time of childhood, preparation, and immaturity. When the time was right, Christ came (Gal. 4:4), bringing the full revelation of mature doctrine and morality. The Old Testament was a period of learning the theological alphabet, of ceremonial ordinances, and of elementary teaching. But now, believers in Christ have received a full revelation and are reckoned as mature heirs. Finally, in Hebrews 1:1–2, the author describes two kinds of revelation: "God, who at various times and in various ways spoke in time past to the fathers by the prophets, has in these last days spoken to us by *His* Son." These examples show that God's truth was not given all at once, but that it was spread over a period of time. In other words, he revealed his truths progressively.

The Priority of the Testaments

Traditional dispensationalists consider the Old and the New Testaments as equally valid. Therefore, when interpreting the Old Testament, traditional dispensationalists' adherence to the grammatical-historical method keeps their referent point in the Old Testament. Johnson writes, "What the individual Old Testament author wrote is a 'type' of the fuller sense of meaning that corresponds to the divine author's sense of meaning communicated in the New Testament."[25] In reference to both testaments, Johnson observes that an "extremely tight correspondence of meaning exists between the words used in the Old Testament and the words used in the New Testament."[26]

The Meaning of "Mystery"

Johannes Louw and Eugene Nida define "mystery" (μυστήριον) as "the content of that which has not been known before but which has been revealed to an in-group or restricted constituency."[27] For example, Jesus explains to His disciples why He spoke to them in parables. He said that "it has been given to you to know the mysteries [τὰ μυστήρια] of the kingdom of heaven" (Matt. 13:11). Similarly, McClain defines mystery as "that which is hidden and secret, what can be known only to those who are specially initiated or taught; ... that which has hitherto been unrevealed."[28]

Israel and the Church

Israel. Louw and Nida define "Israel" ('Ισραήλ) in three ways. The first two relate to this study. First, Israel is the name of "the patriarch Jacob." Second, it refers to "the people/the nation of Israel (Matt. 2:6)." When the word 'Ισραήλ is attached to οἶκος or υἱοί, "house of Israel" or "sons of Israel," it refers to "the people of Israel as an ethnic entity—the people of Israel, the nation of Israel."[29] Arnold Fruchtenbaum also defines Israel as "referring to all descendants of Abraham, Isaac, and Jacob, also known as the Jews, the Jewish people, Israelites, Hebrews, etc." The Scripture clearly states that God elected Israel out from among other nations because of His love. Moses wrote, "The LORD did not set His love on you nor choose you because you were more in number than any other people, for you were the least of all peoples; but because the LORD loves you" (Deut. 7:7–8a). Fruchtenbaum identifies two forms of election: national and individual.[30] Which kind of election is being referred to in this passage? In this context, it is national election, not individual election. Fruchtenbaum contrasts these forms of election by stating that "national election does not guarantee the salvation of every individual. ... But national election guarantees God's purpose(s) for choosing the nation will be accomplished and that the elect nation will always survive as a distinct entity."[31] Conclusively, God has elected Israel as his people forever.

Fruchtenbaum analyzes the usage of the term "Israel" in

the New Testament. He observes that the term "Israel" is used "a total of seventy-three times in the New Testament." He then concludes that the usage of "Israel" in the New Testament refers to "national, ethnic Israel."[32] However, he cites Galatians 6:16, among others, as a passage which non-dispensationalists use to base their arguments for equality between Israel and the church.[33] We will examine this passage later.

The church. The term *church* is the English translation of the Greek word ἐκκλησία. Louw and Nida define ἐκκλησία as a "congregation of Christians, implying interacting membership— congregation, church." ἐκκλησία also refers to believers rather than to a building.[34] For example, Paul writes "to the church of God which is at Corinth" (1 Cor. 1:2). This passage is directed to believers in Corinth. In the Septuagint, ἐκκλησία, which is translated "church,"[35] is equivalent to the Hebrew term קָהָל. Brown, Driver, and Briggs say this term means an "assembly, convocation or congregation." The assembly may convene for evil council (Gen. 49:6); for war or invasion (Num. 22:4); for returning from exile as a group (Neh. 7:66); and lastly, for religious purposes, such as hearing the Word of God (Deut. 5:19). As a congregation, קָהָל refers to Israel as an organized body (Num. 22:3).[36]

Robert Lightner defines church as "an assembly of people called together for specific purpose."[37] Interpreters may use three guidelines to identify the meaning of a Greek word such as ἐκκλησία: etymology, development, and immediate context.[38] According to Radmacher, the word ἐκκλησία comes from a Greek preposition ἐκ (out) and the verb καλέω ("to call" or "to summon"). Therefore, the word ἐκκλησία means "to call out or called out ones."[39] He also notes that the word ἐκκλησία in the New Testament "signified an assembly."[40] He classifies the uses of ἐκκλησία in three ways: nontechnical, technical, and metaphorical. The nontechnical use occurs "where the usage of *ekklesia* [ἐκκλησία] had no etymological association or historical connotation that carried its meaning beyond the idea of a physical assembly."[41] Acts 7:38 is a clear biblical example of this usage: "This is he who was in the congregation [ἐν τῇ ἐκκλησίᾳ] in the wilderness with the Angel who spoke to him on Mount Sinai, and *with* our fathers, the one who received the living oracles to give to us." The phrase τῇ ἐκκλησίᾳ refers to the Old Testament congregation or assembly of Israel. This implies that the term "church" (ἐκκλησία) can be used generally to signify any kind of assembly.

In the technical usage, ἐκκλησία is applied in a restrictive way to an assembly that has a specific nature. The word ἐκκλησια was identified "with a new kind of assembly—an assembly with a spiritual or Christian unity."[42] In this usage, the phrase "of God" is sometimes affixed to the word ἐκκλησία.[43] The technical use of ἐκκλησία with the phrase "of God" occurs twice in the New Testament ("the church of God" [Acts 20:28]; "I will build My church" [Matt. 16:18]). The phrase "My church" denotes ownership or possession by Jesus Christ. Third, the metaphorical use of ἐκκλησία goes beyond the technical sense. These usages are still being investigated. One clear example occurs when Paul portrays himself as having persecuted the ἐκκλησία (Gal. 1:13).[44]

The metaphorical use of the term church as the "body of Christ" deserves attention (1 Cor. 12:12; Eph. 1:22; 3:10, Col. 1:18, 24). Radmacher notes that this phrase is a New Testament concept. He writes, "The church, the body of Christ, must be confined in this dispensation."[45] His argument is based on Christ's victorious work on the cross, which he claim is "by the necessity of the death, resurrection, and ascension of Christ."[46] His point is that Christ died in his body, was resurrected with his body, and finally ascended up in heaven with his body. The body of Christ, which did not exist in the old dispensation, in the new dispensation becomes a living organism, namely, the church. Radmacher notes that this conclusion has important implications: (a) "God raised Christ from the dead. ... The church is also raised unto newness of life, which act is absolutely essential to its existence (Eph.

1:19–20; Col. 3:10)." (b) "God raised Christ to a place of honor at His own right hand. Thus, the body of Christ has the necessary Head to whom it is intimately united and from whom it receives its direction." (c) The ascension of Christ was necessary because he could then give gifts to the church (Eph. 4:8–11). Radmacher supports this implication as follows: "A body without gifts would be incapable of growth and would therefore lack the ability to accomplish one of its primary responsibilities."[47] The Holy Spirit gives gifts to the body of Christ. Therefore, the Spirit's coming on the day of Pentecost made the body of Christ an organism capable of functioning.

Ryrie points out two distinctives of the church as the body of Christ. First, "it is distinct of those who are included within that body (Jews and Gentiles as fellow heirs)." Second, "it is distinct because of the new relationships of being in Christ and of Christ's indwelling the members of that body."[48] The first distinctive of joining these two entities together was not revealed in the previous dispensation. Moreover, the body concept is only revealed in the New Testament (Eph. 3:6). The Jews and Gentiles have been brought together in the body of Christ (Eph. 2:16). Therefore, the body of Christ came into existence after the death of Christ.[49]

As for the second distinctive of the body of Christ ("the indwelling presence of Christ in the members of that body"),[50] Paul writes, "To them God willed to make known what are the riches of the glory of this mystery among the Gentiles: which is Christ in you, the hope of glory" (Col. 1:27). In explaining this verse, Ryrie writes, "The immediate context speaks of the body of Christ three times (vv. 18, 22, 24), leaving no doubt that it is the members of the body who are indwelt by the living Christ. That is what makes the body a living organism, and this relationship was unknown in Old Testament times."[51]

The Nature of the Kingdom

The Davidic kingdom is the kingdom that God promised to establish with David and his descendants. It is also called the messianic kingdom because the Messiah (that is, Christ) will reign over it. Ryrie notes that the Davidic kingdom "will be realized at the Second Advent of Christ when He will establish His kingdom and fulfill those promises made to David."[52] The promise of the Davidic messianic kingdom is stated in 2 Samuel 7:12, 16. This Old Testament passage is crucial because it establishes the Davidic dynasty. David expressed his intent to build a more appropriate structure for the ark of the covenant (2 Sam. 7:2). The prophet Nathan approved of his desire (2 Sam. 7:4–7), but the matter was not settled. It had to come before the Yahweh. He did not approve of David's desire to build the temple, but he did approve the plan through David's son, Solomon, who had not even yet been born. Paul Williamson explains why David's desire was not approved:

> First, Yahweh had not requested any such edifice for himself (2 Sam. 7:5-7); second, the promised "rest" had still not yet been fully realized (2 Sam. 7:8-11); and third, Yahweh had selected another for the task of "building a house for his Name" in the context of the more secure rest in the future (2 Sam. 7:12–13). A fourth reason not stated in this passage is David's military exploits (1 Chr 22:8; 28:3).[53]

Instead, Yahweh made a covenant with David. The Davidic kingdom is part of the Davidic covenant (2 Sam. 7:5–16; cf. 1 Chron. 17:3–15; Psa. 89). The covenant promised an eternal house (vv. 13, 16), an eternal throne (vv. 13, 16), and an eternal kingdom (vv. 13, 16). Yahweh stated it in simple terms, "And your house and your kingdom shall be established forever before you. Your throne shall be established forever" (2 Sam. 7:16).

Revelation 20:1–6 is the key passage in the New Testament that establishes the future earthly messianic kingdom. In this passage, verses 2–6 repeat the word "thousand" five times, which means that the reign will last a thousand years. This why it is also called the millennial kingdom. Numerous Old Testament passages also refer to this kingdom, along with its promises and the certainty of its fulfillment by a descendant of David (cf. Jer. 23:5–8; 33:15–26; Ezek. 39:28). The passage in Jeremiah reads:

> "Behold, *the* days are coming," says the LORD,
> "That I will raise to David a Branch of righteousness;
> A King shall reign and prosper,
> And execute judgment and righteousness in the earth.
> In His days Judah shall be saved,
> And Israel will dwell safely;
> Now this *is* His name by which He will be called:
>
> THE LORD OUR RIGHTEOUSNESS.
>
> "Therefore, behold, *the* days are coming," says the LORD, "that they shall no longer say, 'As the LORD lives who brought up the children of Israel from the land of Egypt,' but, 'As the LORD lives who brought up and led the descendants of the house of Israel from the north country and from all the countries where I had driven them.' And they shall dwell in their own land. (Jer. 23:5–8)

This passage looks forward to the future when God will establish the Davidic dynasty. It also promises safety or peace for Israel, an aspect that Israel presently lacks. Israel is therefore assured of a future restoration by Yahweh when that kingdom is established by a righteous Branch (i.e., descendant). This passage is a messianic reference to Jesus Christ because he alone, in contrast to previous Davidic kings, is the righteous king.

The Davidic kingdom is also revealed in the New Testament. The authors of the New Testament refer to it as a future earthly kingdom that will be established at Jesus Christ's Second Coming. Paul charges Timothy on the basis of the coming kingdom by saying, "I charge *you* therefore before God and the Lord Jesus Christ, who will judge the living and the dead at His appearing and His kingdom: Preach the word!" (2 Tim. 4:1–2a). Dwight Pentecost comments that this kingdom "must refer to the earthly Davidic Kingdom that will be established on earth, since that is the kingdom which will follow the Second Advent of Jesus Christ … (Matt. 25:1–46)."[54] He also notes that 1 Corinthians 15:24 alludes to it. The passage states, "Then *comes* the end, when He delivers the kingdom to God the Father, when He puts an end to all rule and all authority and power." Pentecost further states that "the resurrection program does not come until after the reign of Christ here on earth, following His Second Coming. At the conclusion of that resurrection program, Christ will have delivered up the kingdom to God (v. 24)."[55]

The Hermeneutics of Traditional Dispensationalism

Traditional dispensationalists attempt to adhere to a consistently literal interpretation of the Scripture. Literal interpretation, also known as the grammatical-historical method, has now become a system or pattern of interpretation. Johnson states that the literal system can be used in a connotative sense, which means that the literal system is guided by a presupposition in which *"literal is a commitment to understanding that the Bible's authority is embedded in the meanings expressed in the words of the text."* He claims this concept aligns well with the reality that the Bible is the Word of God written in human words. It reaffirms the words of Jesus, the apostles, and later evangelical interpreters who claimed that the Scriptures are the Word of God. Johnson highlights three pertinent principles that underlie this claim. First, "the Bible speaks with the authority of God."[56] The Bible's authority obligates its adherents to accept its claims. Second, "the authoritative speaking of a written document resides in the type of meanings expressed by the words of the text." Interpreters have no freedom to alter or change what is written in the text. As Johnson notes, "A text should be read word for word, line upon line, as the reader gains a comprehension of the meaning expressed in the text." Third, "The authoritative meanings of the text are understood as messages expressed only if the words are read in context."[57] The immediate context, the book context, and the canonical context are essential to ascertaining a text's true meaning.

Literal interpretation underlies the grammatical-historical method. Johnson writes that grammar is "related to what an author has written—including syntax and literary genre." He notes that history "involves the author and his worldview, the occasion for the original communication, and the original readers and their worldview." To sum it up, Johnson writes that literal interpretation "entails those meanings which the author intended to communicate in the expressions of the text (grammar) in the original setting (historical)."[58] Ryrie also holds to a consistently literal hermeneutic and considers it an essential feature of dispensationalism. He writes, "Literal/historical/grammatical interpretation is not the sole practice of dispensationalists, but the consistent use of it in all areas of biblical interpretation is."[59]

In the following sections we will categorize the results of traditional dispensationalism's hermeneutic into three areas: stable meaning, a distinction between Israel and the church, and the literal fulfillment of the Davidic covenant at the Second Coming of Christ.[60]

Stable Meaning

Unlike other systems that advocate multiple or spiritual meanings, a system that employs literal interpretation arrives at certain conclusions about the meaning of a text. Such a system produces a stable meaning. A stable meaning is the single biblical meaning that the divine author intended to communicate. Johnson lists three reasons why consistently literal interpretation and the stable meaning it produces are indispensable. First, it is necessary "because the Bible claims to be God's communication to men through human writers."[61] Second, "consistent interpretation is indispensable because it provides a normative definition of verbal meaning. This method provides validation of interpretation." Third, this principle "forces the interpreter to consistently consider the text as the basis of the meaning. Only this can satisfy the priority of the Bible in formulating doctrine."[62] In conclusion, when an interpreter carefully follows correct exegetical rules, they are more likely to arrive at a stable meaning.

History plays a major role in determining the stability of meaning, especially regarding the usage of words. Some non-literalists argue that words may expand or lose their meaning over time. If this is true, then it is useless to attempt to produce a stable, consistent meaning. Johnson addresses this issue by asking, "Does a stated meaning about a historical event change or expand when that event is again interpreted with the benefit of a perspective of time?" Some non-dispensationalists respond to this question affirmatively. But Johnson cautions, "To make such a judgment depends upon the stability in meaning of the original statement." In defense of the claim of stability of original statements, Johnson asks, "In the progress of revelation, does the meaning of these statements change or expand due to the perspective of added revelation?"[63] The answer is definitely negative. The two biblical accounts that illustrate these principles are the Exodus and the sign to King Ahaz. Regarding these accounts, Johnson asks,

> Does the meaning of Moses' historical record interpreting the exodus from Egypt change or expand soon after Israel had been deposed from the land again? Or does the meaning of Isaiah's sign given to Ahaz in his unbelief change or expand in light of Matthew's use of that sign to interpret the Virgin Birth?[64]

Because the meanings appear to be stable in the original texts, Johnson concludes therefore that "the meaning of these statements is stable in spite of the perspective gained by further revelation. And the truth of these statements made by the prophets is also stable in spite of subsequent revelation."[65]

Johnson explains how the Exodus event illustrates stable meaning: "The meaning of Moses' historical record of the Exodus is stable even though the reader's understanding may be enriched and deepened by later revelation. It now is clear that Israel's redemption at the Exodus is not complete." And then he adds, "Yet in speaking of what God would do in the future as redemption, this further revelation reflects that the original record of the experience was a true model of what God does. Thus, our understanding has matured in time, but the type of meaning originally expressed has not expanded. It still means 'redemption from Egypt.'"[66]

The next example that illustrates stable meaning is the sign given by Yahweh to Ahaz and the descendants of David through the prophet Isaiah. The passage reads:

> Moreover the LORD spoke again to Ahaz, saying,
> "Ask a sign for yourself from the LORD your God;

ask it either in the depth or in the height above."
But Ahaz said, "I will not ask, nor will I test the
LORD!" Then he said, "Hear now, O house of
David! *Is it* a small thing for you to weary men,
but will you weary my God also? Therefore the
Lord Himself will give you a sign: Behold, the
virgin shall conceive and bear a Son, and shall call
His name Immanuel." (Isa. 7:10–14)

This passage has been interpreted in various ways. In order
to determine its meaning, we must ask, "What is the relationship
between Isaiah 7:14 and the sign to Ahaz?" Johnson has carefully
examined this passage and settled on a convincing argument.
Most views focus on either the word "virgin" (עַלְמָה), which
means "a young woman" (Gen. 24:43; Ex. 2:8; Prov. 30:19; Isa.
7:14), or בְּתוּלָה, which is a specific Hebrew word used for "virgin"
(Gen. 24:16). But neither term implies a time limit that restricts
the historical fulfillment of the sign during Ahaz's life. According
to Johnson, two things define the important components of the
textual meaning: the subject and the complement. Thus he writes:

Isaiah proclaimed a sign that is two-edged. This
is the subject. The Lord granted evidence (signs)
that accompany His Word and vouch for its
validity and reliability. At issue in the context is
the Lord's warning of the certain and near demise
of Damascus and Ephraim (7:7–9a). Included as
well is the warning concerning Ahaz's own future
(7:9b). His future rested on his faith in response
to the Lord's warning.
 Isaiah offered a sign to verify his warnings.
When Ahaz refused to believe (7:12), the sign did
two things. It guaranteed the house of David in

spite of the threat of attack from Israel and Syria, and at the same time it assured the king of his coming demise.

The sign then was in the restatement of the divine Word that promised a divinely enabled birth. In Isaiah's prophecy the sign was in the statement of the promise that pointed to an unusual miracle in the future. The complement expressed something about that two-edged sign. It denied Ahaz, who rejected the sign, a future in the royal line. And yet it affirmed the glorious climax of the Davidic line in spite of imminent judgment by Syria. If this is stated about the עַלְמָה conception, then the conception would exclude Ahaz or his heir from participating in the royal line of David. Thus the type of meaning expresses limits and determines the sense of עַלְמָה and harmonizes completely with the Matthean usage.[67]

Johnson's analysis supports the literal sense of the text and refutes the interpretation the claims double fulfillment. Johnson concludes:

Similarly, Isaiah's statement, which provided a sign for Ahaz, is stable in meaning. That stability is undermined if the sign in the original set of circumstances meant a natural conception, the timing of which is a sign, and if in a later set of circumstances the sign means a supernatural conception, which is the sign. The original sign may be followed by a second sign, but the original sign does not change to become a second sign.[68]

A consistent use of the literal hermeneutic produces a stable single meaning. Thomas correctly argues, "A fundamental principle in grammatico-historical exposition is that the words and sentences can have but one significance in one and the same connection. The moment we neglect this principle we drift out upon a sea of uncertainty and conjecture."[69] The principle of a stable meaning refutes the notion of double fulfillment. In this case, the prophecy of Isaiah 7:14 refers to only one thing—the virgin birth of the Messiah. Johnson's explanation reinforces the traditional dispensationalists' view that, "while the questions of history and the benefits gained in the progress of revelation may introduce added complexity to interpretation, it does not invalidate the principle that literal is what an author intended to communicate through a text."[70]

How one interprets the fulfillment of the Old Testament prophecy can help them achieve stability of meaning. Charles Dyer distinguishes between the fulfillment of the Old Testament text's meaning and a New Testament writer's application of its significance to a later situation. He writes, "If the New Testament writer looks back to the Old Testament and draws significance from the Old Testament for his specific audience, this is application of the Old Testament, not fulfillment of the Old Testament."[71] Meaning and significance are different entities. Traditional dispensationalists hold to a single meaning of a text but more than one possible application. Dyer notes that "meaning focuses specifically on the author's intended understanding of the text." He describes significance as a "reference to the application of a text's meaning to various groups of individuals"[72] and gives an example: "Paul's prediction in 1 Thessalonians 4 has only one single meaning, but it has had significance for believers throughout the ages. ... [This is] because the potential existed for the passage to be fulfilled from Paul's day till today."[73]

Herman Hoyt holds that the Old Testament should be

interpreted literally.[74] John Walvoord also notes, "If interpreted literally, the Old Testament gives a clear picture of the prophetic expectation of Israel. … The premillennial interpretation offers the only literal fulfillment for the hundreds of verses of prophetic testimony."[75] This principle forms the foundation for interpreting the New Testament. Since traditional dispensationalists abide by the principle of single meaning (i.e., sense), it requires that "every Old Testament passage must receive its own grammatical-historical interpretation, regardless of how a New Testament writer uses it."[76] The grammatical-historical method therefore views both testaments as having equal status. For example, the word "Israel" is understood as Israel in its normal sense in both the Old and New Testaments. Ryrie urges, "We must remember that most often the New Testament uses the Old Testament prophecies literally and does not spiritualize them."[77] Ryrie also observes that "hardly ever do New Testament writers not use the Old Testament in a historical-grammatical sense. … The rule is that they interpreted the Old Testament plainly; the exceptions are rare and typological."[78]

Therefore, the Old Testament should be interpreted in its normal, literal sense in every aspect. This method alone guarantees that the interpreter will hold to a literal fulfillment of the Davidic covenant at Christ's Second Coming. In conclusion, the traditional dispensationalist view is that Old Testament prophecies have already been fulfilled literally or await a future literal fulfillment.

The Church as Distinct from Israel

The distinction between Israel and the church is regarded as an essential feature by traditional dispensationalists. Ryrie calls it the *sine qua non* (absolutely indispensable feature) of dispensationalism. The other essential features are a consistently literal hermeneutic and a doxological goal of Scripture.[79] In this section, we will consider seven reasons why dispensationalists make this distinction.

The time of the church's beginning. Traditional dispensationalists distinguish between Israel and the church based on the time of their origins. Evangelicals hold three views as to when the church actually began. Amillennialists and postmillennialists believe the church is continued from the Old Testament. Ultra-dispensationalists hold that the church began with the apostle Paul (citing Acts 28:28). Finally, traditional dispensationalists, such as Ryrie, Fruchtenbaum, and Radmacher maintain that the church started on the day of Pentecost. Fruchtenbaum writes, "The church was born at Pentecost, whereas Israel had existed for many centuries."[80]

Vlach also advocates this view. He writes, "There is a strong biblical reason that views the Church as beginning in the New Testament era and not in the Old Testament." According to Vlach, the verb οἰκοδομήσω used in the phrase, οἰκοδομήσω μου τὴν ἐκκλησίαν ("I will build My church" [Matt. 16:18]), shows that the church was a future entity. The verb οἰκοδομήσω is future indicative tense.[81] Ryrie supports this argument as well. He writes that, after the resurrection, Jesus spoke of the church as yet future,[82] and states that "the inescapable conclusion is that the body of Christ did not come into existence until the day of Pentecost when the first members of the body were joined to the risen Head. If by the stretch of the interpretive imagination the body could be said to have existed before Pentecost, then, it was without a head."[83] Traditional dispensationalists hold, then, that the church began on the day of Pentecost, unlike Israel which had existed from the time of the Exodus.

The events required for the church's beginning. Before the church could function in its organic relationship with Christ as his body, certain events had to occur that did not take place when Yahweh established the nation of Israel. Yahweh prepared Israel to be his nation by allowing them to be in bondage for nearly 400 years, sending the plagues, bringing them across the Red Sea on dry ground, speaking his Law to them from Mt. Sinai, and making his covenant with them (Exodus 1–20). Fruchtenbaum explains the different set of events necessary for the church to exist as the body of Christ: "Certain events in the ministry of the Messiah were essential to the establishment of the Church. These events are the resurrection/ascension of the Messiah to become head of the church."[84] Jesus' resurrection not only gave his followers the hope of an afterlife, it also made the church a living organism. Fruchtenbaum and other traditional dispensationalists believe that the church began after Christ's ascension and that it only functioned after the Holy Spirit had provided necessary gifts to it (Eph. 4:7–11).[85]

The mystery nature of the church. In the Old Testament, God revealed his plan about the nation of Israel to Abraham (Gen. 12:1–3), Jacob (Gen. 25:23), and Judah (Gen. 49:8–10). The church, however, was unrevealed in the Old Testament. But evangelicals disagree as to whether the church as a "mystery" was unrevealed or revealed. The progressive dispensationalists, for instance, claim that because the term "mystery" appears in both the Old and New Testaments, it lacks the idea of hiddenness. Traditional dispensationalists, on the other hand, are firm in their conviction that the church was unrevealed in any form in the Old Testament. For example, Fruchtenbaum defines the term "mystery" as "a truth not revealed in the Old Testament (Eph. 3:3–5, 9; Col. 1:26–27)."[86] This understanding of mystery as something unrevealed in the Old Testament is a major contribution of traditional dispensationalism's theology. To support his definition, Fruchtenbaum identifies four mysteries in the New Testament: (a) the concept of Jewish and Gentiles united in one body (Eph. 3:1–12); (b) the doctrine of Christ indwelling every believer (Col. 1:24–27); (c) the church as the Bride of Christ (Eph. 5:22–32); and (d) the rapture (1 Cor. 15:50–58).[87] Ryrie defines the concept of mystery as follows:

The idea of mystery being something secret
in Old Testament times but revealed in the
New Testament is clearly seen in a passage like
Colossians 1:2. ... Thus the concept of mystery
is basically a secret which only the initiated
share. This includes two ideas: 1) a time when
the secret was not known; and 2) deeper or higher
wisdom which is revealed to the one initiated into
an understanding of the mystery. ... In other
words the mystery concerns Jews and Gentiles as
joint-heirs, in a joint-body, and joint-sharers of the
promise in Christ ... The heart of the mystery is
that there would be a "joint-body" for Jews and
Gentiles.[88]

It is clear that the church is a mystery because it did not exist
in the Old Testament. Abraham was the ancestor of the nation of
Israel, so Israel existed in the old dispensation before the church
was revealed. The notion of the church as redeemed people, saved
by grace through faith in Christ alone, was unrevealed—even to
the prophets. This shows that the church and Israel are distinct.

The unity of the church. The concept of the church as "one new
man" distinguishes the church from Israel. This truth is revealed
in Ephesians 2:15, where Paul writes that Christ abolished the
hatred between Jews and Gentiles "to create in Himself one new
man *from* the two, *thus* making peace" (ἵνα τοὺς δύο κτίσῃ ἐν
αὐτῷ εἰς ἕνα καινὸν ἄνθρωπον ποιῶν εἰρήνην). The concept of
a καινον ἄνθρῶπον ("new humanity") was nonexistent in the
previous dispensation. Jews were separate from Gentiles. Vlach
identifies the unique relationship between Jews and Gentiles in
Ephesians 2:15. He writes that the concept of a "one new man"
is a New Testament revelation.[89] Ryrie, too, supports the concept
that a "new man" in Ephesians 2:15 forms the basis of distinction.
He writes, "That body-church is called a 'new man' (Eph. 2:15),

not a continuation or remaking of Israel, but something new and distinct from the Israel of the Old Testament. ... Just as the redeemed before Abraham's day (like Enoch and Noah) were not a part of Israel, so the redeemed of this age are not either."[90] Israel was therefore the old man (revealed) and the church is the "new man." The new man (i.e., the church) consists of believing Jews and Gentiles. This is why Paul writes that Christ created "one new man *from* the two" in Ephesians 2:15.

The distribution of the word ἐκκλησία. The uneven distribution of the term ἐκκλησία in the New Testament indicates that the church started after the public ministry of Christ. The word occurs 114 times in the New Testament.[91] It occurs three times in the Gospel of Matthew (but not in any other Gospel), twenty-three times in Acts, sixty-two times in Paul's letters, six times in the general epistles, and twenty times in the book of Revelation. Nineteen of the occurrences in Revelation are in the first three chapters, while the other instance is in chapter 22. In summary, the word "church" occurs only three times in the Gospels because the church had not yet been established, while it occurs more often in Acts because the church was started during that time. By the time the rest of the New Testament was written, the church had already been established, which accounts for the remaining eighty-eight occurrences.

The development of a technical meaning for ἐκκλησία. The word ἐκκλησία developed from a nontechnical meaning referring to any assembly to a technical or exclusive meaning referring to believers in Christ. Vlach observes that the New Testament develops the word *"ekklesia* from the nontechnical meaning of 'assembly' or 'gathering' to the technical meaning of the Christian people of God."[92] Radmacher also observes that *ekklesia* is never used in a technical sense in the Septuagint.[93] In other words, even though the word ἐκκλησία basically means an "assembly," the context determines its meaning. In the technical sense, the term ἐκκλήσια is restricted to a group that identifies itself with Jesus

Christ by faith, while the nontechnical sense may be an assembly of any sort. Therefore, the ἐκκλησία in the New Testament is distinct from the קָהֵל of the Old Testament. If the distinction does not exist, then ἐκκλησία and קָהֵל are the same, which supports the concept that the church is a continuation of the people of God in the Old Testament. Radmacher's survey reveals that *ekklesia* was never used in a technical sense in the Septuagint.[94] Table 1 illustrates the notion of the technical and nontechnical senses of ἐκκλησία.

The eternal distinction between Israel and the church. The Scriptures maintain the distinction between Israel and the church in the current age, during the millennium kingdom, and throughout eternity. Stanley D. Toussaint observes that the distinction between the church and Israel extends to the future. Regarding the millennial kingdom, he writes, "The church will reign with Christ during the Messianic kingdom on earth, the distinction between Israel and the church will still stand."[95] But this distinction extends beyond the millennial kingdom. Ryrie quotes Daniel P. Fuller, who writes that "the basic premise of Dispensationalism is two purposes God expressed in the formation of two peoples who maintain their distinctions throughout eternity."[96] The Scriptures support these ongoing distinctions in the following ways:

1) Paul tells the church at Corinth that as saints (cf. 1 Cor. 1:2) they will judge both the world and the angels (1 Cor. 6:2–3). It seems obvious that the "world" includes the Jews and Gentiles who are not part of the church. In the larger context, Paul compares this to a related concept, namely, that the church will reign as kings (1 Cor. 4:8). The idea may be that when they are reigning they will also judge the world because they will have authority over the world along with Christ (cf. 2 Tim. 2:12).

2) In Revelation 2–3, Christ dictates his messages to the first-century local churches in Asia Minor. Regardless of the possibility that these churches were predominately Jewish,[97] we

must remember that they are churches. In one of these messages, Christ promises those members of the church at Thyatira who persevere and obey him to the end that they will have "authority over the nations" (Rev. 2:26). This probably refers to the church's reign with Christ over other Gentile nations.[98] We see this in Matthew 19:28 as well, where Jesus informs the disciples that, in the kingdom, they will judge the twelve tribes of Israel. However, this is not a strong argument because some might say the context is entirely Jewish in view of the fact that the disciples were Jewish. Psalm 2 makes it clear that Christ will rule over the Gentiles, and Revelation 2:27 links the rule of the overcomer with Christ's rule,[99] but nowhere is it said that Israel itself will rule over them. Instead, the Messiah will rule Israel (Ezek. 34:11–31), and they will serve as "a kingdom of priests" (Exod. 19:6), that is, they will be mediators between the Messiah and the nations regarding his pronouncements, but they will not enforce them. The church, therefore, will have a ruling function that Israel will not have.

On the other hand, Christ's promise to those at the church at Laodicea who overcome their lukewarm condition by accepting his righteousness and fellowshipping with him does not refer to reigning (Rev. 3:21). Instead, he says that, when they overcome, he will grant them the right to sit with him on his throne, just as he overcame and sat with his Father on his Father's throne. This points to the fact that he rested from his work (Heb. 1:3) and was being honored (Heb. 1:13).[100] Christ's comparison of the two situations must mean they both have the same cause (overcoming) and the same effect (resting from overcoming and being honored for overcoming).

3) Also, except for the occurrence in Revelation 22:16, which is a closing reference to the churches mentioned in Revelation 2 and 3, the absence of ἐκκλησία from Revelation 4 through 22 points to the book's strong connection with Old Testament prophecies about the nation of Israel (cf. Rev. 10:7). It proves the church will be in heaven during the tribulation, while the nation

of Israel, generally speaking, will be on earth. Only when we come to Revelation 19 and afterward do we find allusions to the church, and even then, it is called "the bride" or "wife" of the Lamb (19:7; 21:2, 9; 22:17). Christ is the Lamb (John 1:29; 1 Pet. 1:19; Rev. 5:6–12). He only had one life to give and he gave it for the church, so he only has one bride—the church (Eph. 5:25–32; cf. 2 Cor. 11:2).

4) The fact that the New Jerusalem is called "the bride, the wife of the Lamb" (Rev. 21:2, 9) also seems to indicate that this city is the residence of the church. This is confirmed by the geographical relationship of Israel and the nations to this city. Whatever its overall shape is vertically, the city and the wall around it form a square (Rev. 21:13, 18). The wall has twelve foundation stones, each with the name of one of the twelve apostles engraved on it (v. 14). This reinforces its relationship to the church as well. However, each of the walls also has three gates for a total of twelve gates, and each gate has the name of a tribe of Israel on it (v. 12). The names of the tribes are not given in this account, but John clearly states that each wall faced toward a particular direction: east, north, south, and west (v. 13). In Numbers 2:2–32, Yahweh tells Moses and Aaron that the Israelites are to camp in a certain order on the four sides of the tabernacle: Judah, Issachar, and Zebulon on the east; Reuben, Simeon, and Gad on the south; Ephraim, Manasseh, and Benjamin on the west; and Dan, Asher, and Naphtali on the north. They were situated around a tent that was only seventy-five feet wide on the east and west sides, and one hundred fifty feet long on the other two sides.[101] The tabernacle only had one gate on the east.

Ezekiel describes the shape and size of Jerusalem in the millennial kingdom and lists the gates that each tribe is to use (Ezek. 48:30–34). Once again, the city is square. The walls on each side are approximately a mile and a quarter long,[102] and each side has three gates in it. The gates for Judah, Reuben, and Levi are on the north; Joseph (one gate for both Ephraim and

Manasseh), Benjamin, and Dan each have their own gate on the east; Simeon, Issachar, and Zebulon enter from separate gates on the south; and Gad, Asher, and Naphtali have their gates on the west. Each tribe has their own land outside the city. The New Jerusalem, on the other hand, is fifteen hundred miles long on each of its four sides (Rev. 21:16, NASB). Each of the three tribes could occupy twenty-five hundred square miles (five hundred miles by five hundred miles) along their side of the city.

But the point is that, if the arrangements described in Numbers 2 and Ezekiel 48 are any indication of the tribes' location in relation to the New Jerusalem, the nation of Israel will be living outside of the city and going into it and out of it through their own gates. The New Jerusalem will not be their residence. But for what may be a primarily Jewish church audience (cf. Revelation 2–3), it will be the city for which they were looking (Heb. 11:9–10).

5) The non-Jewish nations, also, are situated in places other than in the city or even around it. John tells his readers that "the nations of those who are saved shall walk in its light, and the kings of the earth bring their glory and honor into it. Its gates shall not be shut at all by day (there shall be no night there). And they shall bring the glory and the honor of the nations into it." (Rev. 21:24–26). These are Gentiles who lived during a dispensation other than the church age, did not become Jews, but had faith in God. The light emanating from the Lamb will replace the sunlight and the moonlight (v. 23). These two light bearers are generally on opposite sides of the earth at any given time, so a nation could be located on the other side of the earth and still receive the light coming from the Lamb in the New Jerusalem. It will be so bright that it will shine on every nation. This means that these nations do not live in the city, and most likely do not live, or need to live, near it. In addition to this, the city's gates will never be closed so that the kings of the nations can enter the city to glorify and honor God and the Lamb in whatever way is appropriate (vv. 24–26). We can assume that they leave through these gates.

In summary, the church, Israel, and the nations will continue to exist as three distinct groups of people in the new universe by virtue of their geographic relationship to the New Jerusalem and their political and religious relationship to each other.

The Literal Fulfillment of the Davidic Kingdom at Christ's Second Coming

Traditional dispensationalists believe that the promises made to Israel and David will be fulfilled at Christ's Second Coming. Walvoord points out some examples of biblical prophecies that have been fulfilled literally:

> For instance the birth of Christ was to be supernatural. His mother was to be a virgin (Isa. 7:14), His place of birth was Bethlehem, pinpointed in Micah 5:2 about seven hundred years before He was born. He was to be the seed of the woman (Gen. 3:15) who would have victory over Satan. ... The Old Testament abounds with prophetic details about Jesus as prophet, priest, and king (Deut. 18:15–18; 1 Sam. 2:35: Ps. 110:4; cf. Gen. 49:10; 2 Sam. 7:12–16, etc.). Isaiah 9:6–7 summarizes His birth, Person, and deity. All these prophecies have been literally fulfilled. In all these cases the prophetic Scriptures have been fulfilled historically in a literal way.[103]

It then follows that the unfulfilled prophecies will be fulfilled in the same way. Walvoord rightly concludes, "Unfilled prophecies will have the same literal fulfillment, especially when they are couched in terms that make sense literally."[104] Christ will fulfill the Davidic (i.e., messianic) kingdom literally, that is, he will establish a physical kingdom on earth.

Dwight Pentecost believes that the Davidic kingdom will be fulfilled literally. He offers several reasons to substantiate his arguments. First, God has promised to preserve Israel as a nation. Second, God has promised to bring Israel back as a nation to its land of inheritance. This land has geographic boundaries. Third, David's son, Jesus Christ, must return to the earth, bodily and literally, in order to reign over the kingdom God promised in his covenant with David. Finally, the Messiah has no reason to return unless he has a literal earthly kingdom over which to reign.[105]

The Prophesied Postponement of the Messianic Kingdom

We have established that not all the conditions of the Davidic covenant have been met. This is important, as Johnson notes: "A promise is fulfilled when the agreement is *kept*. A covenant is fulfilled only when *all* of the related provisions are *kept*."[106] This is not the case with the Davidic covenant. Only the house (i.e., the dynasty) element of God's promise to David has been fulfilled. The throne and kingdom aspects are not yet fulfilled. The following biblical evidence from the Old and New Testaments substantiates this conclusion. We should note first that the title מָשִׁיחַ ("messiah") is significant. In the Old Testament it is "an awaited or future anointed agent of God."[107] Israel had been waiting for their Messiah for six centuries. Jesus finally came as the promised Messiah, but Israel rejected him and eventually had him killed. As a result, the offer of the messianic kingdom was temporarily withdrawn (Matt. 21:43).

Prophecies unfulfilled at Christ's First Coming. In addition to 2 Sam. 7:11–16, several other scripture passages speak about the messianic kingdom. In the following paragraphs, we will discuss some of the prophecies that have not been fulfilled.

1) Psalm 45. This messianic psalm describes a royal wedding as a metaphor of the future messianic kingdom. Verses 6–7 read,

Your throne, O God, *is* forever and ever;
A scepter of righteousness *is* the scepter of Your kingdom.
You love righteousness and hate wickedness;
Therefore God, Your God, has anointed You
With the oil of gladness more than Your companions. (Psa. 45:6–7).

We know that the anointing of this king is future because he is addressed as "God" and his kingdom will last forever (כִּסְאֲךָ אֱלֹהִים עוֹלָם וָעֶד [Psa. 45:6]), thus making him deity. Furthermore, he loves righteousness and hates wickedness, therefore he will rule righteously. As of the writing of this psalm, no Davidic king met this description. In fact, no Davidic king will ever fit this description except the promised messianic king (cf. Isa. 9:6–7). Therefore, Psalm 45:6–7 speak of the Messiah whose anointing and reigning will take place in the future.

2) Isaiah 11:1–10. This passage is another clear example. In verses 1–2 and 10, the prophet states:

There shall come forth a Rod from the stem of Jesse,
And a Branch shall grow out of his roots.
The Spirit of the LORD shall rest upon Him,
The Spirit of wisdom and understanding,
The Spirit of counsel and might,
The Spirit of knowledge and of the fear of the LORD.
. . . .
And in that day there shall be a Root of Jesse,
Who shall stand as a banner to the people;
For the Gentiles shall seek Him,
And His resting place shall be glorious.

In this passage, God promises that the Davidic dynasty will continue until it ends in a future reign in which the one sitting on the throne displays wisdom, understanding, counsel and might, and the fear of the Lord. Verses 3–9 describe the reign of this Davidic descendant, and verse 10 concludes as follows: "And in that day there shall be a Root of Jesse, …; the Gentiles shall seek Him." According to Joseph A. Fitzmyer, the phrase ("a Root of Jesse") "denotes the succession of David's heir to the throne and God's blessings on him."[108] Therefore, this passage indicates that the messianic kingdom will be instituted in the future when the Messiah reigns. Christ is the "Root of Jesse," that is, he is a descendant of David who will reign.

3) Jeremiah 23:5–6. In this passage, the prophet Jeremiah repeats Isaiah's message and expands on it:

> "Behold, *the* days are coming," says the LORD,
> "That I will raise to David a Branch of righteousness;
> A King shall reign and prosper,
> And execute judgment and righteousness in the earth.
> In His days Judah shall be saved,
> And Israel will dwell safely;
> Now this *is* His name by which He will be called:
>
> THE LORD OUR RIGHTEOUSNESS."

The Davidic heir who is to come from the house of David is called "a Branch of righteousness." He will be raised up "to David," that is, he will be the representative of the house of David.

4) Jeremiah 33:15–17. Regarding the Davidic throne, Jeremiah writes that it will be fulfilled when Israel's Messiah comes. He says,

In those days and at that time
I will cause to grow up to David
A Branch of righteousness;
He shall execute judgment and righteousness in
the earth.
In those days Judah will be saved,
And Jerusalem will dwell safely.
And this *is the name* by which she will be called:

THE LORD OUR RIGHTEOUSNESS.

For thus says the LORD: "David shall never lack
a man to sit on the throne of the house of Israel."
(Jer. 33:15–16)

Jerusalem has not experienced the safety promised in these verses, nor has Israel been restored to her land. The throne of David is also still vacant. The re-establishment of the Davidic throne and Christ's rule over the Davidic kingdom awaits future fulfillment. Furthermore, the consistent testimony of the Scriptures indicates that the Davidic throne is located in Jerusalem, not in heaven, and that Christ will not sit on this throne until he establishes his kingdom (cf. Ps. 110:1; Heb. 10:13).

5) Ezekiel 34:23–24. The prophet Ezekiel also shares a similar message of a future Davidic ruler. He writes, "I will establish one shepherd over them, and he shall feed them—My servant David. He shall feed them and be their shepherd. And I, the LORD will be their God, and my servant David a prince among them; I, the LORD, have spoken" (Ezek. 34:23–24). Here the future Davidic ruler is called "shepherd" (רֹעֶה) and "prince" or "leader" (נָשִׂיא). This future leader is also called a "king" (Ezek. 37:24), and a "prince forever" (v. 25). These titles refer to a future David. The angel Gabriel foretold regarding Jesus that "the Lord God will give Him the throne of His father David. And He will

reign over the house of Jacob forever, and of His kingdom there will be no end" (Luke 1:32–33). Jesus called himself "the good shepherd" (John 10:11). These titles and themes emphasize the roles of the coming ruler in the yet-to-be-established Davidic kingdom. They will help Israel recognize the Davidic leader when the time comes for him to establish the messianic kingdom.

6) Daniel 2:44 and 7:12–13. These two passages provide evidence for a future earthly kingdom. The first passage states, "The God of heaven will set up a kingdom which shall never be destroyed; and the kingdom shall not be left to other people; ... it shall stand forever" (Dan. 2:44). It clearly indicates that there shall be a future kingdom that will be stronger and last longer than any human kingdom. Human kingdoms have a beginning and an end, but this kingdom will last forever. The second text expands on the earlier one. There Daniel writes,

> I was watching in the night visions
> And behold, *One* like the Son of Man,
> Coming with the clouds of heaven!
> He came to the Ancient of Days,
> And they brought Him near before Him.
> Then to Him was given dominion and glory and a kingdom,
> That all peoples, nations, and languages should serve Him.
> His dominion *is* an everlasting dominion,
> Which shall not pass away,
> And His kingdom *the one*
> Which shall not be destroyed. (Dan. 7:13–14)

The two passages have the following content in common: the kingdom will never be destroyed, that is, it will last forever. The clause, "the kingdom shall not be left to other people," means that no other nation will conquer it, in contrast to the preceding empires.[109] The new content is as follows: (a) a human being ("the Son of Man") will rule this kingdom; (b) he will come from heaven ("with the clouds of heaven") to establish his kingdom; (c) he will rule over all nations on earth ("all people, nations, and languages ... serve him"). These have never taken place, but the second point is worth noting. It rules out the possibility of Christ establishing his kingdom at his First Coming. Instead, Christ himself applied this aspect to his future return to earth (Matt. 16:27; 24:29–31; 26:64), as did Luke (Acts 1:11), Paul (2 Thess. 1:7), Jude (quoting Enoch [Jude 14–15]), and John (Rev. 1:7; 19:11–14).

7) Matthew and Luke. The authors of these two Gospels indicate that Israel expected God to fulfill his promise to establish an earthly kingdom literally, with the descendant of David sitting on the throne of David. The genealogies establish Jesus' kingly lineage (Matt. 1:1–17; Luke 3:23–38). The authors give Jesus the titles "Son of Abraham" (Matt. 1:1) and "Son of David" (Matt. 1:1; Luke 1:32). The title "Son of Abraham" identifies Jesus as a descendant of Abraham through Isaac and Israel (i.e., Jacob), and as a leader over the sons of Abraham (i.e., the Israelites). On the other hand, the title "Son of David" recalls God's promise to raise up David's descendant and to establish an earthly kingdom, with his descendant sitting on his throne forever (2 Sam. 7:12–16). The angel's announcement in Luke connects Jesus sitting on the throne of David with his reign over Israel. Luke mentions that Jesus is the Messiah appointed by God to sit "on the throne of His father David" (Luke 1:32b), and that "He will reign over the house of Jacob forever" (Luke 1:33a). This crucial event is yet to be fulfilled.

8) Matthew 19:28. Here Jesus says, "Assuredly I say to you, that in the regeneration, when the Son of Man sits on the throne of His glory, you who have followed Me will also sit on twelve thrones, judging the twelve tribes of Israel." At the time Jesus spoke these words, he was not sitting "on the throne of his glory." Three things are noteworthy in this passage. The first is a

reference to the word "regeneration" (παλιγγενεσία), which means "a new birth."[110] Regarding this word, Plummer notes, "It was the belief of the Jews that the Messiah, after His advent, would create a new heaven and a new earth."[111] The concept of the regeneration caused the Jews to look forward to a future fulfillment. Second, the phrase "Son of Man" is significant. The "Son of Man" sitting upon the throne of his glory alludes to Daniel 7:13–14, where the Ancient of Days gives the kingdom to the "Son of Man." Last, the "twelve tribes" refers to national Israel. Israel will be restored after confessing her sins. This national confession of their sins has not yet taken place. Therefore, this passage is biblical evidence that the Davidic kingdom and the throne, when God shall restore all things, are still future.

10) Luke 19:11–28. Jesus gave the parable of pounds to correct a misconception that the kingdom would come immediately. He explains the reason for its rejection, the interval of its delay, and its future arrival. The passage reads:

> Now as they heard these things, He spoke another parable, because He was near Jerusalem and because they thought the kingdom of God would appear immediately. Therefore He said: "A certain nobleman went into a far country to receive for himself a kingdom and to return. So he called ten of his servants, delivered to them ten minas, and said to them, 'Do business till I come.' But his citizens hated him, and sent a delegation after him, saying, 'We will not have this *man* to reign over us.' And so it was that … he returned, having received the kingdom. (Luke 19:11–15a)

Luke states two purposes for this parable: Jesus was close to Jerusalem, and the disciples thought the kingdom would soon appear. Therefore, the people imagined that this special journey to Jerusalem was for the purpose of establishing the messianic kingdom. But they were mistaken.

This passage is closely connected to verse 10 which states, "for the Son of Man has come to seek and to save that which was lost." Thus, it is possible that the mention of the epitaph, 'Son of Man' having come raised their [disciples] hopes of their earthly expectations. Van Osterzee observes,

> "from ch. xviii. 34 it appears that they were as yet by no means cured of their earthly messianic hopes and were also, as often, there lay a certain truth at the basis of their error that the kingdom of God should become manifest ἀναφαίνεσθαι, was in and of itself subject to no doubt, but that it would come into view at this very point and that in a palpable, sensuous form, in other words, that Christ would be glorified without a previous separation from His own; in that lay the error of which they must be immediately cured.[112]

This parable was therefore given to correct this inaccurate mindset and teach that the Davidic kingdom and its throne are future.

We should note several factors in Luke 19:11–15a. At his First Coming, Jesus was like a nobleman who deserved a kingdom, but he did not enter into his rule. Therefore, he did not sit on David's throne at his First Coming. Second, like the nobleman who went to "receive for himself a kingdom and to return," Jesus left for a far country (heaven [v. 12]). Third, while Jesus is gone to the far country, his servants are to earn money for him with what he gave them. Therefore, the citizens of his country are supposed to be honoring Jesus until he receives the kingdom and returns to reign. However, just as the citizens of the nobleman hated him, the Jewish leaders hated Jesus. They resented him by saying, "We will not have this *man* to reign over us" (v. 14; cf. John 19:15). Fourth, the reign does not start until Christ, after receiving the kingdom, returns to earth. In short, this parable proves that Jesus is gone to a far country. When the Father gives him the kingdom, he will return to rule on earth in his promised kingdom. This parable is strong evidence that Jesus will come again to establish the Davidic kingdom and its throne.

11) Acts 1:6–7. This passage also indicates that the Davidic kingdom is not fulfilled in this age. Jesus' disciples asked him, "'Lord, will You at this time restore the kingdom to Israel?' And He said to them, 'It is not for you to know times or seasons which the Father has put in His own authority.'" The apostles were inquiring about the restoration of a future literal kingdom to Israel because they anticipated such a kingdom. This is implied in Jesus' response. He does not disregard the notion that he would restore the kingdom. He only tells them that they are not given the knowledge of when that will be (Acts 1:7). Ralph A. Gade explains what is happening:

> One of the questions that was going through the minds of the disciples was, "Will thou at this time restore again the kingdom to Israel?" (Acts 1:6). The Lord did not say, "There will be no kingdom—Israel has been put aside." He said, "It is not for you to know the times or the seasons, which the Father hath put in his own power." ... What the Lord is actually telling them is that the kingdom is yet future.[113]

The disciples' question was about time ("When?"), and Jesus responded to that question by saying, "It is not for you to know the times or seasons" (v. 7). The idea of the kingdom being restored to Israel was a settled fact. However, the time when this restoration would take place was not clear. In short, the kingdom of Christ was not set up during Jesus' First Coming but will be established in the future.

12) Acts 15:14–17. The council at Jerusalem also illustrates the early church's understanding of the timing of the fulfillment of the Davidic covenant. In this passage, James appears to say that the Old Testament indicates that there would be a time of Gentile salvation preceding the restoration of Israel. Pentecost summarizes this passage by noting the following:

> First, God visits the Gentiles, taking from them a people for His name. Second, Christ will return— after the outcalling of the Gentiles for His name. … Third, as a result of the coming of the Lord, the tabernacle of David will be built again; that is, the kingdom will be established exactly as promised in the Davidic covenant. Amos clearly declared that this rebuilding will be done "as it used to be" (Amos 9:11).[114]

Benware observes that "the rebuilding of that which is fallen" refers to the throne and kingdom, which was overthrown in the past but will be restored in the future.[115] The ruins refer to Israel, which had been broken and is yet to be restored. The raising up of David's fallen tent looked forward to an eschatological time: "In that day." James quotes this passage (Acts 15:16–17), but no evidence exists that James was equating the tabernacle of David with the church, or that its New Testament use had exhausted the meaning of Amos 9:11–12. Instead, Amos predicted a future time when the Davidic kingdom and the throne would be re-established, but he seems to be using the prophecy from Amos 9:11–12 as an analogy. In other words, if God intends to save Gentiles after the restoration of the kingdom, he can do it prior to that time.

13) Second Timothy 4:1. Paul writes about the promised

future Davidic kingdom: "I charge *you* therefore before God and the Lord Jesus Christ, who will judge the living and the dead at His appearing and His kingdom" (2 Tim. 4:1). His appeal to the return of Christ and the earthly Davidic kingdom Christ will establish following his Second Coming (Matt. 25:1–46) shows that Timothy also believes in it, otherwise Paul's charge would have no effect. Furthermore, the term ἐπιφάνειαν ("appearing" [1 Tim. 6:14; 2 Tim. 4:8; Titus 2:13]) refers to "Christ's second coming."[116] The article ("the appearing" [τὴν ἐπιφάνειαν]) indicates a definite event involving a manifestation of Christ's glory when he appears.[117] This appearance will take place at Christ's Second Coming to rule when he comes to fulfill the Davidic kingdom aspect of the covenant. Paul echoes this thought in 1 Corinthians 15:24, where he writes, "Then *comes* the end, when He delivers the kingdom to God the Father, when He puts an end to all rule and all authority and power." The kingdom referred to here is "the millennium kingdom over which Christ reigns on earth, following his Second Advent."[118] This is a good indication that the kingdom and the throne are yet future.

14) The book of Hebrews. The author of Hebrews presents Christ's current role in heaven as that of a priest. While it is true that Jesus fulfills the three offices of prophet (Heb. 1:2), priest (4:14–16), and king (1:6), the priesthood of Christ is a dominant theme in Hebrews. Ryrie notes that as a king "he shall be worshipped by the angels when He comes again (1:6)."[119] Ryrie goes on to observe that, "regarding the Davidic covenant, the use of Psalm 110:1 is mentioned four times in Hebrews: in Hebrews 1 to show the superiority of Jesus to angels, in Heb. 8 and 10 to show his superiority to Levitical priest; in Heb. 12 it attests the magnitude of His glory."[120] Hebrews mentions the exaltation of Christ as "sitting at the Father's right hand" (Heb. 1:3, 13; 8:1; 10:12; and 12:12). Also, Jesus has been crowned with glory and honor (2:9). After Christ's resurrection, his right to the throne was established.

Hebrews 2:5 also presents a feature of the future earthly kingdom. The verse reads, "For it was not to angels that God subjected the world to come." In the phrase, τὴν οἰκουμένην τὴν μέλλουσαν ("the world to come"), the phrase, "inhabited earth, γη, is supplied" (Heb. 2:5), and refers to "a future world or kingdom to be inhabited by people."[121] Furthermore, the word οἰκουμένην 'inhabited earth' is used instead of κόσμος "system" or 'αἰωνας' ages. This verse implies that there will be an inhabited earth to come. Thus, there will be an earth to come, not the present one, but a future, earthly, Messianic Kingdom. William Lane also notes that "this designation τὴν οἰκουμένην τὴν μέλλουσαν ("the heavenly world to come"), which finds equivalent expression in μέλλοντος αἰῶνος 'age to come' (6:5) or πόλιν ... τὴν μέλλουσαν, 'city to come' (13:14) reflects a class of statements in the psalter that proclaim the stability of the eschatological kingdom of God."[122] This event occurs after Christ has defeated his enemies. Thereafter, he will fulfill the messianic promises (Heb. 1:13; 2:8; 10:13). Philip Hughes notes that the world to come "is the age of the Messiah in which the messianic promises and prophecies of old find fulfillment."[123] The theme of the world to come is also mentioned toward the end of the letter: "For here have we no continuing city, but we seek one to come" (Heb. 13:14). In addition to this, the author of Hebrews indicates that Christ is currently sitting at the right hand of God (Heb. 10:12–13). This does not indicate that Christ has already fulfilled the Davidic throne provision. Instead, it proves that the throne of David is not the same as the throne of God.

15) The book of Revelation. Finally, the book of Revelation also contributes to an understanding of the fulfillment of the Davidic kingdom. Jesus is identified as the Messiah, "the Lion of the tribe of Judah" (Rev. 5:5; cf. Gen. 49:9), "the Root of David" (Rev. 5:5; cf. Isa. 11:1, 10), and "the Root and the Offspring of David" (Rev. 22:16). In Revelation 3:21, Jesus draws a distinction between the Father's throne and his throne. The verse reads, "To

him who overcomes I will grant to sit with Me on My throne, as I also overcame and sat down with My Father on His throne." Jesus is not seated on his throne but the Father's. This refers to a future universal kingdom in which "the kingdoms of this world have become *the kingdoms* of our Lord and of His Christ, and He shall reign forever and ever" (Rev. 11:15). The Lord will therefore rule after the tribulation when all the kingdoms of the world have been demolished. Benware notes that "Jesus has been established as the king but has not yet begun to rule."[124] Revelation ends with Christ establishing the Davidic kingdom (Rev. 20: 2–7). To summarize the preceding discussion, we can say with confidence that the Scriptures indicate repeatedly that the Davidic kingdom and throne have been postponed.

The offer of the kingdom and Israel's rejection of it. Jesus offered the Davidic kingdom to Israel when he presented himself to the nation as their king in the triumphal entry (Matt. 21:9; Mark 11:9–10; Luke 19:37–38; John 12:12–15; cf. Ps. 118:26; Matt. 23:39; Luke 13:35). He taught that the only way to enter the kingdom is by faith in him (John 3:3, 14–15). In the Sermon on the Mount, he taught the moral rules for living in the kingdom (Matt. 5:1–7:29). The kingdom that Jesus offered to Israel was the one concerning which the Old Testament prophets spoke. Both the prophets and Israel expected it to be literal, with the throne of David established in Jerusalem and ruled by a physical descendant of David (Zech. 14:1–21). John the Baptist preached in the wilderness saying, "Repent, for the kingdom of heaven is at hand!" (Matt. 3:2). Soon, Jesus (Matt. 4:17), the twelve apostles (Matt. 10:5–7) and the Seventy (Luke 10:1–12) preached the same message about the earthly Davidic kingdom. The message was meant for the people of Israel (Matt. 10:5, 6). However, the establishment of the kingdom required national repentance on the part of the Israelites.

The Gospels clearly show that Israel rejected the kingdom offer. Israel's sin of rejecting Jesus took place when the Pharisees attributed his miracles to satanic powers (Matt. 12:24–45). The leaders ratified their rejection of the offer at Christ's triumphal entry into Jerusalem (Matt. 21–23), as well as by their decision to hand Christ over to the Romans for crucifixion (Matt. 26–27). The people echoed Israel's religious leaders' rejection when they shouted to Pilate: "'Away with *Him,* away with *Him!* Crucify Him!' Pilate said to them, 'Shall I crucify your King?' The chief priests answered, 'We have no king but Caesar!'" (John 19:15). Thus, John summarizes the situation, "He came to His own, and His own did not receive Him" (John 1:11). Otto Borchert offers convincing arguments as to "why Israel rejected her Messiah": the lowliness of Jesus, his greatness, and his unexpected death as the Messiah. The Messiah was not supposed to die; he was supposed to deliver Israel.[125]

The parables in the Gospels also provide evidence of the offer and rejection of the kingdom. Larry Tyler notes that three parables reveal the conditional offer of the Davidic kingdom: "1) the vineyard and the land (Matt. 21:33–46; Mark 12:1–12; Luke 20:9–18); 2) the wedding banquet (Matt. 22:1–10; Luke 14:16–24); and 3) the investment by the king's slaves (Luke 19:11–27)." We will discuss the third parable in more detail later. Tyler notes that Jesus told the parable of the wedding banquet in response to the statement, "Blessed *is* he who shall eat bread in the kingdom of God!" (Luke 14:15b).[126] Clearly, this parable refers to the kingdom (Matt. 22:2). Those who had been invited (i.e., Israel) "were not willing to come" (Matt. 22:3). Yet this coming depended on whether they accepted the invitation to the banquet. Israel rejected the offer. Though it is an argument from silence, this implies that if Israel had accepted the Messiah, the kingdom would have been established at that time. But the kingdom was postponed because Israel rejected the offer.

The mystery form of the kingdom. After the Davidic kingdom was postponed, God replaced it with the so-called "mystery kingdom," which is in operation during the present age. It is called the "mystery kingdom" because it was not revealed in the Old Testament. Jesus introduced it in Matthew 13:1–58, where he presents eight parables that provide its essential characteristics. He taught that the present age is distinct from the messianic kingdom. Ron Bigalke Jr. notes several contrasts between the mystery kingdom and the messianic kingdom. First, "the messianic kingdom is to be established by decisive, divine intervention, and the destruction of God's enemies (Matt. 13:3–9, 18–23, 36–43)." Second, "during the Messianic Kingdom, any disobedience will be put down with a 'rod of iron' and righteousness will prevail. However, in Matthew 13, Satan is active, the 'sons of the evil one' will exist alongside the 'sons of the kingdom' (13:30, 39–43), and there will be tribulation and persecution because of the Word."[127] Even though the Lord introduced the mystery kingdom, he assured his disciples that he will definitely establish the messianic kingdom (24:27–31; 25:31–33).

The principle of potential fulfillment. Traditional dispensationalists recognize the validity of potential fulfillment. Dyer states, "Fulfillment of prophecy is sometimes conditional on the response of those to whom the prophecy is directed." The book of Jonah illustrates this principle. God sent Jonah to Nineveh to inform the people of Nineveh that Nineveh would be destroyed in forty days (Jonah 3:5). For Jonah, the outcome was startling. Nineveh had not been destroyed after forty days. According to Dyer, Jonah's surprise outcome resulted from the people's response. He writes, "Inherent in God's message was the implicit promise that God could change the outcome based on the response of the people." To illustrate the principle that the prophecy must be fulfilled by the people who were intended also applies to a prophecy of a blessing. Dyer quotes what God said to Jeremiah, "The instant I speak concerning a nation and concerning a kingdom, to pluck up, to pull down, and to destroy *it*, if that nation against whom I have spoken turns from its evil, I will relent of the disaster that I thought to bring upon it" (Jer. 18:9–10).

The sovereign God is committed to his Word in accordance with the way his people act. Dyer notes, "God's fulfillment of blessings or cursing can be conditioned on the response of those to whom the message is given. In effect, some prophecies may or may not be realized, depending on how the people respond to the message."[128]

In conclusion, Dyer states two principles that guide the reader to understand the fulfillment of prophecy. First, "the meaning of prophecy must be determined within its original context." Furthermore, context plays a significant role also in interpreting any passage in the Scriptures, but the interpreter should also bear in mind that "later revelation can add more specificity to a prophecy." Genesis 3:15, the so-called *protevangelium*, is a clear example. The specific meaning of this passage became clear when Jesus overcame the humiliation of the cross: the devil was defeated, and Jesus triumphed and was exalted to the right hand of the Father, as the New Testament indicates in numerous places (e.g., Phil. 2:9). Second, "one must recognize the validity of potential fulfillment of prophecy."[129] How people respond to a specific prophecy is a determining factor. If the prophecy concerned sin and the people repented, then the intent of the prophecy is fulfilled. But if they resist, then they will be punished.

When these two principles are understood, the New Testament account is consistent. In his application of these principles, Dyer notes, "The coming of John the Baptist and Christ signals God's announcement/offer of the kingdom to Israel. But the actual fulfillment was contingent on their acceptance. Israel did not accept Jesus as their Messiah, and the Davidic kingdom promises were not fulfilled."[130] In other words, when the Jewish people rejected the offer of the Davidic kingdom, the prophecy of that kingdom was not fulfilled. but it will be fulfilled when the people receive it in the future. This is why traditional dispensationalists believe that the Davidic covenant will be fulfilled literally at Christ's Second Coming. Steven Waterhouse summarizes their position, "The Davidic Covenant supports the premillennial [traditional dispensationalism] system. Christ will return to bring in a literal/ political dominion over the earth with Jerusalem as its capital."[131]

Traditional Dispensationalism and the Davidic Covenant

For convenience's sake, we will restate the Davidic covenant. It is found in 2 Samuel 7:12–16:

> When your days are fulfilled and you rest with your fathers, I will set up your seed after you, who will come from your body, and I will establish his kingdom. He shall build a house for My name, and I will establish the throne of his kingdom forever. I will be his Father, and he shall be My son. If he commits iniquity, I will chasten him with the rod of men and with the blows of the sons of men. But My mercy shall not depart from him, as I took *it* from Saul, whom I removed from before you. *And your house and your kingdom shall be established forever before you. Your throne shall be established forever.* (italics added for emphasis.)

The Structure of the Davidic Covenant

God promised three essential elements to David in verse 16 that form the structure of the Davidic covenant: an eternal house, an eternal throne, and an eternal kingdom. The psalmists also mention this covenant, especially in regard to the choice and rule of David as a king (Pss. 2:6–7; 89:3–4; 132:11, 17). Although the term "covenant" (בְּרִית) does not occur in the oracle that Nathan delivered to David, it occurs in 2 Samuel 23:5 and in 2 Chronicles 13:5, 21:7, and 23:3. The recurrence of the terms "eternal" or "forever" (עַד־עוֹלָם) is significant. They indicate that the covenant committed God to permanently maintaining the Davidic line.

Renald E. Showers discusses these three elements.[132] The first promise made to David was an eternal "house," that is, a "dynasty." Yahweh states, "Your house … shall be established forever before you" (2 Sam. 7:16). Showers notes, "The term house referred to David's physical line of descent."[133] In other words, "house" refers to a dynastic succession of rulers whereby a son was promised in each generation to rule as king.[134] This promise is especially significant. Showers remarks, "God was promising that David's line of descent would endure forever."[135] The promise that David's house would be eternal is a guarantee that his family line would never end. Pentecost notes, "A line stemming from David would continue indefinitely and would be the divinely recognized royal line."[136]

The second promise assured David a perpetual kingdom. The promise is as follows, "Your kingdom shall be established forever before you" (2 Sam. 7:16). Johnson defines the Davidic kingdom as "a realm or reign which would include a chosen people as descendants of Abraham (2 Sam. 7:16; 1 Chron. 17:9; Ps. 89:15–17)."[137] While it is true that, since the Babylonian exile, no one has reigned over the Davidic kingdom, Showers notes, "God pledged that David's kingdom would never pass away permanently, even though it might not function at all times."[138] This promise guarantees that David's kingdom will once again be restored to permanent status. Pentecost argues, "The term kingdom must refer to the political body David would rule and over which David's descendants would successively reign."[139]

The third promise guaranteed David a "throne." It reads, "Your throne shall be established forever" (2 Sam. 7:16). Showers states that a throne "is a reference to the ruling authority which David exercised as king (2 Sam. 3:10; 1 Kings 1:37, 47)."[140] This ruling authority has not been exercised, which implies that there is a future restoration of the Davidic kingdom at Jesus Christ's Second Coming. This promise is also reiterated in Psalm 89:3–4, where God had sworn to build up David's throne "to all generations." Johnson defines a throne as "a seat, but in its use it is a symbol that refers to the power and authority of that reign, exercised while the king was ruling in that kingdom." The ultimate right of sovereignty would never be transferred to another family regardless of who may have temporarily occupied the throne. The covenant guaranteed that David's family would always exist and that it would always be the rightful royal dynasty with a moral right to the throne. Johnson states, "The power symbolized in David's throne was theocratic, political, and righteous."[141] The fact that a Davidic king is not now ruling in Jerusalem is evidence that the eternal kingdom and eternal throne aspects to the Davidic covenant are unfulfilled.

The Nature of the Davidic Covenant in View of Its Fulfillment

Traditional dispensationalists hold that the Davidic covenant is unconditional. Showers notes, "God stated no conditions in the content of the Davidic covenant when he established it with David."[142] The following features indicate its unconditional nature. First, it is eternal (2 Sam. 7:13, 16; 23:5). Pentecost notes that "the only way it could be called eternal is that it is unconditional and rests entirely on the faithfulness of God for its execution."[143] Second, it was confirmed with an unchanging oath (Ps. 89:3, 35). Third, Waterhouse points out that it was reaffirmed after sin.[144] In other words, God promised to keep the covenant with David despite a cycle of faithless apostasy on Israel's part. Pentecost observes, "If the covenant was conditional based on the obedience or faithfulness of the nation Israel, these reaffirmations could never have been made."[145]

The Abrahamic covenant (Gen. 12:1–2; 15:4–5) and Davidic covenant (2 Sam. 7:12–16, 23) are similar in content because, when David receives the promise from God, he also inherits the following promises given to Abraham: (a) a "name" (2 Sam. 7:9; cf. Gen. 12:2); (b) offspring, that is, "seed ... from your own body" (2 Sam. 7:12; cf. Gen. 15:4–5); (c) a "nation" (2 Sam. 7:23; cf. Gen. 12:2); and (d) "blessing" (2 Sam. 7:29 [as the object of the blessing]; cf. Gen. 12:2–3 [as the origin of the blessing]). These similarities present some unique implications because "they stress the continuity of God's dealing with Israel before and after David's accession to kingship."[146] Therefore, the Davidic covenant is both unconditional and irrevocable, because it is an extension of certain features of the Abrahamic covenant.[147] Johnson also believes that the Davidic covenant is "a unilateral covenant with promises unconditionally assured in their outcome."[148]

The Fulfillment of the Davidic Covenant

In the oracle the prophet Nathan delivered to David, God promised David three important things: an eternal house, an eternal throne, and an eternal kingdom. Traditional dispensationalists believe that these promises will be fulfilled when Christ establishes the millennium at his Second Coming. Traditional dispensationalists do not believe that the Davidic king is now ruling in Jerusalem. When Jesus entered Jerusalem at his triumphal entry, the Jews shouted, "Blessed *is* the kingdom of our father David / That comes in the name of the Lord! Hosanna in the highest!" (Mark 11:10). However, before Jesus' ascension to heaven, the disciples asked him, "Lord, will You at this time restore the kingdom to Israel?" (Acts 1:6). This biblical evidence proves that the kingdom and throne aspects of the Davidic covenant are unfulfilled. Waterhouse states,

> Premillennialists [traditional dispensationalists] believe that the Davidic Covenant is still in force and must yet be fulfilled. A Davidic descendant must usher in a Kingdom and a throne that cannot end. Since no such kingdom exists at the present time, it must be that Jesus Christ, the

Son of David, will bring in this great and eternal
Kingdom at His Second Coming.[149]

Waterhouse also writes that God promised David that his seed
would have a right to rule and would eventually rule over Israel
forever (2 Sam. 7:12). But David's descendants have not ruled
over Israel since before the exile.[150] Traditional dispensationalists
therefore believe that the promise of an eternal throne for David's
son must be fulfilled in the ultimate Son of David, Jesus Christ.
These promises are eternally binding and must come to pass as
the Scriptures attest (Psa. 89:3–4, 28–29, 33–37).

Johnson holds to a two-stage process for the development of
Israel's monarchy: the people's part and Yahweh's part. In regard
to the first factor, the people could choose to have a monarchy
(Deut. 17:14), but in the second part, they had a mandate to
receive God's choice for them (Deut. 17:15).[151] This process was
applied during Yahweh's choice of both Saul (1 Sam. 9:15–16) and
David (1 Sam. 16:1–13). After the people decided they wanted a
king (1 Sam. 8:4), Samuel's part was to communicate God's choice
to the people (1 Sam. 9:16–17; 10:20–24; 16:1–13). The people
had no option but to receive whomever the Lord had appointed.
Johnson writes, "The people's appointment was an official, formal
agreement sealed with an act of anointing by all the people."[152]
Johnson also holds that the provision of the Davidic house "was
inaugurated when the first king [Solomon] was enthroned from
the family of David." Though this situation ceased during the
exile, the provisions of the covenant were observed. The throne
remained vacant until the birth of Jesus Christ. Johnson then
writes, "All four Gospels record Yahweh's anointing of Jesus
with the Holy Spirit and adoption of him as Son (Matt. 3:13–17;
Mark 1:9–11; Luke 3:21–22; John 1:32). Thus the provision of
an eternal house had been kept during the times of the Gentiles,
but the provision of a throne and kingdom awaited the people's
response to God's choice."[153]

Jesus' rightful claim to be a son of David was fulfilled by the pronouncement of the people at the triumphal entry (Matt. 21:9–11). However, his claim to be king led to his crucifixion (Matt. 27:21). The leaders mobilized the crowd to reject him as the king of the Jews and demand that the Romans crucify him (John 19:21). The people, therefore, rejected Jesus' claim to the Davidic throne. Johnson responds to the question of whether the kingdom was actually fulfilled at Christ's First Coming by stating, "The First Advent called for a real decision and provided the real Anointed One from God." The people were required to accept and confess the Son of David before he could usher in the earthly Davidic kingdom they expected. Furthermore, Johnson rejects the idea of an already or inaugurated fulfillment of the kingdom provision. He writes, "It would never have been a realized Davidic Kingdom, let alone an already or inaugurated fulfillment of the Davidic covenant without the Cross first." Johnson believes that Christ's First Coming only fulfilled the provision of the Son of David "in part."[154]

Renald Showers states five reasons for the future fulfillment of the Davidic covenant by Christ "after His Second Coming."[155] However, I am placing them in what I believe is the chronological order of occurrence, rather than Showers' original order.

1) The Messiah's current role. Showers notes that "according to Psalm 110:1–2 Messiah is to sit at the right hand of His Father in Heaven until it is time for Him to rule. Therefore, Messiah's rule as king will not start until after His present session with the Father in Heaven."[156] While it is true Jesus sits at the right hand of the Father now, it is as a priest, not as a ruling king. His prerogative to rule will take place in the future.

2) The Messiah's visible return from heaven. "Daniel 7:13–14 portrayed God's giving the kingdom which lasts forever to the Son of man when that Son comes with the clouds of Heaven."[157] The passage reads,

I was watching in the night visions
And behold, *One* like the Son of Man,
Coming with the clouds of heaven!
He came to the Ancient of Days,
And they brought Him near before Him.
Then to Him was given dominion and glory and
a kingdom,
That all peoples, nations, and languages should
serve Him.
His dominion *is* an everlasting dominion,
Which shall not pass away,
And His kingdom *the one*
Which shall not be destroyed. (Dan. 7:13–14)

Showers lists three features of this portrayal. We will focus on the third point. According to Showers, "from Matt. 24:29–31, Jesus indicated that He will fulfill the Dan. 7:13–14 prophecy in His Second Coming." Jesus says this will take place after the tribulation: "Then the sign of the Son of Man will appear in heaven, and then all the tribes of the earth will mourn, and they will see the Son of Man coming on the clouds of heaven with power and great glory" (Matt. 24:30). Showers writes, "These things indicate the kingdom over which Christ is to rule was not given to Him in conjunction with His first coming. God will not give it to Him until His Second Coming. God will give it to Him at His Second Coming."[158]

3) The prophesied location of the Messiah's return. "Zechariah 14:4 and 9 disclosed the fact that Messiah will be king after His feet touches down on the Mount of Olives at His Second Coming."[159] The Christian community expects this event to take place literally–but in the future, just as the angels told the disciples (Acts 1:9–12).

4) The Messiah's future judgment for admission to the

kingdom. "In Matt. 25:31–46, Jesus declared that He would sit on His throne, judge the Gentiles, and send believers into the kingdom in conjunction with His glorious Second Coming."[160] This implies that the throne and the kingdom await Jesus' Second Coming. This is contrary to those who teach that Jesus is sitting on his throne and reigning as king now.

5) The Messiah's regeneration of the earth. According to Showers, "Jesus stated that He would sit on the throne of His glory as the Son of Man when the earth is regenerated (restored to its prefall condition as the result of the curse of man's sin being lifted from it [Matt. 19:28; cf. Rom. 8:18–22]). This regeneration has not happened as yet." Showers claims this time will come when Jesus is on the earth, but not when He is in heaven (Acts 3:19–21). Christ will not sit on His throne until He has returned to earth at His Second Coming.[161]

An Evaluation of the Traditional Dispensationalist Approach

In this section, we will evaluate traditional dispensationalism's view regard the Davidic covenant and kingdom using the criteria of the grammatical-historical method and the *CSBH*. The evaluation will focus on four areas: stability of meaning, the distinction between the church and Israel, the literal fulfillment of the Davidic kingdom at Christ's Second Coming, and the postponement of the Davidic kingdom.

Stable Meaning

Webster's defines the word "stable" as that which is "firmly established, not easily moved, shaken, or overthrown: solid, steadfast."[162] Stability in meaning is evident in the opinions, statements, or viewpoints of traditional dispensationalist writers. They hold that the text has one meaning with many applications. For instance, Charles Dyer writes, "Meaning focuses specifically on the author's intended understanding of the text. The human author and divine author have one meaning in the text."[163] This approach is capable of arriving at a single meaning. Their principle is in harmony with Article VII of the *CSBH*. It states:

> WE AFFIRM that the meaning expressed in each biblical text is single, definite and fixed.

> WE DENY that the recognition of this single meaning eliminates the variety of its application.[164]

Three words in this affirmation require explanation: single, definite, and fixed. *Webster's* dictionary defines "single" as "that which is free from duplicity or insincerity, frank, honest, and open."[165] "Definite" refers to "having distinct or certain limits: determinate in extent or character, limited or fixed."[166] Last, "fixed" refers to "securely placed or fastened: not adjustable: permanently and definitely located."[167] In relation to Article VII of the *CSBH*, Geisler states,

> It stresses the unity and fixity of meaning as opposed to those who find multiple and pliable meanings. What a passage means is fixed by the author and is not subject to change by readers. ... Meaning is also definite in that there are defined limits by virtue of the author's expressed meaning in the given linguistic forms and cultural context. Meaning is determined by an author; it is discovered by the readers.[168]

Traditional dispensationalists' view of a single meaning is valid. This has implications for some of the central issues. *Progressive revelation.* The previous discussion on stable meaning established that if God makes promises to a specific group such as Israel, then he must fulfill that promise with them. This means that progressive revelation cannot cancel the unconditional promises to Israel, as Feinberg notes, "If an Old Testament prophecy or promise is made unconditionally to a given people and is still unfulfilled even in the New Testament era, then the prophecy must still be fulfilled to them. ... Progressive of revelation cannot cancel unconditional promises."[169] His observation is in harmony with the second sentence in the affirmation of Article XVIII of the *CSBH*, which is limited in its meaning by the first sentence. It states:

> WE AFFIRM that the Bible's own interpretation
> of itself is always correct, never deviating from,
> but rather elucidating, the single meaning of the
> inspired text. The single meaning of a prophet's
> words includes, but is not restricted to, the
> understanding of those words by the prophets
> and necessarily involves the intention of God
> evidenced in the fulfillment of those words.[170]

Geisler makes it clear that the "understanding" has to do with implications, not meaning.[171] The traditional dispensationalists' interpretation of the unconditional nature of the Davidic promises is therefore in harmony with this article. The principle that progressive revelation does not change the single meaning intended in earlier revelation results in a stable meaning.

The priority of the testaments. Concerning the New Testament use of the Old Testament, traditional dispensationalists have maintained that the Old Testament must be interpreted literally. Charles Dyer, Charles Ryrie, John Walvoord, and Elliot Johnson agree on this principle. We have observed that literal interpretation offers literal fulfillment of many Old Testament prophetic passages. Robert Thomas notes, "Every Old Testament passage must receive its own grammatical-historical interpretation, regardless of how a New Testament writer uses it."[172] The literal meaning is the normal or obvious meaning of the statements. The literal approach enables the interpreter to discover the meaning of the text in its grammatical and historical context. Traditional dispensationalists seek to apply Article XV of the *CSBH*. It states:

> WE AFFIRM the necessity of interpreting the Bible according to its literal, or normal, sense. The literal sense is the grammatical-historical sense, that is, the meaning which the writer expressed. Interpretation according to the literal sense will take account of all figures of speech and literary forms found in the text.

> WE DENY the legitimacy of any approach to Scripture that attributes to it meaning which the literal sense does not support.[173]

Literal interpretation is in harmony with the grammatical-historical method of interpretation. The denial in Article XV safeguards against nonliteral interpretation. Geisler states, "The Denial warns against attributing to Scripture any meaning not based in a literal understanding, such as mythological or allegorical interpretations."[174] Traditional dispensationalists have removed this tension by making a clear distinction between the Old and New Testaments. Their focus on a literal interpretation preserves the stable meaning stated in the Davidic covenant. This view repudiates allegorical, spiritual, and mystical interpretation as false and unbiblical. Therefore, the literal approach brings a stable meaning to the text.

Traditional dispensationalists have also maintained that

the New Testament does not change the meaning of the Old Testament. Ryrie writes, "New revelation cannot mean contradictory revelation. Later revelation on a subject does not make the earlier revelation mean something different."[175] This principle is in harmony with Article XVII of the *CSBH*, which states, "WE AFFIRM the unity, harmony and consistency of Scripture and declare that it is its own best interpreter."[176] Four words or phrases in this affirmation deserve attention: "unity," "harmony," "consistency," and "own best interpreter." *Webster's* defines the word "unity" as "the quality or state of being or consisting of one."[177] Harmony refers to "a combination into a consistent whole: integration."[178] Consistency refers to "the condition of standing together or remaining fixed in union."[179] In reference to Article XVII, Geisler notes, "Not only is the Bible always correct in interpreting itself (see Article XVIII), but it is the 'best interpreter' of itself." He goes on to say that "comparing Scripture with Scripture is an excellent help to an interpreter. For one passage sheds light on another."[180] In this case, the Bible text should be consulted first before seeking external sources. Traditional dispensationalists are correct in maintaining that the New Testament revelation does not change, alter, complete, or add anything to the original Old Testament promises. These promises remain stable.

Literal interpretation takes into account matters of history, which upholds the author's view point and thus is capable of producing a stable meaning. For instance, in response to the question as to whether a stated meaning about a historical event changes or expands when that event is again interpreted with the benefit of a later perspective of time, we noted that non-dispensationalists maintain that meaning will change or expand. Article XIV of the *CSBH* alludes to historical interpretation by including the following statement:

WE AFFIRM that the biblical record of events, discourses and sayings, though presented in a variety of appropriate literary forms, corresponds to historical fact.

WE DENY that any event, discourse or saying reported in Scripture was invented by the biblical writers or by the traditions they incorporated.[181]

Therefore, a stable single meaning is guaranteed if historical facts are interpreted at face value. This means that traditional dispensationalism seeks to use grammatical-historical interpretation and be in harmony with the *CSBH*.

Israel and the church. I commend traditional dispensationalists for their attempt to define literally terms related to the fulfillment of the Davidic covenant, such as "Israel" and "church." This approach maintains the rules of grammar and syntax, thereby safeguarding against the spiritual interpretation to which non-dispensationalists often resort and in which they sometimes see these terms as interchangeable synonyms. Traditional dispensationalism has counteracted this tendency, and so their approach is in harmony with a grammatical-historical interpretation in which the interpreter takes words at their normal face value.

The Church as Distinct from Israel

If the grammatical-historical method is followed consistently, then we can expect a literal interpretation. The distinction between Israel and the church is a result of this approach. Furthermore, this principle is in harmony with Article VII of the *CSBH*, which states:

WE AFFIRM that the meaning expressed in each biblical text is single, definite and fixed.

WE DENY that the recognition of this single meaning eliminates the variety of its application.[182]

The term "Israel" always means national or ethnic Israel, never the church as "the New Israel." And the word "church," when used in its technical sense, always refers to the body of Christ, which includes both Jews and Gentiles. It never refers to a "spiritual Israel." The reason is that the biblical meaning is single, fixed, and definite.

How do traditional dispensationalists come to the conclusion that the church is distinct from Israel? They do so by deciding to use a valid hermeneutical method before they interpret the Scriptures. Article IX of the *CSBH* states: "WE AFFIRM that the term hermeneutics, which historically signified the rules of exegesis, may be properly extended to cover all that is involved in the process of perceiving what the biblical revelation means and how it bears on our lives."[183] Hermeneutics follows the rules and principles of exegesis. The rules of exegesis are the basis for a grammatical-historical hermeneutic. Traditional dispensationalists distinguish between the church and Israel because they apply a grammatical-historical hermeneutic. The resulting interpretation establishes the fact that the church originates in the New Testament dispensation. Therefore, traditional dispensationalists are right in concluding that the church does not fulfill the promises made to Israel, in particular, a Davidic throne and kingdom. The promises made to Israel must be fulfilled during the future Davidic kingdom. Traditional dispensationalists recognize that the church is an institution that is distinct from Israel in their origin, their relation to their current status, and the promises God made to them. When an interpreter consistently employs the grammatical-historical method to the relationship between Israel and the church, they achieve results that are clear, normal, and literal. When traditional dispensationalists consistently use the grammatical-historical interpretation, they will realize the following truths:

The true relationship between Israel and the church. First, Toussaint says the interpreter will realize that "the church enters into Israel's millennial promises." Several passages support this conclusion. For instance, "Jesus said to them, "Assuredly I say to you, that in the regeneration, when the Son of Man sits on the throne of His glory, you who have followed Me will also sit on twelve thrones, judging the twelve tribes of Israel" (Matt. 19:28). Then Toussaint notes in connection with this passage, "The apostles, who are part and parcel of the church, are going to reign over Israel in the land during the millennium."[184] The figure of the olive tree in Romans 11: 6–18 is another example. Toussaint writes:

> The root of the tree (11:16) may refer to the patriarchs or to the early church, which was Jewish. In either case, the hopes of each anticipated the millennial kingdom (cf. Acts 3:20; Rom. 9:4–5, 11:26–27). If the wild olive branches are grafted into the olive tree, then it must indicate that the believing Gentiles participate along with believing Jews in earthly blessings.[185]

The last example is the parable that "looks at the Lord returning to reign (Luke 19:11–27). His faithful servants were given responsibilities to rule over cities in His kingdom, depending on their faithfulness in this age."[186] This implies that Israel still possesses the promise of the kingdom. Toussaint concludes that "the reigning of the church with Christ on earth does not blur the distinctions between Israel and the church. They are distinct in this age and they will be in the future millennium."[187]

The New Testament confirmation of the promises to Israel. Vlach suggests, "The New Testament reaffirms the Old Testament promises, and covenants are still the possession of Israel."[188] In his reference to the covenants, Vlach includes the Davidic covenant. This point is in harmony with the *CSBH* Article XVII, which states, "WE AFFIRM the unity, harmony and consistency of Scripture and declare that it is its own best interpreter."[189] Paul writes, "My countrymen according to the flesh... are Israelites, to whom *pertain* the adoption, the glory, the covenants, the giving of the law, the service *of God*, and the promises" (Rom. 9:3b–4). Regarding this passage, Vlach writes, "According to Paul, the 'covenants' and 'promises' and even 'temple service' are still seen as being the possession of Israel even with the church existing and even during a time in which Israel's disobedience is evident. ... 'To them belong' is a present reality."[190]

The recipients of the original promises based on the historical context. Traditional dispensationalists contend that Davidic promises were given historically to Israel and must be fulfilled with them, not the church. Lightner writes:

> Furthermore, most insist that the national promises embodied in these covenants will be realized by the nation to whom they were given. The promises to the Jewish nation have not been, nor will they ever be, transferred to the church. Israel means Israel and her promises have not been fulfilled by the church. Since they have not, they must be fulfilled in the millennium if God's Word is not to be broken.[191]

Toussaint agrees, "The promises were made to Israel, not the church," and notes that "the church only enters into the promises because of their association with and being joined to the promised Messiah (Gal. 3:29)."[192] This conforms to the *CSBH* Article XIV, which states, "WE AFFIRM that the biblical record of events, discourses and sayings, though presented in a variety of appropriate literary forms, corresponds to historical fact."[193] Geisler explains that "this article insists that any record of events presented in Scripture must correspond to historical fact."[194]

The literal fulfillment of other Old Testament prophecies. A literal hermeneutic is an essential feature of traditional dispensationalism. The literal fulfillment of other Old Testament prophecies confirms that Israel is the referent point and is a product of a literal interpretation of Scripture. Ryrie writes, "If the yet unfulfilled prophecies of the Old Testament made in the Abrahamic, Davidic, and New Covenants are to be literally fulfilled, there must be a future period, the Millennium, in which they can be fulfilled, for the church is not now fulfilling them."[195] On one hand, if Davidic promises are interpreted literally, then, these promises demand a future fulfillment by Israel. On the other hand, if Davidic promises are interpreted in a nonliteral sense, then these promises are fulfilled by the church. Traditional dispensationalists maintain that the church is not fulfilling these promises, but that their fulfillment is reserved for the millennium and is one of the principle features of it. This principle correlates well with the *CSBH* Article XV, which states:

> WE AFFIRM the necessity of interpreting the Bible according to its literal, or normal, sense. The literal sense is the grammatical-historical sense, that is, the meaning which the writer expressed. Interpretation according to the literal sense will take account of all figures of speech and literary forms found in the text.[196]

In conclusion, the fact that believing Gentiles are grafted into the place of spiritual blessing in unbelieving Israel's place (Rom. 11:16–20) does not mean that the Davidic covenant with national Israel has been nullified. Paul writes that the removal of Israel is temporary, not permanent:

> Because of unbelief they were broken off, and you stand by faith. Do not be haughty, but fear. For if God did not spare the natural branches, He may not spare you either. Therefore consider the goodness and severity of God: on those who fell, severity; but toward you, goodness, if you continue in *His* goodness. Otherwise you also will be cut off. And they also, if they do not continue in unbelief, will be grafted in, for God is able to graft them in again. (Rom. 11:20–23)

In the fullness of time, national Israel will be restored and God will fulfill all his spiritual, material, and national promises to them. Traditional dispensationalists, then, maintain that Israel and the church are distinct both now and in the future on the basis of a literal interpretation that conforms to the grammatical-historical approach and the articles of the *CSBH*.

Literal Fulfillment of the Davidic Kingdom at Christ's Second Coming

The fulfillment of the Davidic covenant at Christ's Second Coming does not contradict the original meaning as stated in its Old Testament context. Traditional dispensationalists maintain this principle because it is in harmony with the second sentence in Article VI of the *CSBH*, which states, "We further affirm that a statement is true if it represents matters as they actually are, but is an error if it misrepresents the facts."[197] The statement of the Davidic covenant is originally presented in the Old Testament and is therefore God's absolute truth. Furthermore, we have already seen that fulfillment cannot occur unless it occurs with the ones whom God promised to bless—national Israel. History attests to the fact that Israel rejected their Messiah and that the promises were put on hold, but that does not rule out their fulfillment. Traditional dispensationalists find no evidence that Jesus sat on the throne of David and ruled over the kingdom of Israel. Therefore, the traditional dispensationalists' premise that the establishment of the Davidic throne and Christ's rule over the kingdom awaits a literal future fulfillment appears to be valid. This principle is in harmony with the biblical texts and the *CSBH* Article XVIII:

> WE AFFIRM that the Bible's own interpretation of itself is always correct, never deviating from, but rather elucidating, the single meaning of the inspired text. The single meaning of a prophet's words includes, but is not restricted to, the understanding of those words by the prophet and necessarily involves the intention of God evidenced in the fulfillment of those words.
>
> WE DENY that the writers of Scripture always understood the full implications of their own words.[198]

Unlike other evangelical views, only traditional dispensationalists contend for a strictly future literal fulfillment of the Davidic covenant with Israel at Christ's Second Coming. Other evangelical interpretations argue for either a completed fulfillment in the church at Christ's First Coming or an "already" and "not-yet" fulfillment, beginning with the church at his First Coming and concluding with Israel at the Second Coming. This is because traditional dispensationalists are the only group that tries to adhere to both a grammatical-historical hermeneutic and the articles of the *CSBH*. These criteria correlate well with the unconditional nature of the Davidic promises, as John Feinberg notes, "If an OT prophecy or promise is made unconditionally to a given people and is still unfulfilled to them even in the NT era, then the prophecy must still be fulfilled to them. ... Progress of revelation cannot cancel unconditional promises."[199] God's unconditional promises guarantee that the unfulfilled promises regarding Israel will yet be fulfilled at Christ's Second Coming, a claim that is in harmony with Article XVII of the *CSBH*. This article states that

> WE AFFIRM the unity, harmony and consistency of Scripture and declare that it is its own best interpreter.

> WE DENY that Scripture may be interpreted in such a way as to suggest that one passage corrects or militates against another. We deny that later writers of Scripture misinterpreted earlier passages of Scripture when quoting from or referring to them.[200]

The Prophesied Postponement of the Davidic Kingdom

The term "postponement" brings to mind the concept of "interruption in fulfillment."[201] This delay or withdrawal is only temporary. It will only last until Jesus returns to set up the kingdom. In this section, we will consider six major objections other evangelicals raise against the traditional dispensationalist proposal regarding the postponement of the Davidic kingdom.

The potential results if Israel had accepted the kingdom.

Opponents to the traditional dispensationalist view rightly point out that a bona fide offer of the kingdom could have ended with Israel accepting Jesus as their Messiah and the establishment of the Davidic kingdom. Erich Sauer concludes that, "if Israel had accepted Christ and the kingdom established, Golgotha (the cross) would have been bypassed or impossible."[202] In response to this objection, Charles Feinberg points out that the cross was something Jesus had to do. It was not an obstacle to "the predicted kingdom."[203] He further notes, "If Israel had accepted Christ, then Isaiah 53 and other passages would have proved false."[204] Ryrie, too, in responding to the objection that Israel accepting the Davidic kingdom at Christ's First Coming "makes the Cross theoretically unnecessary or that it detracts from the glory of the church," writes:

> But it will be asked, if the Davidic kingdom is postponed that means that had it been received by the Jews it would not have been necessary for the Lord Jesus to have been crucified. The postponement of the kingdom is related primarily to the question of God's program in this age through the Church and not to the necessity of the crucifixion. The crucifixion would have been necessary as foundational to the establishment of the kingdom even if the church age had never been conceived in the purposes of God. The question is not whether the crucifixion would have been avoided but whether the Davidic kingdom was postponed.[205]

In saying this, Ryrie indicates that the cross does not depend on the kingdom occurring, but on the program of God. Therefore, the cross does not in any way minimize the teaching of the postponement of the kingdom. Ryrie continues, "Postponement relates to the outworking of God's purpose in the church, the body of Christ, and certainly the Cross is central to this work of God. Furthermore, even if there had been no church as a part of God's program, the Cross was necessary to the establishment of the Messianic kingdom—the Cross is basic."[206]

The spiritual emphasis in the offer of the kingdom. The second objection is that the kingdom "at hand" was not an earthly, visible, and political kingdom, but a spiritual kingdom.[207] Furthermore, this kingdom was not withdrawn, but is manifested today through salvation. In response, Showers does not deny the spiritual offer of the messianic kingdom through salvation but adds that the spiritual kingdom concept does not cancel the eschatological, earthly, political kingdom that God promised to David. Showers offers several biblical arguments for an earthly and visible kingdom:

> First, according to Zechariah 14:4 and 9, after Messiah's feet have touched down on the Mount of Olives at the Second Coming, He will be King "over all the earth." Christ will rule, not just over the Church or individual human hearts yielded to Him, but over the entire earth (cf. Ps. 72:8; Zech. 9:10; Dan. 2:35, 44–45).
>
> Second, Jeremiah 23:5–8 promised that when Messiah, a righteous Branch of David reigns as King, He will execute judgment and justice "in the earth." During the days of His rule, the people of Israel will "dwell safely" and will "dwell in their own land." The language of this passage implies an earthly kingdom rule of Christ.[208]

Several Old Testament passages state that there would be an earthly and visible kingdom over which the Son of Man is to rule (Jer. 23:5; Dan. 2:34–35, 44–45; 7:13–14; Zech. 14:9). Furthermore, when Jesus was born, Israel lived in anticipation of the coming Messiah on a widespread scale, as is seen by Simon and Anna waiting in the temple for "the Consolation of Israel" (Luke 2:25–27). Moreover, wise men came from the east, inquiring, "Where is He who has been born King of the Jews?" When these wise men found Jesus, they worshipped him with gifts, especially gold, which symbolizes the fact that he was born to be a king (Matt. 2:1–4).[209]

John the Baptist, Jesus' forerunner, came to "prepare the way of the Lord" (Matt. 3:3; cf. Isa. 40:3). What does "prepare the way of the Lord" imply? It does not refer to the cross, but to the establishment of the kingdom. Toussaint notes, "The kingdom is indeed at hand."[210] John the Baptist's question also implies the same thing. He asked Jesus, "Are You the Coming One [σὺ εἶ ὁ ἐρχόμενος], or do we look for another?" (Matt. 11:3). Ὁ ἐρχόμενος was a widely known title among the Jewish community.[211] Toussaint further notes, "Jesus responded to John's questions by pointing to His miraculous works which were anticipated when the Messiah comes (Isa. 35:1–3), and were proofs of Christ's Messiahship."[212] Jesus telling John's disciples to report his works (i.e., his miracles) is proof that both John and Jesus had the earthly messianic kingdom in mind. It was strongly held that when the Messiah comes, he would perform such works in order to establish his kingdom. Therefore, John the Baptist, the disciples, and Jesus' proclamations were references to the messianic kingdom, not a spiritual kingdom.

The disciples were also expecting Jesus to set up a visible, earthly kingdom. James and John's request that one sit at the right hand of Jesus and the other at his left hand in the kingdom is evidence of this (Mark 10:35–37). Jesus denied their request but not the idea of the kingdom. He confirmed the reality of a physical kingdom by saying that "to sit on My right hand and on My left is not Mine to give, but *it is for those* for whom it is prepared by My Father" (Matt. 20:23).

The current reign of Jesus from heaven. Those who object to a postponement of the Davidic kingdom claim that "Jesus is reigning now as the Davidic king."[213] Progressive dispensationalists and postmillennialists claim that Jesus is currently fulfilling three offices to which he has been anointed: priest, king, and prophet.[214] Those who make this objection further claim that Jesus will not have the same level of authority at any other time than he has now. But this claim is not valid for the following reasons. First, anointing is not a guarantee of immediate kingship. For example, Samuel anointed David in anticipation of his becoming king. It took forty years until Saul's death before David become king and sat on the throne. Likewise, even though Jesus was born "king of the Jews," he will not become king until he actually takes the throne.

Another example concerns Jesus' miracle of the fish and loaves (John 6:15). After the multitude had witnessed the miracle, they attempted to take him by force and make him a king. Jesus avoided this incident by slipping away through the multitude. He was repudiating the idea of receiving a kingdom by the will of the people. Even though he was king, his time to reign in a visible kingdom had not come. His Kingship was also revealed during his triumphal entry. The people shouted "Hosanna," which means "save us now," when he rode into Jerusalem on a donkey on Palm Sunday in fulfillment of the prophecy (Zech. 9:9; John 12:12–14). Jesus was also crucified with this phrase on His cross, "King of the Jews" (Matt. 27:37). Again, Pilate asked Jesus, "Are You the King of the Jews?" Jesus evaded the question but admitted that He was indeed a king, and had been born for that purpose, but that his kingdom was "not of this world" (John 18:33–35). The author of the book of Hebrews emphasizes Christ's current session as high priest at God's right hand (Heb. 1:3; 8:1; 10:12; 12:20). These passages indicate that Christ is not seated on the earthly Davidic throne. Jesus is not currently a king, but is currently serving as the high priest for the church.

The argument from silence. The fourth objection to a theory of the postponement of the Davidic kingdom concerns "the silence of the Bible."[215] Erich Sauer writes, "In the whole Bible there is no single place which speaks distinctly of such an 'offer' and 'postponement' of the earthly kingdom. Rather do all the explanations related to this idea rest upon exact attention to the wording of certain passages of Scripture or upon inferences drawn from them."[216] Toussaint partly concedes, but then refutes this objection by writing:

> It is true, the word "offer" is not used in the Gospels in the connection with the kingdom, but has been explained in the preceding section, it is a necessary implication from the Lord's words. The temporary nearness of the kingdom, the national judgment because of lack of repentance, the laments of Christ, and the parable of judgment all teach this doctrine.[217]

The lack of a prerequisite for the kingdom. Sauer points to the fact that repentance is not stated as a condition in either John the Baptist or Jesus' preaching about the kingdom. Instead, they only said, "Repent, for the kingdom of heaven is at hand" (Matt. 3:2; 4:17). In other words, repentance was not a condition for the kingdom to come because it was already near. Sauer writes, "They did not say, '*If* you repent *then* the kingdom of the heavens will draw near.' The repentance of man was not the condition for the coming of the kingdom, but the coming of the kingdom was the ground of the demand for repentance."[218] Toussaint responds by noting that "these two ideas are not mutually exclusive. The people of Israel were to repent in order for them individually to enter the kingdom, but they were also to repent for the kingdom to come."[219] The kingdom was limited to them, but for them to receive it, they had to amend their ways. John the Baptist emphasized repentance (Matt. 3:1, 2); Christ stressed repentance (Matt. 4:17); the twelve disciples preached repentance (Matt. 10:5–7); and the Seventy were sent to heal the sick and condemn those who did not repent (Luke 10:1, 9–16).

The foreordination of Israel's rejection of the kingdom. Toussaint lists several passages that indicate Israel would reject her Messiah (Isa. 53:1–10; Dan. 9:26; Zech. 12:10) and says that some claim that "the offer of the kingdom was not valid because God had foreordained Israel's rejection."[220] But McClain responds, "Those who cavil at the idea of an offer which is certain to be rejected betray an ignorance, not only of Biblical history (cf. Isa. 6:8–10 and Ezek. 2:3–7), but also the important place of the legal proffer in the realm of jurisprudence."[221] In other words, if a bona fide offer had not been made, Israel could have claimed they had no choice. The Scripture indicates that Israel is invited to trust in Christ just like anyone else (Rom. 10:9). Therefore, this objection does not hold.

Conclusion

I have established that traditional dispensationalists adhere to a grammatical historical hermeneutic and the *CSBH* as criteria for understanding the biblical text. The consistent application of literal interpretation is the feature of this view. This approach is more consistent because of its stable meaning in the interpretation of Scripture. They argue that subsequent revelation may clarify previous revelation but not alter it. They also maintain that the Davidic covenant must be fulfilled with those to whom God made the promise, that is, Israel. Since the provision of the Davidic house was fulfilled literally in Jesus Christ, the remaining provisions are yet be fulfilled literally as well. This reasoning is supported in the Scripture and is therefore a valid one.

Traditional dispensationalists hold that truth is objective and absolute. This position is in harmony with the affirmation of Article VI of the *CSBH*:

> WE AFFIRM that the Bible expresses God's truth in propositional statements, and we declare that biblical truth is both objective and absolute. We further affirm that a statement is true if it represents matters as they actually are, but is an error if it misrepresents the facts.[222]

Traditional dispensationalists claim that truth is objective. Therefore, biblical truth has one meaning. It is fixed and consistent, and thus it is objective and absolute. This is traditional dispensationalism's strongest affirmation. This approach adopts the grammatical-historical method, which leads the interpreter to find the meaning of words in the Scriptures. The interpreter has no right to force their meaning into the text. The context of a passage, especially the immediate context, should guide the exegete in determining the meaning. The exegete who adopts this method maintains that authority resides in the words of the text and not with the interpreter. They argue that the text of the Davidic covenant indicates that national Israel is the referent to whom God made the promises.

In summary, traditional dispensationalism maintains that God will fulfill the promises of the Davidic kingdom in the future. According to this view, Jesus offered the kingdom to the Jewish nation, but they rejected it. As a result, the kingdom was put on hold. This kingdom will be established in the future when Jesus sits on the throne of David in the messianic kingdom. At that time, the Jewish people will repent and accept Jesus as their king after recognizing that he was the Messiah they originally rejected. God will fulfill all the unfulfilled promises pertaining to Israel. This guarantee of the fulfillment of Israel's promises is due to a consistent use of the literal interpretation, which is the foundation of the principles of the grammatical-historical method. By using this method, Ryrie, Walvoord, and Johnson concluded that the prophecies of Jesus' First Coming were fulfilled literally and, therefore, that the unfulfilled prophecies pertaining to Israel and the Davidic kingdom will also be fulfilled literally at Jesus' Second Coming. This view maintains that the church is distinct from Israel. In that case, the church is not fulfilling the promises to Israel. This is a summary of the traditional dispensationalist view. Finally, traditional dispensationalism complies with the principles of the grammatical-historical hermeneutic (see table 4).

---

1   Ryrie, *Dispensationalism*, 47.

2   Johnson, "A Traditional Dispensational Hermeneutic," in *Three Central Issues*, 64-5.

3   Ryrie, Dispensationalism, 46-48. Traditional dispensationalists are committed to three essentials: the distinction between the church and Israel, the literal meaning of the Scriptures, and the doxological purpose of God as opposed to a purpose that is soteriological (postmillennialist) or Christological (progressive dispensationalist).

4   Ryrie, *Dispensationalism*, 39-40.

5   Johnson, "Covenants in Traditional Dispensationalism," in *Three Central Issues*, 134, 135, and 155. Johnson claim that traditional dispensationalists maintain that God has not fulfilled the grant covenants (i.e., the Abrahamic, Davidic, and New covenants) during the church age, but that he will fulfill them in the future to the restored nation of Israel.

6   Refer to Appendix 1 of the *Chicago Statement of Biblical Hermeneutics*, 200.

7   Ryrie, *Dispensationalism*, 71–74.

8   Ryrie, *Dispensationalism*, 74–77.

9   Ryrie, *Dispensationalism*, 77–79.

10 Larry V. Crutchfield, *The Origins of Dispensationalism: The Darby Factor* (Lanham, MD: University Press of America, 1992), 50–60. [This book

is in the PIU Library.] Cf. Ryrie (*Dispensationalism*, 39–42), who claims traditional dispensationalists hold to these same characteristics.

11 Ryrie, *Dispensationalism*, 76–77, 79. Cf. Cliff R. Loriot, "John Nelson Darby's Dispensationalism" (unpublished manuscript, February 28, 2012), Microsoft Word file: "Appendix: Darby's Dispensational System Illustrated," 23. [I'm sending this page as an attachment. You have my permission to use it.]

12 Gary L. Nebeker, "John Nelson Darby and Trinity College, Dublin: A Study in Eschatological Contrasts," *Fides et Historia* 34, no. 2 (April 1 2002): 107 [You should look this up and provide an access date and URL. Page range: 87–108].

13 Chafer's influence is seen in his role as a founding president and professor at Dallas Theological Seminary, https://www.dts.edu/about/history/, accessed 6/9/18.

14 Bock ("Hermeneutics of Progressive Dispensationalism," 98-99) claims the term *normative dispensationalist* tends to aggravate the situation and does not accurately represent dispensationalism's historical development. Cf. Ryrie, *Dispensationalism*, 190. Craig A. Blaising ("The Extent and Varieties of Dispensationalism," 22-23) also refers to the period in which essential dispensationalists held the dominant view (i.e., 1950-1990) as the *revised period*.

15 Refer to chapter 5, pages 195-6 on the weakness of traditional dispensationalism. Consider also Ron J. Bigalke Jr., Progressive Dispensationalism: An Analysis of the Movement and Defense of Traditional Dispensationalism (Lanham, MD: University Press of America, 2005), 106.

16 Christopher Cone, "Presuppositional Dispensationalism," *Conservative Theological Journal* 10, no. 29 (May 2006): 75–94, esp. 87–93, http://www.galaxie.com/article/ctj10-29-06; Cone, "Hermeneutical Ramifications of Applying the New Covenant to the Church: An Appeal to Consistency," *Journal of Dispensational Theology* 13, no. 40 (December 2009): 5–22, http://www.galaxie.com/article/jodt13-40-01.

17 Ryrie, *Dispensationalism*, 89.

18 Ryrie, *Dispensationalism*, 36-37.

19 Charles C. Ryrie, *Basic Theology* (Wheaton, IL: Victor, 1999), 130.

20 Thomas D. Bernard, *The Progress of Doctrine in the New Testament*, The Bampton Lectures of 1864 (Grand Rapids: Eerdmans, 1949), 20.

21 Zuck, *Basic Bible Interpretation*, 73.

22 Plummer, *The Gospel according to S. Matthew*, 75.

23 Thomas D. Ice, "Global Proclamation of the Gospel," *Article Archives*, 76 (2009), accessed April 30, 2018, http://digitalcommons.liberty.edu/pretrib_arch/76.

24 Kenneth Boa, "John–Chapter 1, Part 2," Studies in the Book of John (December 2009), *Bible.org*, accessed March 15, 2015, https://bible.org/seriespage/john-chapter-1-part-2.

25 Herbert Bateman, "Dispensational Yesterday and Today," in *Three Central Issues*, 39. (cf. Elliot E. Johnson, "Author's Intention and Biblical Interpretation," in Hermeneutics, Inerrancy, and the Bible: [papers from ICBI Summit II], ed.

26 Bateman, "Dispensational Yesterday and Today," in *Three Central Issues*, 39.

27 Louw and Nida, *Greek-English Lexicon*, §28.77, s.v. "μυστήριον."

28 Alva J. McClain, *The Greatness of the Kingdom: An Inductive Study of the Kingdom of God* (Winona Lake, IN: BMH Books, 1959), 324.

29 Louw and Nida, *Greek-English Lexicon*, §11.58, s.v. "Ἰσραήλ, ὁ."

30 Arnold G. Fruchtenbaum, "Israel and the Church," in *Issues in Dispensationalism*, ed. Wesley R. Willis, John R. Master, and Charles Caldwell Ryrie (Chicago: Moody Press, 1994), 113.

31 Fruchtenbaum, "Israel and the Church," 114.

32 Fruchtenbaum, "Israel and the Church," 118.

33 Fruchtenbaum, "Israel and the Church," 120.

34 Louw and Nida, *Greek-English Lexicon*, §11.32, s.v. "ἐκκλησία."

35 LXX, Deuteronomy 4:10, "10 ... τῇ ἡμέρᾳ τῆς ἐκκλησίας, ὅτι εἶπε Κύριος πρός με· ἐκκλησίασον πρός με τὸν λαόν, ..." Cf., Deut. 9:10, 18:16; 23:1, 3, 8; 31:30. https://www.septuagint.bible/deuteronomy/-/asset_publisher, accessed 6/9/2018. However, 'ekklessia' could mean 'congregation, evil gathering, or assembly." In the New Testament, it means 'the body of Christ."

36 Francis Brown, S. R. Driver, and Charles A. Briggs, *The Drivin Driver-Briggs Hebrew and English Lexicon: With an Appendix Containing the Biblical Aramaic* (Oxford Clarendon Press, 1907), s.v. "קָהָל."

37 Robert P. Lightner, *Evangelical Theology: A Survey and Review* (Grand Rapids: Baker Book House, 1986), 217.

38 A. T. Robertson, *A Grammar of the Greek New Testament in the Light of Historical Research* (Nashville, TN: Broadman, 1934), 31–48, 388–89.

39 Earl D. Radmacher, *The Nature of the Church* (Haysville, NC: Schoettle, 1996), 116.

40 Radmacher, *The Nature of the Church*, 131.

41 Radmacher, *The Nature of the Church*, 134-142.

42   Radmacher, *The Nature of the Church*, 138.
43   Radmacher, *The Nature of the Church*, 139.
44   Radmacher, *The Nature of the Church*, 143.
45   Radmacher, *The Nature of the Church*, 207.
46   Radmacher, *The Nature of the Church*, 216.
47   Radmacher, *The Nature of the Church*, 216.
48   Ryrie, *Dispensationalism*, 144.
49   Ryrie, *Dispensationalism*, 145.
50   Ryrie, *Dispensationalism*, 145.
51   Ryrie, *Dispensationalism*, 145.
52   Ryrie, *Basic Theology*, 461.
53   Paul Williamson, *Sealed with an Oath: Covenant in God's Unfolding Purpose*, New Studies in Biblical Theology 23 (Downers Grove, IL: InterVarsity Press, 2007), 125.
54   Dwight Pentecost, "The Relationship of the Church to the Kingdom of God," in *When the Trumpet Sounds*, ed. Thomas Ice and Timothy J. Demy (Eugene, OR: Harvest House, 1995), 175.
55   Pentecost, "The Relationship of the Church to the Kingdom of God," 175.
56   Elliot E. Johnson, "Literal Interpretation: A Plea for Consensus," in *When the Trumpet Sounds*, 213; italics orig.
57   Johnson, "Literal Interpretation," 214.
58   Johnson, "A Traditional Dispensational Hermeneutic," 65.
59   Ryrie, *Dispensationalism*, 47.
60   Larry Tyler, "An Analysis of Amillennialism, Historic Premillennialism, Progressive Dispensationalism, and Traditional Dispensationalism: A Hermeneutical Analysis of the Fulfillment of the Abrahamic, Davidic, and New Covenants in Contemporary Evangelical Research" (PhD diss., Southeastern Baptist Theological Seminary, 2006), 180, accessed July 15, 2015, https://search.proquest.com/docview/304910319?accountid=165104.
61   Elliot E. Johnson, "A Traditional Dispensational Hermeneutic," 71.
62   Johnson, "A Traditional Dispensational Hermeneutic," 66.
63   Johnson, "A Traditional Dispensational Hermeneutic," 66.
64   Johnson, "A Traditional Dispensational Hermeneutic," 66-67.
65   Johnson, "A Traditional Dispensational Hermeneutic," 67.
66   Johnson, "A Traditional Dispensational Hermeneutic," 67.
67   Elliott E. Johnson, "Dual Authorship and the Single Intended Meaning of Scripture," *Bibliotheca Sacra* 143, no. 571 (July 1986): 226, accessed January 27, 2016, http://www.galaxie.com /article/bsac143-571-03.
68   Johnson, "A Traditional Dispensational Hermeneutic," 67.
69   Thomas, "The Principle of Single Meaning," 141.

70 Johnson, "A Traditional Dispensational Hermeneutic," 67.

71 Charles H. Dyer, "Biblical Meaning of 'Fulfillment,'" in *Issues in Dispensationalism*, 67.

72 Dyer, "Biblical Meaning of 'Fulfillment,'" 66.

73 Dyer, "Biblical Meaning of 'Fulfillment,'" 67.

74 Herman A. Hoyt, "Dispensational Premillennialism," in *The Meaning of the Millennium*, 67.

75 John F. Walvoord, *The Millennial Kingdom* (Findlay, OH: Dunham, 1959), 114.

76 Robert L. Thomas, *Evangelical Hermeneutics: The New Versus the Old* (Grand Rapids: Kregel, 2002), 242.

77 Ryrie, *Basic Theology*, 131.

78 Ryrie, *Basic Theology*, 131.

79 Ryrie, *Dispensationalism*, 46-48.

80 Fruchtenbaum, "Israel and the Church," 116.

81 Vlach, *Has the Church Replaced Israel?*, 209.

82 Charles C. Ryrie, "The Mystery in Ephesians 3," *Bibliotheca Sacra* 123, no. 439 (January 1966):29, accessed January 25, 2016, http://www.galaxie.com/article/bsac123-489-03.

83 Ryrie, "The Mystery in Ephesians 3," 27-28.

84 Fruchtenbaum, "Israel and the Church," 117.

85 Fruchtenbaum, "Israel and the Church," 117.

86 Fruchtenbaum, "Israel and the Church," 117.

87 Fruchtenbaum, "Israel and the Church," 118.

88 Ryrie, "The Mystery in Ephesians 3," 25.

89 Vlach, *Has the Church Replaced Israel?*, 210.

90 Ryrie, "The Mystery in Ephesians 3," 28.

91 Vlach, *Has the Church Replaced Israel?*, 208.

92 Vlach, *Has the Church Replaced Israel?*, 209.

93 Radmacher, *The Nature of the Church*, 115.

94 Radmacher, *The Nature of the Church*, 134-35.

95 Stanley D. Toussaint, "Israel and the Church of a Traditional Dispensationalist," in *Three Central Issues in Contemporary Dispensationalism*, 252.

96 Daniel P. Fuller, "The Hermeneutics of Dispensationalism" (ThD diss., Northern Baptist Theological Seminary, 1957), 25, quoted in Ryrie, *Dispensationalism*, 46.

97 Cf. Matthew McGee, "The Seven Churches of Revelation," *Wielding the Sword of the Spirit*, accessed April, 14, 2018, http://www.matthewmcgee.org/7church.html; Don Samdahl, "Understanding the Book of Revelation," *Doctrine.org*, accessed April 14, 2018, https://

doctrine.org/understanding-the-book-of-revelation; Hillel ben David, Micah ben Hillel, and Poriel ben Avraham, "Revelation and the Seven Congregations," *The Watchman*, updated March 26, 2018, accessed April 14, 2018, http://www.betemunah.org/revelation1.html.

98 Ronald D. McCune, *A Systematic Theology of Biblical Christianity*, 3 vols. (Allen Park, MI: Detroit Baptist Theological Seminary, 2010), 3:389.

99 Leon Morris, *The Revelation of St. John: An Introduction and Commentary*, Tyndale New Testament Commentaries, ed. R. V. G. Tasker (Grand Rapids: Eerdmans, 1969), 74.

100 Morris, *The Revelation of St. John*, 85.

101 Walter C. Kaiser Jr., "Exodus," in *The Expositor's Bible Commentary*, 2:463.

102 E. M. Cook ("Weights and Measures," in *The International Standard Bible Encyclopedia*, rev. ed., ed. Geoffrey W. Bromiley [Grand Rapids: Eerdmans, 1988], 4:1049) says a cubit is 17.5 inches. According to Ezek. 48:30–34, each of the four sides is four thousand five hundred cubits long, which is approximately 1.24 miles.

103 John F. Walvoord, "Basic Considerations in Interpreting Prophecy," in *Vital Prophetic Issues: Examining Promises and Problems in Eschatology*, Vital Issues Series 5, ed. Roy B. Zuck (Grand Rapids: Kregel, 1995), 19-20.

104 Walvoord, "Basic Considerations in Interpreting Prophecy," 19-20.

105 J. Dwight Pentecost, *Thy Kingdom Come: Tracing God's Kingdom Program and Covenant Promise Throughout History* (Grand Rapids: Kregel, 1995), 148.

106 Elliott E. Johnson, "Covenants in Traditional Dispensationalism," in *Three Central Issues in Contemporary Dispensationalism*, 135; italics orig.

107 Joseph A. Fitzmyer, *The One Who Is to Come* (Grand Rapids: Eerdmans, 2007), 8.

108 Fitzmyer, *The One Who Is to Come*, 8.

109 Leon J. Wood, *A Commentary on Daniel* (Eugene, OR: Wipf and Stock, 1973), 73; Stephen R. Miller, *Daniel: An Exegetical and Theological Exposition of Scripture*, The New American Commentary 18, ed. E. Ray Clendenen (Nashville, TN: B and H Publishing Group, 1994), 100.

110 Gingrich, *Shorter Lexicon of the Greek New Testament*, s.v. "παλιγγενεσια."

111 Plummer, *The Gospel According to S. Matthew*, 212.

112 J[ohannes]. J[acobus]. Van Osterzee, *The Gospel According to Luke: An Exegetical and Doctrinal Commentary*, Lange's Commentary on the Holy Scripture, ed. John Peter Lange and Philip Schaff (Grand Rapids, MI: Zondervan Publishing House, 1980), 289.

113 Ralph M. Gade, "Is God Through with the Jews?" *Grace Journal* 11, no. 2 (Spring 1970): 21-33.

114 Pentecost, *Thy Kingdom Come*, 145.

115 Paul N. Benware, *Understanding End Times Prophecy: A Comprehensive Approach* (Chicago: Moody Press, 2006), 62.

116 Thomas D. Lea and Hayne P. Griffin Jr., *1, 2 Timothy, Titus: An Exegetical and Theological Exposition of Holy Scripture*, The New American Commentary 34, ed. E. Ray Clendenen (Nashville, TN: Broadman Press, 1992), 242.

117 Daniel Wallace, *Greek Grammar Beyond the Basics*, 205.

118 Pentecost, "Relationship of the Church to the Kingdom of God," 177.

119 Charles C. Ryrie, *Biblical Theology of the New Testament*, 2nd ed (Dubuque, IA: ECS Ministries, 2005), 241.

120 Ryrie, *Biblical Theology of the New Testament*, 89.

121 Gingrich, *Shorter Lexicon of the Greek New Testament*, 137.

122 William L. Lane, *Hebrews 1-8*, Word Biblical Commentary, v. 47 (Dallas, TX: Word Book Publisher, 1991), 41-42.

123 Philip Edgcumbe Hughes, *A Commentary on the Epistle to the Hebrews* (Grand Rapids: Eerdmans, 1977), 82.

124 Benware, *Understanding End Times Prophecy*, 66-67.

125 Otto Borchert, *The Original Jesus*, trans. L. M. Stalker, Lutterworth Library 1 (London: Lutterworth Press, 1933), 23-37.

126 Tyler, "A Hermeneutical Analysis of the Fulfillment of the Abrahamic, Davidic, and New Covenants," 206.

127 Bigalke, *Progressive Dispensationalism*, 106.

128 Dyer, "Biblical Meaning of 'Fulfillment,'" 67.

129 Dyer, "Biblical Meaning of 'Fulfillment,'" 67.

130 Dyer, "Biblical Meaning of 'Fulfillment,'" 71.

131 Steven Waterhouse, *Not by Bread Alone: An Outlined Guide to Bible Doctrine*, 3rd ed. (Amarillo, TX: Westcliff Press, 2007), 478.

132 Ronald F. Showers, *There Really is a Difference: A Comparison of Covenant and Dispensational Theology* (Bellmawr, NJ: Friends of Israel Gospel Ministry, 1990), 85-97.

133 Showers, *There Really is a Difference*, 86.

134 Johnson, "Covenants in Traditional Dispensationalism," 127.

135 Showers, *There Really Is a Difference*, 86.

136 Pentecost, *Thy Kingdom Come*, 142.

137 Johnson, "Covenants in Traditional Dispensationalism," 128.

138 Johnson, "Covenants in Traditional Dispensationalism," 128.

139 Pentecost, *Thy Kingdom Come*, 142.

140 Showers, *There Really is a Difference*, 86-87.

141 Johnson, "Covenants in Traditional Dispensationalism," 128.

142 Showers, *There Really Is a Difference*, 87.

143 Pentecost, *Thy Kingdom Come*, 144.

144 Waterhouse, *Not by Bread Alone*, 479-80.

145 Pentecost, *Thy Kingdom Come*, 144.

146 T. Desmond Alexander and Brian S. Rosner, eds., *New Dictionary of Biblical Theology*, IVP Reference Collection (Downers Grove, IL: InterVarsity Press, 2000), 181.

147 McClain, *The Greatness of the Kingdom*, 156.

148 Johnson, "Covenants in Traditional Dispensationalism," 127.

149 Waterhouse, *Not by Bread Alone*, 312.

150 Waterhouse, *Not by Bread Alone*, 312.

151 Johnson, "Covenants in Traditional Dispensationalism," 139.

152 Johnson, "Covenants in Traditional Dispensationalism," 140.

153 Johnson, "Covenants in Traditional Dispensationalism," 141.

154 Johnson, "Covenants in Traditional Dispensationalism," 142.

155 Showers, *There Really Is a Difference*, 90.

156 Showers, *There Really Is a Difference*, 92.

157 Showers, *There Really Is a Difference*, 90-91.

158 Showers, *There Really Is a Difference*, 91.

159 Showers, *There Really Is a Difference*, 91.

160 Showers, *There Really Is a Difference*, 91.

161 Showers, *There Really Is a Difference*, 92.

162 *Webster's*, s.v. "Stable."

163 Dyer, "Biblical Meaning of 'Fulfillment,'" 67.

164 Geisler, *Summit II Hermeneutics*, 21.

165 *Webster's*, s.v. "Single."

166 *Webster's*, s.v. "Definite."

167 *Webster's*, s.v. "Fixed."

168 Geisler, *Summit II Hermeneutics*, 7.

169 Feinberg, "Systems of Discontinuity," 76.

170 Geisler, *Summit II Hermeneutics*, 23.

171 Geisler, *Summit II Hermeneutics*, 14.

172 Thomas, *Evangelical Hermeneutics*, 242.

173 Geisler, *Summit II Hermeneutics*, 23.

174 Geisler, *Summit II Hermeneutics*, 12.

175 Ryrie, *Dispensationalism*, 95.

176 Geisler, *Summit II Hermeneutics*, 23.

177 *Webster's*, s.v. "Unity."

178 *Webster*, s.v. "Harmony."

179 *Webster*, s.v. "Consistency."

180 Geisler, *Summit II Hermeneutics*, 13.

181 Geisler, *Summit II Hermeneutics*, 22.

182 Geisler, *Summit II Hermeneutics*, 21.

183 Geisler, *Summit II Hermeneutics*, 21.

184 Toussaint, "Israel and the Church of a Traditional Dispensationalist," 250.

185 Toussaint, "Israel and the Church of a Traditional Dispensationalist," 250.

186 Toussaint, "Israel and the Church of a Traditional Dispensationalist," 250.

187 Toussaint, "Israel and the Church of a Traditional Dispensationalist," 251.

188 Vlach, *Has the Church replaced Israel?*, 93.

189 Geisler, *Summit II Hermeneutics*, 23.

190 Vlach, *Has the Church Replaced Israel?*, 193.

191 Lightner, *Evangelical Theology*, 262.

192 Toussaint, "Israel and the Church of a Traditional Dispensationalist," 252.

193 Geisler, *Summit II Hermeneutics*, 11.

194 Geisler, *Summit II Hermeneutics*, 22.

195 Ryrie, *Dispensationalism*, 171-2.

196 Geisler, *Summit II Hermeneutics*, 23.

197 Geisler, *Summit II Hermeneutics*, 21.

198 Geisler, *Summit II Hermeneutics*, 23–24.

199 Feinberg, "Systems of Discontinuity," 76.

200 Geisler, *Summit II Hermeneutics*, 23.

201 J. Randall Price, "Prophetic Postponement in Daniel 9 and Other Texts," in *Issues in Dispensationalism*, 133.

202 Erich Sauer, *From Eternity to Eternity: An Outline of the Divine Purposes* (Grand Rapids: Eerdmans, 1994), 175.

203 Charles Feinberg, "The Eternal Kingship of Christ," in *Jesus the King is Coming*, ed. Charles Feinberg (Chicago: Moody Press, 1973), 188.

204 Feinberg, "The Eternal Kingship of Christ," 188.

205 Ryrie, *Biblical Theology of the New Testament*, 88.

206 Ryrie, *Dispensationalism*, 177.

207 Gentry, *He Shall Have Dominion*, 170.

208 Showers, *There Really Is a Difference*, 93, cf. 93-95

209 Ryken, Wilhoit, and Longman, *Dictionary of Biblical Imagery*, 341.

210 Toussaint, *Behold the King*, 59.

211 Toussaint, *Behold the King]*, 148; Fitzmyer, *The One Who Is to Come*, 135-138.

212 Toussaint, *Behold the King*, 148.

213 Blaising, "The Fulfillment of the Biblical Covenants," 175.

214 Gerry Breshears, "The Body of Christ: Prophet, Priest, and King" in *Journal Evangelical Theological Studies*, 37/1 (March, 1994): 6, 7, 26.

215 Sauer, *From Eternity to Eternity*, 175-76.

216 Sauer, *From Eternity to Eternity*, 175.

217 Stanley D. Toussaint, "The Contingency of the Coming of the Kingdom," in *Integrity of Heart, Skillfulness of Hands: Biblical Leadership Studies in Honor of Donald K. Campbell*, ed. Charles H. Dyer and Roy B. Zuck (Grand Rapids: Baker Books, 1994), 237.

218 Sauer, *From Eternity to Eternity*, p. 176.

219 Toussaint, "The Contingency of the Coming of the Kingdom," 236.

220 Toussaint, "The Contingency of the Coming of the Kingdom," 236.

221 McClain, *Greatness of the Kingdom*, 344.

222 Geisler, *Summit II Hermeneutics*, 21.

CHAPTER 5

Conclusions

We have investigated three evangelical viewpoints regarding the interpretation of the Davidic kingdom in an attempt to answer the question: "Which evangelical hermeneutical system— postmillennialism, progressive dispensationalism, or traditional dispensationalism—best explains the fulfillment of the messianic kingdom?" The information we gathered was sufficient to reach a conclusion. In this chapter, we will summarize each approach, state their strength(s) and weakness(es), and offer some final thoughts.

First, I will summarize each chapter. In chapter 1, we discussed Israel's expectation of a messianic kingdom, the problem regarding the fulfillment of that hope, my approach to finding the answer, and the importance of this study. In chapters 2–4, we analyzed in detail three evangelical views regarding whether, or to what extent, the Davidic kingdom has or has not been fulfilled. Next, we will discuss the strength(s) and weakness (es) of each view. I will conclude this chapter with some final thoughts about the whole issue.

Summary of the Research

The three elements that Yahweh promised to David in his covenant with him are a house (dynasty), a throne, and a kingdom (2 Sam. 7:12, 16). All three of the evangelical groups we discussed unanimously agree that Jesus fulfills the promised eternal house (dynasty) during his First Coming. He fulfills the promise that the Messiah would be a descendant of David (2 Sam. 7:12, 13; cf. Matt. 1:1). The Davidic dynasty had been vacant for almost six centuries following the exile, but Matthew begins his Gospel by writing, "The book of the genealogy of Jesus Christ, the Son of David, the Son of Abraham" (Matt. 1:1). The title, "the Son of David," points toward the Davidic covenant, but Matthew further emphasizes Jesus' royal character by reversing the historical sequence, that is, by putting David before Abraham. We have established that Jesus now fills the void of the awaited Davidic descendant (i.e., the house or dynasty). Whether the other two elements have been fulfilled (i.e., the throne and the kingdom) is still debated. Evangelical scholars have not reached a consensus regarding the *time* and *manner* in which these elements are fulfilled. In the following sections, I summarize each of the three evangelical group's views of the fulfillment of the Davidic throne and kingdom. I then summarize their view of the fulfillment of the house (dynasty), throne, and kingdom aspects of the Davidic covenant in tables 2 and 3.

Postmillennialism

A throne. Postmillennialists maintain that Jesus is sitting on his throne now. Mathison writes, "Jesus the Messiah has been seated at the right hand of God and has been given universal authority over all of heaven and earth. He has been given dominion. ... He is now the ruler of the nations of the earth."[1] Postmillennialists, therefore, teach that Jesus has full authority now. This authority is defined in the Great Commission in which Jesus states, "All authority has been given to Me in heaven and on earth" (Matt. 28:18). Mathison indicates that Jesus' authority is based in his resurrection and ascension. He writes, "In Peter's sermon on the Day of Pentecost, he explicitly points to Christ's resurrection and exaltation to the right hand of God as the fulfillment of the promise made to David (Acts 2:29–36; cf. Dan. 7:13–14)."[2] Postmillennialists claim that there is no other time when Jesus will have full authority other than now. Therefore, they deny the notion of a future reign on a physical throne, and maintain instead that Jesus currently sits on his throne in heaven and reigns in the hearts of believers.

A kingdom. Just like progressive dispensationalists, postmillennialists "maintain that the Messianic Kingdom was inaugurated during Jesus' First Advent." Mathison lists a couple of passages in which the Old Testament "indicates the beginning of the kingdom at the First Advent (Dan. 2:44; 7:13; Zech. 9:9–10)." Then he adds, "The New Testament confirms that these prophecies were fulfilled (Matt. 2:2; 28:18–20; Luke 1:32–33; Acts 2:29–36; 17:7; I Cor. 15:23–25; Col. 1:13; Rev. 1:5)."[3] He concludes by saying that the inaugurated kingdom, which postmillennialists hold is redemptive in nature, "will be consummated at the Second Coming of Christ."[4]

Progressive Dispensationalism

A throne. Progressive dispensationalists teach that the Davidic throne aspect of the covenant was partly fulfilled after Jesus' death-resurrection-ascension event in which he has been exalted to sit at the right hand of the Father. However, they equate the throne of Christ in heaven with the throne of David. Saucy writes, "The meaning of the right hand of God in Psalms 110:1 and Acts 2:33 is, therefore, the position of messianic authority. It is the throne of David."[5] Again, Saucy notes, "The messianic throne has been transferred from Jerusalem to heaven, and Jesus has begun His messianic reign as the Davidic king."[6] Blaising and Bock also maintain that Jesus sat on the Davidic throne after conquering death. They write, "Repeatedly, He is portrayed as enthroned at the right hand of God in fulfillment of the promises that belong to God's covenant with David. His enthronement and present authority is messianic."[7]

A kingdom. Because progressive dispensationalists maintain that Jesus is already reigning from the David's throne in heaven, they logically conclude that he has inaugurated the Davidic kingdom. This is why Saucy writes, "The exaltation of Jesus to the right hand of God in fulfillment of the Davidic messianic promise therefore allows for the inaugural fulfillment of those promises in distinction from the total postponement of the Davidic promise in traditional dispensationalism."[8] As a result, progressive dispensationalists argue for the inaugural fulfillment of a spiritual kingdom in which Christ is reigning over the church. They believe that the kingdom is fulfilled in both an "already" and a "not-yet" aspect. The "already" aspect is the current inaugural fulfillment, while the "not-yet" aspect is the consummation of the kingdom promise at Christ's Second Coming. Saucy notes that "even though Jesus spoke of the futurity of the kingdom, His message included the presence of the kingdom as well. The presence of the kingdom was in the form of the Holy Spirit, evident by Jesus' working of miracles (Matt. 12:28)."[9]

Traditional Dispensationalism

A throne. Traditional dispensationalists interpret 2 Samuel 7 to mean that the throne God promised to David was earthly and literal, and so they anticipate a future fulfillment because they maintain that Jesus has not sat on it. The Davidic throne aspect of the covenant will be fulfilled when Jesus sits on it and reigns for a thousand years. Andy Wood offers the following arguments to indicate that Jesus is not currently sitting on the throne of David:

> First, the Old Testament consistently depicts the Davidic Throne as in terrestrial rather than celestial terms. Second, because of this scriptural portrayal of the Davidic Throne, to argue that the Davidic Throne is now manifesting itself in this age from heaven is to contort the notions of progress of revelation and literal or normal, grammatical, historical hermeneutics. Third, no New Testament verse or passage, including those frequently appealed to in early Acts, clearly puts Christ on David's Throne in the present age.[10]

Therefore, the Davidic throne is currently vacant. This aspect of the Davidic covenant is yet to be fulfilled in the future.

A kingdom. Yahweh promised an eternal kingdom in the Davidic covenant (2 Sam. 7:12–16; 1 Chron. 17:14). Traditional dispensationalists maintain that this kingdom will be fulfilled literally at Christ's Second Coming. When Jesus came the first time, he offered the promised Davidic kingdom to Israel, but they rejected the offer. As a result, the kingdom was put on hold but it will be established in the future. Ryrie notes the following in regard to this issue:

> Because the king was rejected, the Messianic, Davidic kingdom was (from a human viewpoint) postponed. Though he never ceases to be king and, of course, is king today as always, Christ is never designated the king of the church … This awaits His second coming. Then the Davidic kingdom will be realized (Matt 25:31; Rev 19:15; 20).[11]

Pentecost agrees with Ryrie. He writes, "David's son, the Lord Jesus Christ, must return to the earth, bodily and literally, in order to reign over David's covenanted kingdom. The allegation that Christ is seated on the Father's throne reigning over a spiritual kingdom, the Church, simply does not fulfill the promises of the covenant."[12]

Tables 2 and 3 summarize the views of each of the three groups regarding the fulfillment of the primary aspects of the Davidic covenant: a house (a dynasty), a throne (the right to rule), and a kingdom (a realm over which to rule). The first column lists each of these elements. Table 2 gives the references for the prophecy in the Old Testament, the reference regarding its fulfillment in the New Testament, and each position's hermeneutical approach. Table 3 indicates their resulting views regarding the three elements' nature, form, and current status.

The Strengths and Weaknesses of Each View

In the following sections, I will draw some conclusions regarding the strength(s) and weakness(es) of each of the positions in reference to the fulfillment of the Davidic kingdom

Postmillennialism

Strength. The strength of this view lies in its confidence in the power of the gospel and its belief in the primacy of preaching. Postmillennialists remind the church that biblical truth has the power to transform our cultures and societies. Therefore, in some sense the reign of God is indeed a present reality. As Jesus said, "Lo, I am with you always" (Matt. 28:20).

Weaknesses. In teaching that the world will be Christianized through the preaching of the gospel and enjoy a long period of peace and prosperity prior to Christ's Second Coming, postmillennialists face dilemmas regarding the following issues:

1) The imminent return of Christ. Post millennialists implicitly deny the New Testament teaching that Christ could return at any moment. The return does not depend on any human effort, such as spreading the gospel, but on Christ himself (Matt. 24:42–44, 25:13; 1 Thess. 5:6; Luke 21: 28, 31; Rev. 3:11, 16:15, 22:12, 13). In refuting postmillennialism, Vern Poythress notes, "Most postmillennialists appear to me not merely to have this gospel optimism, but to claim that the second coming cannot take place just yet, because we have not yet seen a sufficiently broad and deep triumph of Christianity worldwide."[13]

2) The purpose of the gospel. Postmillennialism is inconsistent with the biblical fact that the cataclysmic return of Christ, rather than the preaching of the gospel and gradual human progress, brings in the kingdom (Revelation 19–20). The purpose of preaching the gospel in the current age is to gather saints for the coming kingdom. Furthermore, an increase in the number of Christian converts has not resulted in a transformational socio-cultural influence. In fact, cultural regression has often taken place. Such thinking by postmillennialists falls far short of the Old Testament description of the actual conditions of the kingdom (cf. Isa. 2:1–4; Jer. 23:3–8).

3) The beginning of the kingdom. Postmillennialists teach that the Davidic kingdom was established during Christ's First Coming but nowhere does the New Testament teach that this kingdom came into existence at that time. It does, however, say that during Christ's ministry "the kingdom of heaven is at hand" (Matt. 3:2; Mark 1:15), "the kingdom of God has come near to you" (Luke 10:9; cf. v 11), "the kingdom has come upon you" (Luke 11:20), and "the kingdom of God is in your midst" (Luke 17:21, NASB), but it stops short of saying that it arrived during his First Coming.

4) World conditions. Postmillennialists expect the world to improve and deny the obvious decline of Christian influence and presence in the world today (Matt. 24:9–14). Instead, they suggest

that Christianity is having a positive influence. However, their assertion is not true, as Hal Lindsey notes, "No self-respecting scholar who looks at the world conditions and the accelerating decline of Christian influence is a postmillennialist."[14] If this trend continues, the whole system of postmillennialism will prove to be unrealistic and fatally flawed.

5) The nature of the last days. Finally, postmillennialists fail to reflect on the New Testament descriptions of the end times. Postmillennialists take an optimistic view, while the Scriptures paint a pessimistic picture in stating that the spiritual and moral condition of individuals will decline as the end comes (Matt. 24:4–7; Luke 18:8; 2 Tim. 3:1–5).[15] These weaknesses invalidate postmillennialism's view of the Davidic kingdom.

Progressive Dispensationalism

Strength. Though progressive dispensationalism's approach is dualistic (i.e., "already" and "not-yet"), its adherents maintain that Jesus will establish his millennial kingdom after his Second Coming. During the millennium, he will restore national Israel and fulfill the promises God made to them through David. This element of their position is in harmony with biblical teaching (Zech. 12:10).

Weaknesses. However, progressive dispensationalism's hermeneutic is flawed with regard to their view of the following matters:

1) The New Testament's complementary use of the Old Testament. Blaising and Bock claim that "the New Testament includes or expands the Old Testament promises."[16] They further note, "The additional inclusion of some in the promise does not mean that the original recipients are therefore excluded."[17] This conclusion is illogical. God was pleased in his wisdom to grant the covenants to Israel exclusively, so all the grant covenants belong to Israel by divine right (i.e., the Abrahamic covenant [Gen.

15:5–18], the Davidic covenant [2 Sam. 7:12–16], and the New covenant [Jer. 31:31]). Because the Bible does not warrant their assertions, Blaising and Bock appear to manipulate God's Word through speculation and conjecture.

2) Expansion of meaning. Progressive dispensationalists advocate an expansion of meaning rather than stability in meaning. Regarding progressive revelation, Bock claims that the "expansion of meaning does not change meaning."[18] This claim cannot be true because Bock has already noted that the New Testament changes, alters, or expands the meaning of statements in the Old Testament. He claims the expansion of meaning involves the inclusion of Gentiles in the grant covenants. Therefore, Bock's statements are ambiguous and contradict his position.

3) Ambiguity. Progressive dispensationalists promote ambiguity in their hermeneutic. They try to distance themselves from amillennialists or postmillennialists who clearly spiritualize prophecy by denying that they use a spiritual hermeneutic, but in practice they employ ambiguity by giving a statement two referents. Consider the following examples. First, Saucy claims that "the throne of David has been transferred from Jerusalem to heaven."[19] Bock holds that "the kingdom of David has had an initial fulfillment through the 'already' or near aspect (Luke 10:9, 18–19; 11:20–23; 17:21; 19:14–15), ... when in reality this kingdom will be future,"[20] and advocates multiple meaning by stating that "the text cannot be limited to one meaning."[21] Blaising and Bock write that "the Seed of Abraham is not limited to Israel, but also comprises all those who are in Christ (Gal. 3:29)."[22] In this case, they imply that salvific union supersedes any distinction between national Israel and believing Gentiles. This conclusion is incorrect because Christ is the true seed and the church inherits his status through its union with him. Finally, Saucy claims that the church fulfills Israel's grant promises.[23] All these examples indicate that they employ a spiritual hermeneutic. Therefore, progressive dispensationalists are committed to the

complementary hermeneutic they claim to use and interpret the Scriptures in a manner consistent with it.[24]

4) The "already" and "not-yet" interpretation. The progressive dispensationalists' dualistic hermeneutic of eschatology is artificial and unbiblical. They interpolate meaning into the text with their analogy of the "already" and "not-yet" aspect of the kingdom. This approach is flawed in two ways. If the kingdom is already here in any form, as progressive dispensationalists claim, then it does not need to be anticipated. Furthermore, the "already" aspect of the kingdom is unrelated to the "not-yet" kingdom to be revealed. The "already" does not bring in the "not-yet," nor is the "not-yet" the result of the "already." They are two entirely separate entities. The messianic kingdom does not come in pieces, but as a unit. The Bible never teaches an "already" aspect of the messianic kingdom apart from fulfilling the "not-yet" aspect. We can conclude, then, that progressive dispensationalism's complementary hermeneutic is flawed.

Traditional Dispensationalism

Strengths. The following strengths concerning the fulfillment of the Davidic kingdom characterize traditional dispensationalism:

1) An attempt to consistently apply a hermeneutic based on the normal laws of language. Traditional dispensationalism's primary strength lies in a consistently literal approach to the interpretation of the Scripture. We should note that traditional dispensationalists are as much finite, sinful human beings as are postmillennialists and progressive dispensationalists. Therefore, they are also subject to arriving at flawed interpretations of the Scriptures. However, traditional dispensationalists are more consistent in the use of a literal hermeneutic than are the other two evangelical groups.

2) Stable meaning. We saw previously that literal interpretation guarantees a stable meaning. As a result, a consistently literal hermeneutic points to the future fulfillment of prophecy. For instance, the Old Testament prophecies regarding

Christ's First Coming, including his life, ministry, death, and resurrection, were fulfilled literally. It follows therefore that the unfulfilled prophecies about Jesus Christ would be fulfilled literally at his Second Coming. Traditional dispensationalists maintain that he will institute the millennial kingdom and reign for a thousand years. This claim has multiple attestation in the Scriptures (Isaiah 11; 65:20–25; Dan. 7:13–14; Rev. 20:2–7). It is significant that the Scriptures state no less than six times in six sequential verses that Christ will reign for a literal thousand years (Rev. 20:2–7).

3) Proper application of the Scriptures. Traditional dispensationalists maintain that the primary application of an Old Testament passage is to the original audience, which upholds the historical interpretation of the Old Testament. Although postmillennialists and progressive dispensationalists observe this principle regarding many Old Testament passages, prophecy is the distinguishing factor. For instance, Yahweh makes it clear in 2 Samuel 7:10–13 that the kingdom he promises to David and his descendants pertains only to Israel and the land Yahweh has given them. Postmillennialism and progressive dispensationalism both ignore this strict application.

4) A scripturally based optimism. While traditional dispensationalists are pessimistic regarding the last days of the current age, they teach that the promise of Christ's Second Coming to establish the messianic kingdom gives believers the hope they need to endure through the difficulties of this life (2 Thess. 1:4–12; 2 Tim. 2:12). In fact, the difficulties and dismal outlook of this age cause them to cry out, "Even so come, Lord Jesus" (Rev. 22:20), because they will find comfort and recompense when Christ returns to reign (1 Cor. 9:25; 2 Tim 4:8; Jas. 1:12).

Weakness. Traditional dispensationalists commonly hold that Jesus offered Israel the literal Davidic kingdom, but when Israel rejected their Messiah, the offer of the kingdom was put on hold. They also agree that it will be established in the future. However, traditional dispensationalists do not agree on the status of the kingdom during the current age. Some contend that the kingdom exists in a mystery form (Matt. 13:11), while others deny this notion by simply stating that the kingdom mysteries represent new truths concerning the kingdom that were undisclosed in the previous dispensation. Therefore, we must conclude that, even though traditional dispensationalists are not in practice always entirely consistent with their hermeneutic, the principles of the approach should enable the interpreter to conform to the grammatical-historical method of hermeneutics, as well as the articles of the *CSBH*. Consequently, only the principles of the traditional dispensationalist hermeneutic can serve as the basis for a more consistent dispensational hermeneutic.

The New Testament confirms God's promise to David of an earthly kingdom (Rev. 20:1–6). The fulfillment of the Davidic kingdom is anchored in God's nature. He keeps his covenants (Deut. 7:9; 1 Kings 8:23; Dan. 9:4; Neh. 1:6; 9:32; Luke 1:67–79). As the prophet Isaiah reminds Israel, Yahweh promised to watch over his Word to ensure that it will be fulfilled, "So shall My word be that goes forth from My mouth; It shall not return to Me void, But it shall accomplish what I please, And it shall prosper *in the thing* for which I sent it" (Isa. 55:11, cf. Jer. 1:12). He will do just that at Christ's Second Coming to establish the messianic kingdom he promised to David. This promise may be delayed from a human point of view, but Christ's coming is imminent, as the apostle John writes, "He who testifies to these things says, 'Surely I am coming quickly.' Amen. Even so, come, Lord Jesus!" (Rev. 22:20). God fulfills his promises (Num. 23:19; Isa. 55:8; 2 Cor. 1:20), and so he is committed to fulfilling his promises to Israel. In conclusion, traditional dispensationalism's compliance with the grammatical-historical method and the *CSBH* best explains the fulfillment of the Davidic kingdom as stated in 2 Samuel 7:12–16. This is the eschatology taught in the

New Testament: an eschatology that demands a future literal fulfillment of Yahweh's covenant promises to Israel alone.

Adherence to the Principles of the *CSBH*

Table 4 compares the three viewpoints regarding their adherence to the principles of a grammatical-historical hermeneutic. More specifically, in view of their interpretation of the fulfillment of the Davidic covenant, the question is whether they comply with the principles contained in the articles of the *CSBH* (see appendix 1).[25] The three positions appear in the first column, and the following columns list the answers regarding their adherence to the relevant principles. Each column represents one of the criteria for evaluation discussed in chapter 1. Briefly restated, they are as follows: (a) "Grammar" refers to how the grammatical function of a term in the statement affects its meaning.[26] (b) "Historicity" looks at how the historical-cultural background of the term or statement influences its meaning.[27] (c) "Genre" takes into consideration the way in which the kind of literature in which the term or statement occurs affects its meaning.[28] (d) "Figures of speech" are unique ways of conveying meaning, but ultimately express a literal meaning.[29] (e) "Context" is based on the principle that the Scriptures are their own best commentary.[30] The context includes the paragraph, section, and book in which the statement occurs, as well as the rest of Scripture.[31]

Table 4 indicates that neither postmillennialists nor progressive dispensationalists comply with the principles of grammatical-historical interpretation. Only traditional dispensationalists adhere to this method. Therefore, the hermeneutical methods the other positions adopt are invalid.

Patrick W. Nasongo

A Topic for Further Study

After analyzing the three views of the fulfillment of the Davidic kingdom, it is apparent that a fresh exegesis of Matthew 13:1–58 regarding the concept of a mystery kingdom is in order. The primary question we must answer is as follows: "Do the eight parables mentioned by Jesus in Matthew 13 support the idea of a mystery form of the kingdom or do they present a truth undisclosed in the Old Testament (e.g., the distinction between different kinds of "believers" in the parable of the sower [13:1–9, 18–23] and the separation of believers and non-believers in the parable of the wheat and the tares [13:24–30, 36–43])?" This question presents a challenge to traditional dispensationalists in particular.

I believe it is a grave mistake to think that the parables reveal a present spiritual form of the kingdom known as the "mystery form" of the kingdom. The Scriptures do not support this view. In the parables, Jesus did not speak about the "mystery form" of the kingdom but the "mysteries of the kingdom of heaven" (Matt. 13:11). Furthermore, a spiritual kingdom such as this supports the non-dispensational hermeneutics of the "kingdom now theology." Furthermore, a mystery form of the kingdom is illogical in view of Daniel's prophecy of the seventy weeks (Dan. 9:24–27). The church is in the parenthetical period between the sixty-ninth and seventieth weeks.[32] It is not the spiritual or mystery form of the kingdom. If the above suggested areas are clarified exegetically, then any future controversies about the mystery kingdom will be settled according to the Scriptures. Therefore, I recommend that traditional dispensationalists re-examine the context and interpretation of Matthew 13 in order to clarify any misconceptions about a spiritual or mystery form of the kingdom.

Final Thoughts

Postmillennialism, progressive dispensationalism, and traditional dispensationalism hold many beliefs in common, such as the authority of the Bible; the physical, glorious return of Christ at his Second Coming; salvation by grace through Jesus Christ alone; and some form of consummative eschatology. This can only mean that the adherents of each viewpoint are fellow Christians. Therefore, this analysis is not meant to condemn any individual. Instead, my purpose is to promote biblical scholarship among fellow believers. My prayer is that these findings will contribute to a better understanding of the Word of God and create cordial relations among believers of differing millennial views. We know this for certain: regardless of who is right, when the Lord carries out his sovereign plan, we will be like him and will not condemn anyone who was honestly mistaken. Finally, at that point we will not care who was right. We will be with our Lord. And so our prayer always should be, "Even so come, Lord Jesus."

---

1   Mathison, *Postmillennialism*, 191.
2   Mathison, *Postmillennialism*, 200.
3   Mathison, *Postmillennialism*, 190.
4   Mathison, *Postmillennialism*, 192.
5   Saucy, *The Case for Progressive Dispensationalism*, 72.
6   Saucy, *The Case for Progressive Dispensationalism*, 70.
7   Craig A. Blaising, "The Kingdom of God in the New Testament," in *Progressive Dispensationalism*, 257.
8   Saucy, *The Case for Progressive Dispensationalism*, 76.
9   Robert L. Saucy, "The Presence of the Kingdom and the Life of the Church," *Bibliotheca Sacra* 145, no. 577 (January–March 1988): 36, accessed August 21, 2015, http://www.galaxie.com.proxy1.athensams. net/article/bsac145-577-03.
10 Andy Wood, "The Coming Kingdom," *Pre-TribResearchCenter*, accessed June 15, 2015, http://www.pre-trib.org/articles/view/ the-coming-kingdom-27.

11   Ryrie, *Basic Theology*, 259.

12   Pentecost, *Things to Come* (Findlay, OH: Dunham, 1958), 114.

13   Vern Sheridan Poythress, "Currents Within Amillennialism," *Presbyterian* 26, no. 1 (January 2002): 22.

14   Hal Lindsay, *The Late Great Planet Earth* (New York: Bantam Books, 1973), 164-65.

15   Lindsay, *The Late Great Planet Earth*, 87.

16   Bock, "How Texts Speak to Us," 103.

17   Bock, "How Texts Speak to Us," 103.

18   Bock, "Current Messianic Activity," 72.

19   Saucy, *Case for Progressive Dispensationalism*, 70.

20   Darrell L. Bock, "Evidence from Acts," in *The Coming Millennial Kingdom: A Case for Premillennial Interpretation*, ed. Donald K. Campbell and Jeffrey L. Townsend (Grand Rapids: Kregel, 1997), 184.

21   Bock, "How We Read Texts," 68.

22   Bock, "How Texts Speak to Us," 101.

23   Saucy, *The Case for Progressive Dispensationalism*, 79.

24   Blaising, "Development of Dispensationalism by Contemporary Dispensationalists," 272.

25   Geisler, *Summit II Hermeneutics*, 19–25.

26   Fee, *New Testament Exegesis*, pp. [In the first edition, this is pp. 30–32. It includes Fee's steps 5–7.]

27   Fee, *New Testament Exegesis*, pp. [In the 1st ed., this is step 8.]

28   Zuck, *Basic Bible Interpretation*, 135.

29   Bullinger, *Figures of Speech Used in the Bible*, xv; Radmacher, "The Current Status of Dispensationalism and Its Eschatology," 167.

30   Geisler, *Summit II Hermeneutics*, 13.

31   Zuck, *Basic Bible Interpretation*, 106–112, 122.

32   Alva J. McClain, *Daniel's Prophecy of the 70 Weeks*, 3rd ed. (orig. pub. 1959; Winona Lake, IN: BMH Books, 2007), 31–45.

The Chicago Statement on Biblical Hermeneutics

Articles of Affirmation and Denial

Article I.   WE AFFIRM that the normative authority of Holy Scripture is the authority of God Himself, and is attested by Jesus Christ, the Lord of the Church.

WE DENY the legitimacy of separating the authority of Christ from the authority of Scripture, or of opposing the one to the other.

Article II.   WE AFFIRM that as Christ is God and Man in one Person, so Scripture is, indivisibly, God's Word in human language.

WE DENY that the humble, human form of Scripture entails errancy any more than the humanity of Christ, even in His humiliation, entails sin.

Article III.   WE AFFIRM that the Person and work of Jesus Christ are the central focus of the entire Bible.

WE DENY that any method of interpretation which rejects or obscures the Christ-centeredness of Scripture is correct.

Article IV.   WE AFFIRM that the Holy Spirit who inspired Scripture acts through it today to work faith in its message.

WE DENY that the Holy Spirit ever teaches to any one anything which is contrary to the teaching of Scripture.

Article V.   WE AFFIRM that the Holy Spirit enables believers to appropriate and apply Scripture to their lives.

WE DENY that the natural man is able to discern spiritually the biblical message apart from the Holy Spirit.

Article VI.   WE AFFIRM that the Bible expresses God's truth in propositional statements, and we declare that biblical truth is both objective and absolute. We further affirm that a statement is true if it represents matters as they actually are, but is an error if it misrepresents the facts.

WE DENY that, while Scripture is able to make us wise unto salvation, biblical truth should be defined in terms of this function. We further deny that error should be defined as that which willfully deceives.

Article VII.   WE AFFIRM that the meaning expressed in each biblical text is single, definite and fixed.

WE DENY that the recognition of this single meaning eliminates the variety of its application.

Article VIII.   WE AFFIRM that the Bible contains teachings and mandates which apply to all cultural and situational contexts and other mandates which the Bible itself shows apply only to particular situations.

WE DENY that the distinction between the universal and particular mandates of Scripture can be determined by cultural and situational factors. We further deny that universal mandates may ever be treated as culturally or situationally relative.

Article IX.   WE AFFIRM that the term hermeneutics, which historically signified the rules of exegesis, may be properly extended to cover all that is involved in the process of perceiving what the biblical revelation means and how it bears on our lives.

WE DENY that the message of Scripture derives from, or is dictated by, the interpreter's understanding. Thus we deny that the "horizons" of the biblical writer and the interpreter might rightly "fuse" in such a way that what the text communicates to the interpreter is not ultimately controlled by the expressed meaning of the Scripture.

Article X.   WE AFFIRM that Scripture communicates God's truth to us verbally through a wide variety of literary forms.

WE DENY that any of the limits of human language render Scripture inadequate to convey God's message.

Article XI.   WE AFFIRM that translations of the text of Scripture can communicate knowledge of God across all temporal and cultural boundaries.

WE DENY that the meaning of biblical texts is so tied to the culture out of which they came that understanding of the same meaning in other cultures is impossible.

Article XII.   WE AFFIRM that in the task of translating the Bible and teaching it in the context of each culture, only those functional equivalents which are faithful to the content of biblical teaching should be employed.

WE DENY the legitimacy of methods which either are insensitive to the demands of cross-cultural communication or distort biblical meaning in the process.

Article XIII.   WE AFFIRM that awareness of the literary categories, formal and stylistic, of the various parts of Scripture is essential for proper exegesis, and hence we value genre criticism as one of the many disciplines of biblical study.

WE DENY that generic categories which negate historicity may rightly be imposed on biblical narratives which present themselves as factual.

Article XIV.   WE AFFIRM that the biblical record of events, discourses and sayings, though presented in a variety of appropriate literary forms, corresponds to historical fact.

WE DENY that any event, discourse or saying reported in Scripture was invented by the biblical writers or by the traditions they incorporated.

Article XV.   WE AFFIRM the necessity of interpreting the Bible according to its literal, or normal, sense. The literal sense is the grammatical-historical sense, that is, the meaning which the writer expressed. Interpretation according to the literal sense will take account of all figures of speech and literary forms found in the text.

WE DENY the legitimacy of any approach to Scripture that attributes to it meaning which the literal sense does not support.

Article XVI.   WE AFFIRM that legitimate critical techniques should be used in determining the canonical text and its meaning.

WE DENY the legitimacy of allowing any method of biblical criticism to question the truth or integrity of the writer's expressed meaning, or of any other scriptural teaching.

Article XVII.   WE AFFIRM the unity, harmony and consistency of Scripture and declare that it is its own best interpreter.

WE DENY that Scripture may be interpreted in such a way as to suggest that one passage corrects or militates against another. We deny that later writers of Scripture misinterpreted earlier passages of Scripture when quoting from or referring to them.

Article XVIII.   WE AFFIRM that the Bible's own interpretation of itself is always correct, never deviating from, but rather elucidating, the single meaning of the inspired text. The single meaning of a prophet's words includes, but is not restricted to, the understanding of those words by the prophet and necessarily involves the intention of God evidenced in the fulfillment of those words.

WE DENY that the writers of Scripture always understood the full implications of their own words.

Article XIX.   WE AFFIRM that any preunderstandings which the interpreter brings to Scripture should be in harmony with scriptural meaning and subject to correction by it.

WE DENY that Scripture should be required to fit alien preunderstandings, inconsistent with itself, such as naturalism, evolutionism, scientism, secular humanism, and relativism.

Article XX.   WE AFFIRM that since God is the author of all truth, all truths, biblical and extrabiblical, are consistent and cohere, and that the Bible speaks truth when it touches on matters pertaining to nature, history, or anything else. We further affirm that in some cases extrabiblical data have value for clarifying what Scripture teaches, and for prompting correction of faulty interpretations.

WE DENY that extrabiblical views ever disprove the teaching of Scripture or hold priority over it.

Article XXI.   WE AFFIRM the harmony of special with general revelation and therefore of biblical teaching with the facts of nature.

WE DENY that any genuine scientific facts are inconsistent with the true meaning of any passage of Scripture.

Article XXII. WE AFFIRM that Genesis 1–11 is factual, as is the rest of the book.

WE DENY that the teachings of Genesis 1–11 are mythical and that scientific hypotheses about earth history or the origin of humanity may be invoked to overthrow what Scripture teaches about creation.

Article XXIII. WE AFFIRM the clarity of Scripture and specifically of its message about salvation from sin.

WE DENY that all passages of Scripture are equally clear or have equal bearing on the message of redemption.

Article XXIV. WE AFFIRM that a person is not dependent for understanding of Scripture on the expertise of biblical scholars.

WE DENY that a person should ignore the fruits of the technical study of Scripture by biblical scholars.

Article XXV. WE AFFIRM that the only type of preaching which sufficiently conveys the divine revelation and its proper application to life is that which faithfully expounds the text of Scripture as the Word of God.

WE DENY that the preacher has any message from God apart from the text of Scripture.

Progressive Dispensationalism's View of the Kingdom of God

In the following quote, Blaising and Bock explain their view of the kingdom of God in detail. They see Christ's current messianic reign at the Father's right hand, his literal messianic thousand-year reign on earth, and the eternal kingdom of the Father as aspects of a unified whole that is centered on Christ. They hold that the eternal kingdom is the key to understanding the two previous kingdoms. Each phase leads to the next, culminating in the eternal kingdom. They claim this is only revealed in the New Testament. Figure 1 illustrates their view.

> ***The Kingdom of God.*** The theme of the kingdom of God is much more unified and more central to progressive dispensationalism than it is to revised dispensationalism. Instead of dividing up the different features of redemption into self-contained "kingdoms," progressive dispensationalists see one promised eschatological kingdom which has both spiritual and political dimensions. That kingdom is always centered in Christ. The progressive revelation of one or

another aspect of the eschatological kingdom (whether spiritual of political) prior to the eternal reign of Christ, follows the history of Jesus Christ and is dependent on Him as He acts according to the will of the Father. Whether or not certain features of the eschatological kingdom (whether spiritual or political) will be enacted or revealed prior to the full establishment of that kingdom is not to be determined by reasoning from full-orbed descriptions of Old Testament prophets alone. Rather, it is a matter of the Father's will for this and any intervening dispensation, a matter which is discerned through New Testament revelation. The New Testament clarifies how the kingdom predicted by the Old Testament prophets is being revealed today, how it will in fact be in a millennial form, and how this contributes to that everlasting kingdom in which all prophecies will be fulfilled. Progressive dispensationalists put primary emphasis on the eternal kingdom for understanding all previous forms of the kingdom including the millennium. They make no substantive distinction between the terms kingdom of heaven and kingdom of God. And they see Christ's present relationship to the church today as a form of the eschatological kingdom which affirms and guarantees the future revelation of the kingdom in all its fullness.[1]

---

1   Blaising, "The Extent and Varieties of Dispensationalism," 54–55.

Bibliography

Alexander, Desmond T., and Brian S. Rosner, eds. *New Dictionary of Biblical Theology*. IVP Reference Collection. Downers Grove, IL: InterVarsity Press, 2000.

Bahnsen, Greg L. "Double Jeopardy: A Case Study in the Influence of Christian Legislation," *The Journal of Christian Reconstruction*, vol.2, no. 2 (Winter, 1975): 57.–77. Accessed 6/27/2018: https://chalcedon.edu/store/40091-jcr-vol-2-no-2-symposium-on-biblical-law.

Bateman, Herbert W., IV. *Three Central Issues in Contemporary Dispensationalism: A Comparison of Traditional and Progressive Views*. Grand Rapids: Kregel, 1999.

ben David, Hillel, Micah ben Hillel, and Poriel ben Avraham. "Revelation and the Seven Congregations." *The Watchman*. Updated March 26, 2018 Accessed April 14, 2018. http://www.betemunah.org/revelation1.html.

Benware, Paul N. *Understanding End Times Prophecy: A Comprehensive Approach*. Chicago: Moody Press, 2006.

Berkhof, Louis. *Principles of Biblical Interpretation: Sacred Hermeneutics*. Grand Rapids: Baker Book House, 1950.

Bernard, Thomas D. *The Progress of Doctrine in the New Testament*. The Bampton Lectures of 1864. Grand Rapids: Eerdmans, 1949.

Bigalke, Ron, Jr. *Progressive Dispensationalism: An Analysis of the Movement and Defense of the Traditional Dispensationalism.* Lanham, MD: University Press of America, 2005.

Blaising, Craig A. "Developing Dispensationalists Part 2: Development of Dispensationalism by Contemporary Dispensationalists," *Bibliotheca Sacra* 145, no. 579 (July 1988): 254–80. http://www.galaxie.com/article/bsac145-579-02. Accessed 6/14/2018.

Blaising, Craig A. and Darrell L. Bock. *Dispensationalism, Israel and the Church: The Search for Definition.* Grand Rapids: Zondervan, 1992.

Blaising, Craig A., and Darrell L. Bock. *Progressive Dispensationalism.* Wheaton, IL: BridgePoint, 1993.

Boa, Kenneth. "John–Chapter 1, Part 2." Studies in the Book of John (December 2009). *Bible.org.* Accessed March 15, 2015, https://bible.org/seriespage/john-chapter-1-part-2.

Bock, Darrell L. "Current Messianic Activity and OT Davidic Promise: Dispensationalism, Hermeneutics, and Fulfillment," *Trinity Journal* 15, no 1(Spring 1994): 55–84. http://www.galaxie.com/article/trinj15-1-04.

Bock, Darrell L. "Evidence from Acts." In *The Coming Millennial Kingdom: A Case for Premillennial Interpretation.* Edited by Donald K. Campbell and Jeffrey L. Townsend, 181–198. Grand Rapids: Kregel, 1997.

Bock, Darrell L. "The Son of David and the Saints' Task: The Hermeneutic of Initial Fulfillment." *Bibliotheca Sacra* 150 (October–December 1993): 440-57. Accessed April 6, 2015. http://web.a.ebscohost.com/ehost/pdfviewer?.

Boettner, Loraine. *The Millennium.* Philadelphia: Presbyterian and Reformed, 1957.

Borchert, Otto. *The Original Jesus.* Translated by L. M. Stalker. The Lutterworth Library 1. London: Lutterworth Press, 1933.

Breshears, Gerry. "The Body of Christ: Prophet, Priest, and King." in *Journal Evangelical Theological Studies,* 37/1 (March, 1994): 6—26.

Bright, John. *The Kingdom of God: The Biblical Concept and Its Meaning for the Church.* Nashville, TN: Abingdon Press, 1953.

Brown, Francis, S. R. Driver, and Charles A. Briggs. *The Brown-Driver-Briggs Hebrew and English Lexicon: With an Appendix Containing the Biblical Aramaic.* Oxford: Clarendon Press, 1907.

Bullinger, E. W. *Figures of Speech Used in the Bible: Explained and Illustrated.* Reprint. Orig. pub. 1898; Grand Rapids: Baker Book House, 1968.

Carroll, John T. *Response to the End of History: Eschatology and Situation in Luke-Acts.* Society of Biblical Literature Dissertation Series 92. Atlanta, GA: Scholars Press, 1988.

Chilton, David. *Paradise Restored: A Biblical Theology of Dominion.* Fort Worth, TX: Dominion Press, 1987.

Clouse, Robert G., ed. *The Meaning of the Millennium: Four Views.* Downers Grove, IL: IVP Academic, 1977.

Cone, Christopher. "Hermeneutical Ramifications of Applying the New Covenant to the Church: An Appeal to Consistency," *Journal of Dispensational Theology* 13, no. 40 (December 2009): 5–22. http://www.galaxie.com/article/jodt13-40-01.

Cone, Christopher. "Presuppositional Dispensationalism." *Conservative Theological Journal* 10, no. 29 (May 2006): 75–94. http://www.galaxie.com/article/ctj10-29-06.

Couch, Mal, ed. *Dictionary of Premillennial Theology: A Practical Guide to the People, Viewpoints, and History of Prophetic Studies.* Grand Rapids: Kregel, 1996.

Crutchfield, Larry V. *The Origins of Dispensationalism: The Darby Factor.* Lanham, MD: University Press of America, 1992.

Davis, John Jefferson. *Foundations of Evangelical Theology.* Grand Rapids: Baker, 1984.

Davis, John Jefferson. *The Victory of Christ's Kingdom: An Introduction to Postmillennialism.* Moscow, ID: Canon Press, 1996.

DeJong, James A. *As the Waters Cover the Sea: The Millennial Expectations in the Rise of Anglo-American Missions 1640–1810.* Kampen, Neth.: Kok, 1970.

DeMar, Gary. *Last Days Madness: The Folly of Trying to Predict When Christ Will Return.* Brentwood, TN: Wolgemuth and Hyatt, 1991.

Erickson, Millard J. *A Basic Guide to Eschatology: Making Sense of the Millennium.* 2nd ed. Grand Rapids: Baker Books, 1998.

Farrell, Hobert K. "The Eschatological Perspective of Luke-Acts." PhD diss., Boston University, 1972.

Fee, Gordon D. *New Testament Exegesis: A Handbook for Students and Pastors.* 3rd ed. Louisville, KY: Westminster John Knox Press, 2002.

Feinberg, Charles L. "The Eternal Kingship of Christ." In *Jesus the King is Coming.* Edited by Charles Feinberg. Chicago: Moody Press, 1973.

Feinberg, John S., ed. *Continuity and Discontinuity: Perspectives on the Relationship Between the Old and New Testaments—Essays in Honor of S. Lewis Johnson Jr.* Westchester, IL: Crossway, 1988.

Fitzmyer, Joseph A. *The One Who Is to Come.* Grand Rapids: Eerdmans, 2007.

Gade, Ralph M. "Is God through with the Jews?" *Grace Journal* 11, no. 2 (Spring 1970): 21–33.

Gaebelein, Frank E., ed. *The Expositor's Bible Commentary.* 12 vols. Grand Rapids: Zondervan, 1976–1992.

Geisler, Norman L. *Summit II Hermeneutics: Understanding God's Word—A Commentary.* With Exposition by J. I. Packer. ICBI

Foundation Series 6. Oakland, CA: International Council on Biblical Inerrancy, 1983.

Gentry, Kennedy L. "Recent Developments in the Eschatological Debate." *Reformation Online.* "Theology" (May 30, 2018). Accessed October 9, 2015, http://www.reformationonline. com/debate.htm.

Gentry, Kenneth Jr. "The Postmillennial Vision of Christian Eschatology." *Criswell Theological Review* 11, no. 1 (Fall 2013): 89–102.

Gentry, Kenneth L., Jr. "Postmillennialism." In *Three Views on the Millennium and Beyond.* Counterpoints: Bible and Theology. Edited by Darrell Bock and Stanly N. Gundry, 11–57. Grand Rapids: Zondervan, 1999.

Gentry, Kenneth L., Jr. *He Shall Have Dominion: A Postmillennial Eschatology.* Draper, VA: ApologeticsGroup Media, 2009.

Gentry, Kenneth L., Jr. *Postmillennialism Made Easy.* Draper, VA: Apologetic Group Media, 2009. Kindle.

George, Timothy. *Galatians: An Exegetical and Theological Exposition of Holy Scripture.* The New American Commentary 30. Edited by E. Ray Clendenen. Nashville, TN: Broadman and Holman, 1994.

Gingrich, Wilbur F. *Shorter Lexicon of the Greek New Testament.* 2nd ed. Edited by Frederick W. Danker. Chicago: The University of Chicago Press, 1983.

Gowan, Donald E. *Eschatology in the Old Testament.* Philadelphia: Fortress, 1986.

Greidanus, Sidney. *The Modern Preacher and the Ancient Text: Interpreting and Preaching Biblical Literature.* Grand Rapids: Eerdmans, 1988.

Gundry, Robert H. *Matthew: A Commentary on His Literary and Theological Art.* Grand Rapids: Eerdmans, 1982.

Hagner, Donald A. *Matthew 1–13.* Word Biblical Commentary 33A. Edited by Bruce Metzger. Nashville, TN: Thomas Nelson, 1993.

Harless, Hal. *How Firm a Foundation: The Dispensations in the Light of the Divine Covenants*. Studies in Biblical Literature 63. New York: Peter Lang, 2004.

Hodge, Charles. *Systematic Theology*. 3 vols. Peabody, MA: Hendrickson, 1999.

Hughes, Philip Edgcumbe. *A Commentary on the Epistle to the Hebrews*. Grand Rapids: Eerdmans, 1977.

Hulse, Erroll. *The Restoration of Israel*. 3rd ed. Worthing, Sussex: Henry E. Walter, 1982.

Ice, Thomas D. "Global Proclamation of the Gospel." *Article Archives*, 76 (2009). Accessed April 30, 2018. http://digitalcommons.liberty.edu/pretrib_arch/76.

Ice, Thomas, and Timothy J. Demy, eds. *When the Trumpet Sounds*. Eugene, OR: Harvest House, 1995.

Ice, Thomas. "Elijah is Coming." *Pre-TribResearchCenter*. Paper presented at the 26th Annual Conference, December 4–6, 2017. Accessed March 3, 2018. http://www.pre-trib.org/articles/view/elijah-is-coming.

Ice, Thomas. "The Unscriptural Theologies of Amillennialism and Postmillennialism." *Pre-TribResearchCenter*. Paper presented at the 26th Annual Conference, December 4–6, 2017. March 20, 2018. http://www.pre-trib.org/articles/view/unscriptural-theologies-of-amillennialism-and-post millennialism.

Johnson, Elliot E. "Dual Authorship and the Single Intended Meaning of Scripture." *Bibliotheca Sacra* 143, no. 571 (July 1986): 218–227. Accessed January 27, 2016. http://www.galaxie.com/article/bsac143-571-03.

Kaiser Jr., Walter C. "Kingdom Promises as Spiritual and National," in Continuity and Discontinuity: Perspectives on the Relationship Between the Old and New Testaments— Essays in Honor of S. Lewis Johnson Jr., ed. John S. Feinberg (Westchester, IL: Crossway Books, 1988), 290

Kalt, Edmund, ed. *Herder's Commentary on the Psalms.* Westminster, MD: Newman Press, 1961.

Lane, William L. *Hebrews 1-8*, Word Biblical Commentary, v. 47. Dallas, TX: Word Book Publisher, 1991.

LaSor, William Sanford. *Israel: A Biblical View.* Grand Rapids: Eerdmans, 1976.

Lea, Thomas D. and Hayne P. Griffin Jr. *1, 2 Timothy, Titus: An Exegetical and Theological Exposition of Holy Scripture,* The New American Commentary 34. Edited by E. Ray Clendenen. Nashville, TN: Broadman Press, 1992.

Lightner, Robert P. *Evangelical Theology: A Survey and Review.* Grand Rapids, MI: Baker Book House, 1986.

Lindsay, Hal. *The Late Great Planet Earth.* New York: Bantam Books, 1973.

Louw, Johannes P. and Eugene A. Nida, eds. *Greek-English Lexicon of the New Testament: Based on Semantic Domains.* 2nd ed. 2 vols. New York: United Bible Societies, 1989.

Mathison, Keith A. *Dispensationalism: Rightly Dividing the People of God?* Phillipsburg, NJ: P and R Publishing, 1995.

Mathison, Keith A. *Postmillennialism: An Eschatology of Hope.* Philipsburg, NJ: P and R Publishing, 1999.

Mathison, Keith. "The Davidic Covenant—The Unfolding of Biblical Eschatology." *Ligonier Ministries: The Teaching Fellowship of R. C. Sproul* (March 5, 2012). Accessed May 18, 2015. http://www.ligonier.org/blog/davidic-covenant-unfolding-biblical-eschatology.

McClain, Alva J. *Daniel's Prophecy of the 70 Weeks.* 3rd ed. Orig. pub. 1959. Winona Lake, IN: BMH Books, 2007.

McClain, Alva J. *The Greatness of the Kingdom: An Inductive Study of the Kingdom of God.* Winona Lake, IN: BMH Books, 1959.

McCune, Ronald D. *A Systematic Theology of Biblical Christianity.* 3 vols. Allen Park, MI: Detroit Baptist Theological Seminary, 2008–2010.

McGee, Matthew. "The Seven Churches of Revelation." *Wielding the Sword of the Spirit.* Accessed April, 14, 2018. http://www.matthewmcgee.org/7church.html

McLeod, Alexander. *Messiah, Governor of the Nations.* Elmwood Park, NJ: Reformed Presbyterian Press, 1992.

Miller, Stephen R. *Daniel: An Exegetical and Theological Exposition of Scripture.* The New American Commentary 18. Edited by E. Ray Clendenen. Nashville, TN: B and H Publishing Group, 1994.

Morris, Leon. *The Revelation of St. John: An Introduction and Commentary.* Tyndale New Testament Commentaries. Edited by R. V. G. Tasker. Grand Rapids: Eerdmans, 1969.

Murray, Iain. *The Puritan Hope.* Edinburgh: Banner of Truth, 1971.

Nasongo, Patrick W. "A Hermeneutical and Exegetical Analysis of the Fulfillment of the Davidic Kingdom in the New Testament from the Perspectives of Traditional Dispensationalism, Progressive Dispensationalism, and Postmillennialism." (PhD diss., Piedmont International University, 2016).

Nebeker, Gary L. "John Nelson Darby and Trinity College, Dublin: A Study in Eschatological Contrasts." *Fides et Historia* 34, no. 2 (April 1 2002): 87–108. Accessed 06/08/2018. http://brethrenhistory.org/qwicsitePro/php/docsview.php?docid=585.

North, Gary. "The Economics Thought of Luther & Calvin," *The Journal of Christian Reconstruction* vol. ii, no. 1 (Summer, 1975): 97–136. Accessed 6/27/2018. https://chalcedon.edu/store/40089-jcr-vol-2-no-1-symposium-on-christian-economics.

North, Gary. *Millennialism and Social Theory.* Tyler, TX: Institute for Christian Economics, 1990.

Osterzee, Van J. J. *The Gospel According to Luke: An Exegetical and Doctrinal Commentary,* Lange's Commentary on the Holy Scripture, ed. John Peter Lange and Philip Schaff. Grand Rapids, MI: Zondervan Publishing House, 1980.

Pentecost, Dwight J. *Things to Come*. Findlay, OH: Dunham, 1958.

Pentecost, Dwight J. *Thy Kingdom Come: Tracing God's Kingdom Program and Covenant Promise Throughout History*. Grand Rapids: Kregel, 1995.

Plummer, Alfred. *An Exegetical Commentary on the Gospel According to S. Matthew*. New York: Charles Scribner's Sons, 1910.

Poythress, Vern Sheridan. "Currents Within Amillennialism." *Presbyterian 26*, no. 1 (January 2002): 21–25.

Radmacher, Earl D. "The Current Status of Dispensationalism and Its Eschatology." In *Perspectives on Evangelical Theology: Papers from the Thirtieth Annual Meeting of the Evangelical Theological Society*. Edited by Kenneth S. Kantzer and Stanley M. Gundry, 167–176. Grand Rapids: Baker Book House, 1979.

Radmacher, Earl D. *The Nature of the Church*. Haysville, NC: Schoettle, 1996.

Ridderbos, Herman. *The Coming of the Kingdom*. Philadelphia: Presbyterian and Reformed, 1962.

Robertson, A. T. *A Grammar of the Greek New Testament in the Light of Historical Research*. Nashville, TN: Broadman, 1934.

Rushdoony, Rousas John. *God's Plan for Victory: The Meaning of Post Millennialism: A Chalcedon Study*. Fairfax, VA: Thoburn Press, 1977.

Rushdoony, Rousas John. *Thy Kingdom Come: Studies in Daniel and Revelation*. Fairfax, VA: Thoburn Press, 1970.

Ryken, Leland, James C. Wilhoit, and Tremper Longman III, eds. *Dictionary of Biblical Imagery*. Downers Grove, IL: InterVarsity Press, 1998.

Ryrie, Charles C. "The Mystery in Ephesians 3." *Bibliotheca Sacra 123*, no. 439 (January 1966): 24–30. Accessed January 25, 2016. http://www.galaxie.com/article/bsac123-489-03.

Ryrie, Charles C. *Basic Theology*. Wheaton, IL: Victor, 1999.

Ryrie, Charles C. *Biblical Theology of the New Testament.* 2nd ed. Dubuque, IA: ECS Ministries, 2005.

Ryrie, Charles C. *Dispensationalism.* 3rd ed. Chicago: Moody Press, 2007.

Samdahl, Don. "Understanding the Book of Revelation." *Doctrine.org.* Accessed April 14, 2018. https://doctrine.org/understanding-the-book-of-revelation.

Sandlin, Andrew. *A Postmillennial Primer.* Vallecito, CA: The Chalcedon Foundation, 1997.

Saucy, Robert L. "The Presence of the Kingdom and the Life of the Church." *Bibliotheca Sacra* 145, no. 577 (January–March 1988): 30–46. Accessed August 21, 2015. http://www.galaxie.com.proxy1.athensams.net/article/bsac145-577-03.

Saucy, Robert L. *The Case for Progressive Dispensationalism: The Interface Between Dispensationalism and Non-Dispensational Theology.* Grand Rapids: Zondervan, 1993.

Sauer, Erich. *From Eternity to Eternity: An Outline of the Divine Purposes.* Grand Rapids: Eerdmans, 1994.

Showers, Renald E. *There Really is a Difference: A Comparison of Covenant and Dispensational Theology.* Bellmawr, NJ: The Friends of Israel Gospel Ministry, 1990.

Smith, David P., and June Corduan. *B. B. Warfield's Scientifically Constructive Theological Scholarship.* The Evangelical Society Monograph Series 10. Eugene, OR: Pickwick, 2011.

Snowden, James H. *The Coming of the Lord: Will it be Premillennial?* 2nd ed. Reprint. Orig. pub. 1919. Whitefish, MT: Kessinger, 2007.

St. Augustine. *The City of God.* Translated by Marcus Dods. New York: The Modern Library, 1950.

Strawbridge, Gregg. "An Exegetical Defense of Postmillennialism from 1 Corinthians 15:25–26: The Eschatology of the DIXIT DOMINUS." Paper presented at the 51st Annual Meeting of the Evangelical Theological Society. Danvers, MA:

November 17–19, 1999. http://www.wordmp3.com/files/gs/postmill.htm.

Tan, Paul Lee. *Literal Interpretation of the Bible*. Rockville, MD: Assurance Publishers, 1978.

Thomas, Robert L. *Evangelical Hermeneutics: The New Versus the Old*. Grand Rapids: Kregel, 2002.

Toussaint, Stanley D. "The Contingency of the Coming of the Kingdom." In *Integrity of Heart, Skillfulness of Hands: Biblical Leadership Studies in Honor of Donald K. Campbell*. Edited by Charles H. Dyer and Roy B. Zuck, 222-237. Grand Rapids: Baker Books, 1994.

Toussaint, Stanley D. *Behold the King: A Study of Matthew*. Grand Rapids: Kregel, 1980.

Tyler, Larry. "An Analysis of Amillennialism, Historic Premillennialism, Progressive Dispensationalism, and Traditional Dispensationalism: A Hermeneutical Analysis of the Fulfillment of the Abrahamic, Davidic, and New Covenants in Contemporary Evangelical Research." PhD diss., Southeastern Baptist Theological Seminary, 2006. Accessed July 15, 2015. https://search.proquest.com/docview/304910319?accountid=165104.

VanGemeren, Willem. "Psalms," in *The Expositor's Bible Commentary*, 12 vols., ed. Frank E. Gaebelein. Grand Rapids: Zondervan, 1991.

Vlach, Michael J. *Has the Church Replaced Israel?* Nashville, TN: B and H Academic, 2010.

Wallace, Daniel B. *Greek Grammar Beyond the Basics: An Exegetical Syntax of the New Testament*. Grand Rapids: Zondervan, 1996.

Walvoord, John F. "Basic Considerations in Interpreting Prophecy." In *Vital Prophetic Issues: Examining Promises and Problems in Eschatology*. Vital Issues Series 5. Edited by Roy B. Zuck, 14–22. Grand Rapids: Kregel, 1995.

Walvoord, John F. "Eschatological Problems VII: The Fulfillment of the Davidic Covenant." *Bibliotheca Sacra* 102, no. 406 (April 1945): 153–66. Accessed 04/18/2016. http://www.galaxie.com/article/bsac102-406-03.

Walvoord, John F. *The Millennial Kingdom*. Findlay, OH: Dunham, 1959.

Warfield, Benjamin B. *The Inspiration and Authority of the Bible*. Philipsburg, NJ: Presbyterian and Reformed, 1948.

Waterhouse, Steven. *Not by Bread Alone: An Outline Guide to Bible Doctrine*. 3rd ed. Amarillo, TX: Westcliff Press, 2007.

Williamson, Paul R. *Sealed with an Oath: Covenant in God's Unfolding Purpose*. New Studies in Biblical Theology 23. Downers Grove, IL: InterVarsity Press, 2007.

Willis, Jim, and Barbara Willis. *Armageddon Now: The End of the World A to Z*. Detroit: Visible Ink Press, 2006.

Willis, Wesley R., John R. Master, and Charles Caldwell Ryrie, eds. *Issues in Dispensationalism*. Chicago: Moody Press, 1994.

Wood, Andy. "The Coming Kingdom." *Pre-TribResearchCenter*. Accessed June 15, 2015. http://www.pre-trib.org/articles/view/the-coming-kingdom-27.

Wood, Leon J. *A Commentary on Daniel*. Eugene, OR: Wipf and Stock, 1973.

Zuck, Roy B. *Basic Bible Interpretation: A Practical Guide to Discovering Biblical Truth*. Wheaton, IL: Victor, 1973.

Tables

	Text	Phrase	Classification	
			T	N-T
1	Matt. 16:18	οἰκοδομήσω μου τὴν ἐκκλησίαν	T	
2	Matt. 18:17	εἰπὲ τῇ ἐκκλησίᾳ	T	
3	Acts 5:11	φόβος μέγας ἐφ᾽ ὅλην τὴν ἐκκλησίαν	T	
4	Acts 7:38	ἐν τῇ ἐκκλησίᾳ ἐν τῇ ἐρήμῳ	T	
5	Acts 8:1	διωγμὸς μέγας ἐπὶ τὴν ἐκκλησίαν	T	
6	Acts 11:26	συναχθῆναι ἐν τῇ ἐκκλησίᾳ καὶ διδάξαι	T	
7	Acts 19:32	γὰρ ἡ ἐκκλησία συγκεχυμένη		N-T
8	Acts 19:39	ἐν τῇ ἐννόμῳ ἐκκλησίᾳ ἐπιλυθήσεται		N-T
9	Acts 19:41	ἀπέλυσεν τὴν ἐκκλησίαν		N-T

Note: T = Technical; N-T = Nontechnical

Table 2.	Views of the Three Elements in the Davidic Covenant: Texts and Hermeneutic				
Element	View	OT Texts		NT Texts	Hermeneutic
House	PM	2 Sam. 7:12, 13, 16		Matt. 1:1	spiritual
	PD	2 Sam. 7:12, 13, 16; 1 Chron. 17:11–15		Luke 3:3	complementary
	TD	2 Sam. 7:12, 13, 16		Matt. 1:1	literal
Throne	PM	Ps. 110:1		1 Cor. 15:25	spiritual
	PD	2 Sam. 7:12–13; Isa. 9:7; Ps. 110:1		Luke 1:32–33	complementary
	TD			Luke 1:32–33. Matt. 1:2	literal
Kingdom	PM	Dan. 2:44; 7:13–14		Matt. 12:28; Mk 1:15	spiritual
	PD	2 Sam. 7:16; Ps. 89:26–28		Luke 10:9, 2; Tim. 4:1	complementary
	TD	2 Sam. 7:16		Acts 1:6	literal

Note: PM = Postmillennialism; PD = Progressive Dispensationalism; TD = Traditional Dispensationalism

Table 3.	Views of the Three Elements in the Davidic Covenant: Nature, Form, and Status			
Element	View	Nature	Form	Status
House	PM	eternal	spiritual	fulfilled
	PD	eternal	spiritual	fulfilled
	TD	eternal	literal (future)	fulfilled
Throne	PM	conditional	spiritual	fulfilled
	PD	conditional	spiritual	fulfilled
	TD	unconditional	physical	unfulfilled
Kingdom	PM	spiritual redemptive	spiritual	inaugurated
	PD	conditional	progressive	already and not-yet
	TD	unconditional	political	unfulfilled

Note: PM = Postmillennialism; PD = Progressive Dispensationalism; TD = Traditional Dispensationalism

Table 4. Adherence of Each View to Relevant *CSBH* Principles

View	Grammar	Historicity	Genre	Figures of Speech	Context
			CSBH Principles		
PM	No	No	No	No	No
PD	No	No	No	No	No
TD	Yes	Yes	Yes	Yes	Yes

Note: PM = Postmillennialism; PD = Progressive Dispensationalism; TD = Traditional Dispensationalism

Figure 1. Progressive Dispensationalism's View of the Kingdom of God

THE KINGDOM OF GOD IN PROGRESSIVE DISPENSATIONALISM					
DIVINE PRESENCE AND POWER REVEALED IN PROGRESS OF REDEMPTION					
		The Eschatological Kingdom of God			
The Kingly Act of God	The Kingdom of God	In the Person of Christ	In the Community of Christ (The Church)	In the Millennium Empire of Christ	In Eternal Fulfillment
				Christ Descended	
Past Dispensations	Jesus Christ	Present Dispensations	(Millennial)	(Eternal)	
			Future Dispensations		

Source: Adapted from Craig A. Blaising, "The Extent and Varieties of Dispensationalism," in Craig A. Blaising and Darrell L. Bock, *Progressive Dispensationalism* (Wheaton, IL: BridgePoint, 1993), 54–55. Used by permission.

Index of Scripture References

Index of Subjects

Printed in the United States
By Bookmasters